WORD AND CHURCH

WORD AND CHURCH

Essays in Christian Dogmatics

John Webster

T&T CLARK
EDINBURGH & NEW YORK

T&T CLARK LTD

A Continuum imprint

59 George Street	370 Lexington Avenue
Edinburgh EH2 2LQ	New York 10017–6503
Scotland	USA
www.tandtclark.co.uk	www.continuumbooks.com

First published 2001

ISBN 0 567 08818 9

British Library Cataloguing-in-Publication Data
A catalogue record for this book is available from the British Library

Typeset by Fakenham Photosetting Ltd, Fakenham, Norfolk
Printed and bound in Great Britain by MPG Books, Bodmin

In memoriam

GEORGE SCHNER, S.J.

1946–2000

συνεργός τοῦ θεοῦ ἐν τῷ εὐαγγελίῳ τοῦ Χριστοῦ

CONTENTS

Acknowledgments   ix

Introduction   1

Scripture

1   The Dogmatic Location of the Canon   9

2   Hermeneutics in Modern Theology: Some Doctrinal
    Reflections   47

3   Reading the Bible: The Example of Barth and
    Bonhoeffer   87

Christ and the Church

4   Incarnation   113

5   Jesus in Modernity: Reflections on Jüngel's
    Christology   151

6   The Self-organizing Power of the Gospel of Christ:
    Episcopacy and Community Formation   191

7   Christ, Church and Reconciliation   211

Ethics

8   God and Conscience   233

9   Eschatology and Anthropology   263

Index of Names   287

ACKNOWLEDGMENTS

Some of the essays in this volume have been previously published as follows:

'The Dogmatic Location of the Canon', *Neue Zeitschrift für Systematische Theologie* 43 (2001), pp. 17–43.

'Hermeneutics in Modern Theology: Some Doctrinal Reflections', *Scottish Journal of Theology* 51 (1998), pp. 307–41.

'Jesus in Modernity: Reflections on Jüngel's Christology' as 'Jesus in the Theology of Eberhard Jüngel', *Calvin Theological Journal* 32 (1997), pp. 43–71.

'God and Conscience', *Calvin Theological Journal* 33 (1998), pp. 104–24.

'Eschatology and Anthropology' as 'Eschatology, Anthropology and Postmodernity', *International Journal of Systematic Theology* 2 (2000), pp. 13–28.

INTRODUCTION

The essays assembled here, written over the course of the last
five years, form a set of working studies in Christian dogmatics,
that delightful activity in which the church praises God by
ordering its thinking towards the gospel of Christ. They cluster
around three themes. The first of these themes is the nature of
Holy Scripture and its interpretation. Recent theology has
happily witnessed the gradual narrowing of the gap between
systematic theology and biblical studies, as first hermeneutical
theory and then renewed appreciation for pre-critical interpretative practices have begun to cure some of the myopia
of critical-historical exegesis. Yet, from the point of view of
Christian dogmatics, the large and often (too) sophisticated
literature on post-critical hermeneutics is not wholly satis-
factory. One major reason for this is that there has been
remarkably little attention paid to doctrinal description of the
nature of Scripture, with the result that central topics –
concerning the perfection, perspicuity, sufficiency and, above
all, inspiration of the Bible – remain scarcely explored by post-
critical theologians. Partly, also, theological dissatisfaction
arises from the way in which, in the absence of dogmatic
exposition of the nature of Scripture, other discourses quickly
acquire considerable profile. Extensive and elaborate use is
often made, for example, of philosophical accounts of the
nature of interpretation, literary theory, or the sociology of
texts, correlated rather loosely with doctrinal considerations
and often, in fact, assuming the lead voice. This is true even in
the initially promising recent explorations of the relation
between the notion of Holy Scripture and, on the one hand,
the practices of the ecclesial community, and, on the other

hand, the virtues of the Christian reader. For all their evident superiority to the abstract, historicist handling of the Bible which has so afflicted Christian theology, ecclesial or virtue-oriented accounts remain dogmatically underdeveloped, threaten to confuse 'church' and 'sociality', and often presuppose an Aristotelian anthropology which is not easy to coordinate with a Christian understanding of revelatory grace. By contrast, the essays here appeal much more directly to dogmatic categories in giving an account of Scripture and its readers. They suggest that topics such as canonicity or the nature of reading in the community of the church are to be approached as extensions of a Christian theological treatment of the saving self-communication of the triune God, in particular of the theology of Word and Spirit. Language about God's self-communication, they suggest, is the only really secure barrier against the de-eschatologizing of the Bible which historicism fostered and from which even much post-critical 'ecclesial' exegesis has yet to free itself.

A second theme is that of the place of Jesus in modern intellectual culture and, by consequence, in theological discourse about the church. One illuminating way of writing the history of modernity would be to envisage it as the story of the steady eclipse of belief in Jesus' presence – as the gradual erosion of confidence in the basic Christian conviction that, *sub specie resurrectionis,* everything looks different. As that conviction is eroded, and Jesus is no longer acknowledged as axiomatically and catholically real and true, then he is no longer the conditioning factor in all occurrence, but a contingent episode in the history of the world. Two essays – that on incarnation, and that on Jüngel's Christology – map some of the questions. In the course of a dogmatic reflection on the credal confession of the being of Jesus Christ, the first sketches a pathology of modern anxieties (methodological and substantive) about the doctrine of the incarnation. The second offers a reading of a major contemporary dogmatician who – *mirabile dictu* – finds himself inhibited by some of the same anxieties. The second pair of essays tries to show that, once Jesus is no longer considered as a presently operative and communicative figure but rather as inert and silent, other doctrinal areas expand to fill the gap vacated by his removal. Chief among the contenders for more space is ecclesiology, which can inflate itself to do work which in a more orderly dogmatics would be appropriated directly to the risen Jesus in his offices as prophet, priest and king. Both essays are exercises in 'negative ecclesiology', in that both try to win back to Christology territory which has been annexed by accounts of ministry, liturgical action, morals or spirituality; and thereby both make a claim about the permanent centrality of the divine Word (self-communicative presence) for an understanding of the church and its action.

The final theme is anthropological and ethical. A judicious Christian anthropology has to steer a tricky course between, on the one hand, modern inflation of anthropology into the *ratio essendi et cognoscendi* of all other Christian teaching, and, on the other hand, deconstructive postmodern repudiations of substantial and enduring human selfhood and agency. Part of what is involved in breaking free from the modern trajectory is the discipline of fashioning an account of human personhood thoroughly integrated into a trinitarian theology of God's saving self-manifestation. An extension of this is a dogmatic psychology which will inhibit the hypertrophy of a topic such as conscience by placing moral consciousness within a larger field of moral reality which is the space in which there takes place the drama of redemption. But a dogmatic anthropology or psychology, precisely because it is rooted in talk of the God who is creator, reconciler and perfecter, is *humane*. It testifies to the real character of human flourishing in fellowship with God, and so resists the dissolution of humanity by insisting that we are not a mere trace in the sand, but those made and remade by God for praise, love, hope and action.

Undergirding these papers are a conception of the task of Christian theology and a reading of the present situation in which that task is undertaken. Christian theology is rational speech about the Christian gospel. As *rational speech*, it is an attempt to articulate a set of responsible theological judgments. Such judgments are 'responsible' in the sense that they are intellectual (and therefore moral and spiritual) acts in which we struggle to order our thinking and speaking in response to reality, and so to think and speak truthfully. To understand the rational character of theology in this way is, of course, to enter into dispute with some dominant modern conventions, according to which rationality is a critical epistemological directive rather than an obedient following of given nature. That dispute is only tangentially engaged in these essays, but it is implicit in all that follows.[1] As rational speech *about the Christian gospel*, theology directs itself to the declaration which lies at the heart of Christian faith and common life, the announcement that in and as the man Jesus Christ, who is present in the power of the Spirit, God creates, reconciles and perfects all things. Set in the midst of the praise, repentance, witness and service of the people of God, theology directs the church's attention to the order of reality declared in the gospel and attempts responsibly to make it a matter of thought. Conceived in this way, Christian theology is not a spontaneous undertaking but ordered towards a *positum*. It takes its rise in an act done *to* the church rather than *by* the church; it does not attempt to run ahead of or peep behind that act; it does not consider itself competent to inquire into whether there is or ought to be such an act. It arises out of the devastatingly eloquent and gracious self-presence of God, by which it is endlessly astonished and to which it never ceases to turn in humility and hope.

What of the situation in which Christian theology goes about its business? All theology is occasional: bound up in its conception of its own calling is a certain reading of the circumstances into which it speaks. The term 'occasional' is much to be preferred to the more familiar 'contextual'. Talk of theology as 'contextual' readily suggests that contexts are given, transparent and self-evident to those who operate in them, and that

---

[1] For an attempt to explicate this understanding of theology, see J. Webster, *Theological Theology* (Oxford: Clarendon Press, 1998).

they require no theology for their elucidation; and it can also, more alarmingly, make context into a fate before which theological reflection is passive, to which it must adapt or reconcile itself if it wants to survive. At its best, of course, attention to 'context' can remind theology that there is no pure language of Zion, and that theology's conceptual equipment is borrowed from elsewhere. But at its worst it is a form of mental and spiritual laziness, an unwillingness to admit that theology must go about its own business if it is to speak prophetically and compassionately about the gospel to its neighbours. Much better, therefore, simply to speak of the 'occasions' towards which theology directs itself.

Theology is responsible for articulating a theological reading of these occasions. It needs to learn to interpret its present situation, not merely as a set of cultural norms or constraints or opportunities, but as an episode in the history of the gospel's dealing with humanity, as one further chapter in the history of holiness and its overcoming of disorder, wickedness and unbelief. This – the progress of the gospel through the occasions of human life – is theology's context, which is properly spiritual and therefore properly a matter for theological description. Yet the obstacles into which the theologian stumbles in trying to do just that – describe theology and its contexts theologically – are very considerable. Not only is there the resistance generated by the instinctive conservatism of the theological establishment (especially of the liberal establishment) but also the theologian encounters within him- or herself a resistance to the necessary losses sustained by those whom the gospel besieges. There is a certain temper of mind and soul from which the theologian must be set free, a sense of competence in the matter of the Christian faith, an inordinate and unstable desire for intellectual stimulus, the witty avoidance of the wounds which the truth inflicts on our self-sufficiency. Good dogmatics is a mode of holiness: chastened, unassuming, sanctified speech. It has nothing of genius about it; it is simply apostolic. And one of the fruits of apostolic holiness is coming to perceive where we are – in the history of grace, in the wake of the Spirit's presentation of Christ.

Recently British systematic theologians have sometimes given the impression of being rather comfortably self-congratulatory: twenty years ago, times were hard, whereas now there are grounds for confidence that the discipline is enjoying renewed vigour and prestige. I am hesitant about that judgment. That things have progressed since the wearisome days of doctrinal criticism is incontrovertible; a great debt of gratitude is owed to some skilful practitioners who laboured on with little encouragement. Yet – with a handful of exceptions – positive dogmatics is notable only by its absence. The shift in the last two decades has not been towards a recovery of the dogmatic task in and for and by the church, but largely a shift from critical scepticism towards a soft correlationism chastened by a bit of Barth, a sparkling but Christianly not very specific conversation which has lost the rough edges of the gospel. If one finds that one cannot follow this direction, the risk is of casting oneself in the role of a theological Ishmael: Genesis 16.12. The essays which follow are certainly sharply critical of much in which other theologians rejoice, and vigilant at points where others are cheerfully relaxed. All one can do is – following the example of the grand old man of Basel, or of those *ressourcement* theologians who pored over Migne for years looking for buried treasure – dig deeply and lovingly into the thoughts of the church thinkers of the past and above all into Holy Scripture, and say as clearly and vividly and generously as one can what one finds, in the hope that it may well prove to be just what church and culture really need.

SCRIPTURE

1

THE DOGMATIC LOCATION
OF THE CANON

Any attempt to locate the canon doctrinally must do so in the face of two powerful considerations, both of which have contributed to its mislocation. The first is that, as a consequence of the explanatory successes of the application of critical-historical and comparative methods, the Christian canon has been drawn firmly within the sphere of religious history. As with the theology of the Bible generally, so with the canon: once it comes to be viewed as part of the history of religions, the term 'holy' seems less and less appropriate. The success of such explanations, of course, depends not only on their intrinsic fruitfulness, nor even on acceptance, tacit or explicit, of the spiritual and intellectual basis of a culture devoted to critical inquiry. It also depends upon the second consideration, which lies deep within the history of modern Christian theology, namely the distortions introduced into Christian theology of Scripture in the post-Reformation era by its *dogmatic* mislocation. In crude, shorthand terms, the mislocation occurs when the Christian theology of Scripture is transplanted out of its proper soil – essentially, the saving economy of the triune God – and is made to do duty as a foundational doctrine. Scripture, and therefore the canon, share the same fate as the doctrine of revelation. Instead of being a consequential doctrine (consequential, that is, upon logically prior teaching about the prevenience of God in God's dealings with the creation), it shifts to becoming a relatively isolated piece of epistemological teaching. This process shifts the location of the doctrine, forcing it to migrate to the beginning of the dogmatic corpus and to take its place alongside, for example, philosophical arguments for the existence of God. And the process also modifies its content, as it becomes largely disconnected from its setting in trinitarian, pneumatological and ecclesial doctrine.

The extent to which this process is a natural result of the Reformation insistence upon *sola scriptura* is debatable; it is, I believe, more plausible to see it as the result of the abstraction of *sola scriptura* from the other Reformation exclusive particles *solus Christus, sola gratia* and *solo verbo* (all of which are extensions of the primary principle *solus Deus*), which, in effect, tied Reformation teaching about Scripture to a wider set of doctrinal materials and thereby ensured its integration into the scope of dogmatics. What is clear, nonetheless, is that as the canon is lifted out of the network of doctrines within terms of which it makes sense it becomes patent of naturalistic explanation, whether of the more traditional historical-critical variety or of a socio-political cast. Moreover, as I shall try to show, most recent attempts to reintroduce doctrinal description of the canon tend to repeat its mislocation by rendering 'canon' as an ecclesial concept, and operating with very minimal appeal to, for example, soteriology or pneumatology.

My suggestion, then, is that, if the canon is not to be seen as (at best) an arbitrary or accidental factor in Christian religious history or (at worst) an instrument of political wickedness, it requires careful dogmatic articulation. At the very least, this will involve appeal to a variety of doctrinal materials: an account of revelation as the self-communicative presence of the triune God; an account of the mediation of that self-communication through creaturely forms and activities ('means of grace'), including texts, which are annexed and sanctified by God; an account of the church, in particular, the doctrinal specification of the processes of 'canonization'; and an account of the sanctified or faithful reader of the canon.

The account which follows is frankly dogmatic. It assumes the truth of the church's confession of the gospel, regarding that confession as a point from which we move rather than a point towards which we proceed. Readers disposed to anxiety about the viability of such an exercise will find little here to still their hearts. *Theologia non est habitus demonstrativus, sed exhibitivus.* In the matter of the canon we are in the sphere of dogmatics: of faith, church, creed, prayer, holiness. Whether it is worth pitching one's tent in such a sphere is something which cannot be argued here; but we can at least try to exhibit some of the benefits of what at first looks very unpromising indeed.

II

Harnack spoke of the canon as a creative act: 'No greater creative act can be mentioned in the whole history of the Church than the formation of the apostolic collection and the assigning to it of a position of equal rank with the Old Testament'.[1] His words identify what remains a fundamental problem for any doctrinal account of the canon, namely, the 'natural' character of the canon and canonization. Four aspects of inquiry into the canon's 'natural history' can be distinguished.

1. First, *critical-historical* inquiry into the canon, using the same tools of critical analysis as were developed for looking at individual biblical texts, offers an account of the canon in terms of its *Entstehungsgeschichte*, that is, its religio-historical conditions of possibility, such as the church's response to Marcion. Historians differ as to whether such accounts are merely a necessary or, in fact, a sufficient explanation of the canon, but the effect of such inquiry remains the same: the canon is in some measure de-sacralized, and so shares the same fate as Harnack's other two basic features of catholic, ecclesiastical Christianity – creed and episcopacy: it comes to be seen as a contingent and in some measure arbitrary ecclesial process, and not as part of the providential ordering of the church. The doctrinal effect of such historicizing of the canon is, clearly,

---

[1] A. von Harnack, *History of Dogma* (New York: Dover, 1961), vol. 2, p. 62 n. 1.

further to erode confidence in the possibility of distinguishing the biblical writings from other texts by the application of the notion of 'inspiration'. Such historical accounts indicate that canonization involves a good deal more than the recognition of some property in the texts: to talk of texts as 'canonical' Scripture is not to identify a latent characteristic in certain writings which precedes canonization, but rather to indicate a status acquired through usage and eventual inclusion in the canon. With that admission, the boundary between inspired/non-inspired or apostolic/non-apostolic becomes very porous. In effect, the canon shifts from the category of 'Scripture' to that of 'tradition', precisely because Scripture and tradition are so difficult to distinguish with any clarity. And thereby the dogmatic principle of *sola scriptura* becomes increasingly difficult to operate.

2. Critical study of the biblical canon draws the canon into the sphere of religious history. Further impetus in this direction is given by *comparative approaches* to canon and canonization,[2] which have reinforced and refined the 'immanent' accounts of canonicity found in critical-historical studies of the formation of the biblical canon. Most of all, this has been achieved by specifying that 'canon' is a socio-cultural concept which describes the processes of religious societies rather than intrinsic attributes of texts. Thus, 'being scripture is not a quality inherent in a given text, or type of

[2] For an overview, see G. T. Sheppard, 'Canon', in M. Eliade, ed., *The Encyclopaedia of Religion* (New York: Macmillan, 1987), vol. 3, pp. 62–9. Two collections of texts are important here: J. Assman and A. Assman, eds., *Kanon und Zensur* (Munich: Fink, 1987); A. van der Kooij and K. van der Toorn, eds., *Canonization and Decanonization* (Leiden: Brill, 1998). In the last volume, the essays by J. Z. Smith ('Canons, Catalogues and Classics', pp. 295–311) and H. J. Adriaanse ('Canonicity and the Problem of the Golden Mean', pp. 313–30) are particularly fruitful; the collection also contains a very full annotated bibliography (pp. 435–506). See, further, J. Z. Smith, 'Sacred Persistence. Toward a Redescription of Canon', *Imagining Religion. From Babylon to Jonestown* (Chicago: University of Chicago Press, 1982), pp. 36–52; W. Cantwell Smith, *What Is Scripture? A Comparative Approach* (London: SCM Press, 1993); and K. W. Folkert's classic analysis 'The "Canons" of "Scripture"', in M. Levering, ed., *Rethinking Scripture. Essays from a Comparative Perspective* (Albany, NY: SUNY Press, 1989), pp. 170–9. P. J. Griffiths, *Religious Reading. The Place of Reading in the Practice of Religion* (Oxford: Oxford University Press, 1999), gives a sharply critical appraisal of some comparativist approaches.

text, so much as an interactive relation between that text and a community of persons'.[3] Talking of a text as 'Scripture' (and therefore as 'canonical') is not to describe the text but its place and use in a community. Hence, to elucidate the notion of Scripture we have to refer primarily to 'the universe and human life – with the texts as mediating, and in effect secondary'.[4] Crucially, this means that:

> *There is no ontology of scripture.* The concept has no metaphysical, nor logical, referent; there is nothing that scripture finally 'is' . . . [A]t issue is not the texts of scripture that are to be understood and about which a theory is to be sought, but the dynamic of human involvement with them . . . Scripture has been . . . a human activity: it has been also a human propensity, a potentiality. There is no ontology of scripture; just as, at a lower level, there is no ontology of art, nor of language, nor of other things that we human beings do, and are. Rather than existing independently of us, all these are subsections of the ontology of our being persons.'[5]

Though Cantwell Smith's concern is broader than canonicity, the application of what he has to say to canon is clear enough: the referent of 'canon' is modes of relation between texts and their religious users; no 'metaphysics' of canon is required, in the sense that no account need be offered of any transcendent divine action generating or guiding canonization. Canon is what Jonathan Smith calls human 'repertoire'.[6] In terms of the Christian canon this means, quite simply that:

> [t]here is no such thing as *the* canon. There are canons, each of them with normative claims which, as a matter of fact, are mostly conflicting with the claims of other canons. Consequently, a canon must be understood as a socio-cultural phenomenon.'[7]

Neither of these first two factors in the naturalization of the canon necessarily urges the abandonment of the canon; they merely

---

[3] W. Cantwell Smith, *What Is Scripture?*, p. ix.

[4] Ibid., p. 223.

[5] Ibid., p. 237.

[6] J. Z. Smith, 'Canons, Catalogues and Classics', p. 304.

[7] Adriaanse, 'Canonicity and the Problem of the Golden Mean', p. 327.

suggest that it may be explained as immanent within communal religious activity. Two other factors, though less directly connected to the study of biblical or religious texts, have a much more critical impact.

3. *Socio-political theorists of canon*[8] emphasize that a canon of texts is not simply a bearer of value (aesthetic or religious) but is at one and the same time a product of and a medium for social relations. Canon is 'cultural capital'; giving an account of a canon must therefore involve description of the circumstances and agents of its production, and of its 'institutional presentation'.[9] That is to say, an account of canon which failed to give attention to the socio-political and economic processes of the production and imposition of normative texts would be deficient. For Guillory (whose concern is with literary canons) this requires the devotion of critical attention to the school as the site of the canon's invention and reinforcement. 'Canonicity is not a property of the work itself but of its transmission, its relation to other works in a collocation of works – the syllabus in its institutional locus, the school.'[10] And so:

> what is required … is an analysis of the institutional location and mediation of such imaginary structures as the canon in order first to assess the real effects of the imaginary, and then to bring the imaginary itself under more strategic political control'.[11]

So far, little attention has been devoted by practitioners of the critical history of Christian doctrine to the analysis of the function of the biblical canon as a normative element in the social imaginary, although *Ideologiekritik* is now an established aspect of much biblical interpretation, whether new historicist or feminist.[12] Such lines of analysis are not unrelated to the work of earlier

---

[8] The most important text here is J. Guillory, *Cultural Capital. The Problem of Literary Canon Formation* (Chicago: University of Chicago Press, 1993).

[9] Ibid., p. ix.

[10] Ibid., p. 55.

[11] Ibid., p. 37.

[12] See D. Jobling and T. Pippin, eds., *Ideological Criticism of Biblical Texts* (Atlanta: Scholars Press, 1992); R. P. Carroll, 'An Infinity of Traces', *Journal of Northwest Semitic Languages* 21 (1995), pp. 25–43.

scholars (Marxsen or Werner, for example)[13] who argued that the canon, as an aspect of *Frühkatholizismus*, was part of the de-eschatologizing of Christianity and its settlement into normative forms. Recent application of theories of ideology to canonicity turn on more than simply a rather crude dichotomy of charismatic/institutional, and have a much more direct concern with the '*politics* of canonical violence'.[14] That is, the question to put to the text is (in the words of one of the few recent attempts to apply *Ideologiekritik* to the early development of Christian doctrine), 'In whose interest does this text work?', for:

> A surviving text is a successful text ... which means that it has served what turned out to be a successful interest. To understand it fully, we need to be aware of what it does not say, what it controverts, what it represses or suppresses'.[15]

And pursuing such questions means, of course, bidding farewell to the innocence of the canon; canon is poetics, and therefore politics, and therefore power.

4. If ideology critics dissolve the canon's givenness into strategies of power, postmodern repudiations of textual determinacy dissolve the canon into acts of reading – whether through one or other theory of reception, or, more radically, by abandoning the category of 'book' in favour of 'text' or 'intertext'. Both lines of critique assimilate the canon to power, but, rather than seeking political oversight of the social imaginary, postmodernism recommends a shift from the book as a stable totality, a presentation of normative authorial meaning, to the text as a shifting field of play:

> Tradition 'begins' with speech and 'ends' with writing. As 'The Ruler of Reality,' tradition regulates and regularizes by establishing a normative canon. A κανών is a measuring rod or a

---

[13] W. Marxsen, 'Das Problem des NT Kanons', *Neue Zeitschrift für Systematische Theologie und Religionsphilosophie* 2 (1960), pp. 144ff.; M. Werner, *The Formation of Christian Dogma* (London: Black, 1957), pp. 64ff.

[14] D. Jasper, *Readings in the Canon of Scripture. Written for Our Learning* (Basingstoke: Macmillan, 1995), p. 9.

[15] R. Williams, 'Doctrinal Criticism: Some Questions', in S. Coakley and D. Pailin, eds., *The Making and Remaking of Christian Doctrine. Essays in Honour of Maurice Wiles* (Oxford: Clarendon Press, 1993), p. 244.

rule. A rule, in turn, is a *regula*, which is a straight stick, bar, ruler, or pattern. A canon provides the rule by which to distinguish proper from improper and gives the standard against which to judge anomalies and measure transgressions. Though a tradition can, at least for a time, remain oral, a canon tends to be 'fixed' by writing. Canon and book, therefore, are closely related. Once agreed upon, the canon forms the book by which all other books are to be judged and furnishes the rule with which every 'lesser' work is measured. In short, the canon constitutes the masterpiece that rules the tradition. As such, it must be the paradigmatic work of a/The Master.[16]

Once, however, the static metaphysics of origin, intention, presence, 'text-in-itself' are repudiated, then 'canon' loses any force, and is dispersed, for:

> Without a founding origin and an organizing centre, no work can be a masterpiece. The codependence of texts precludes both the mastery of one text by another and the subservience of one text to another. Scriptural relativity breaks the rule of canon and disperses authoritative tradition. Insofar as canon and tradition extend the circle of the book, the end of one is the dissolution of the other. On the one hand, when the book is breached, canon explodes and tradition shatters. On the other hand, when the rule of canon is broken and the line of authority disrupted, the book disintegrates. With the unravelling of the book, canon, and tradition, scripture becomes free to drift endlessly.[17]

The force of all four lines of inquiry is to work against ideas of the canon as a durable *verbum externum* through which the stability of the church can be secured from without. The historicity of the canon, its naturalization or transposition into history, whether the history be that of antique religion, the dynamics of political and economic society or anarchic, undirected freedom, means that it comes to be seen as product, not norm. On the one hand, this attitude can be expressed as a

---

[16] M. C. Taylor, *Erring. A Postmodern A/theology* (Chicago: University of Chicago Press, 1984), p. 88.
[17] Ibid., p. 179.

critical relation to the canon, which is no longer viewed as bearing an irreducible authority but as a further object for transcendental inquiry. On the other hand, the changed relation can be expressed in terms of a sense that the canon is co-constituted by us; community tradition, or a humanly-generated economy of cultural commodities, and acts of reading and reception, are ingredients within the logic of canonicity. In the end, that is, the canon does not transcend us; we transcend the canon.

Where does this leave the possibility of a dogmatic portrayal of the canon?

III

One obvious response to the naturalization of the canon has been to accept it, abandon any claims to the canon's transcendental status, and envisage the canon as simply an immanent social resource for the construction of common meaning.

> The particular canon we have received is a matter of contingent fact ... But the recognition that its precise contours do not correspond to any set of determinable criteria should not lead us to suggest the abandonment or the modification of the canon as such.

For, first, 'the existence of an agreed canon helps to provide a common sensibility for the Christian community as a whole'; and, second,

> the canon's distinctive status enables it to stand apart in its historic singularity from the changing patterns of Christian belief, and so to serve as a potential source of prophetic correction against the ever-present danger of Christians being carried along uncritically by the beguiling streams of contemporary thought.[18]

[18] M. Wiles, 'Scriptural Authority and Theological Construction. The Limitations of Narrative Interpretation', in G. Green, ed., *Scriptural Authority and Narrative Interpretation* (Philadelphia: Fortress Press, 1987), pp. 53f. For further elaboration of this, see M. Wiles, 'The Uses of "Holy Scripture"', in *Explorations in Theology 4* (London: SCM Press, 1979), pp. 73–82. A similar account is offered in J. Barr, 'The Bible as a Document of Believing Communities', in *Explorations in Theology 7* (London: SCM Press, 1980), pp. 111–33.

Such accounts fail to satisfy for a couple of reasons. First, their proposal about the functioning of the canon, though correct in linking the canon to community formation, gives only the most abstract depiction of that link, a depiction whose generality is such that it could not count as a rich or persuasive account of how Christian believers view and use the canon in practice. 'Common sensibility' and (for example) 'the mind of Christ' are concepts of a different order. Second, these accounts do not provide any non-arbitrary reasons for the use of the canon by the church. But a canon which is *only* a useful accident, *only* tradition, cannot *rule*. Or, if it does rule, its rule is perilously exposed to the charge of – political – caprice.

An initially more fruitful, if in the end insufficient, way forward can be seen in a cluster of recent accounts of the canon which have sought to relocate the notions of 'canon' and 'canonicity' within a theological theory of ecclesial existence, thereby making 'canon' and 'community' correlative concepts. Though these accounts resist the drift to naturalism by retaining some aspects of theological language, the marked tendency to make ecclesiology *the* basic doctrine can introduce some of the dogmatic distortions found in nineteenth-century theologies of moral community, and can thereby find it hard to resist the steady move towards immanence.

An initial example is Charles Wood's admirable study of Christian hermeneutics, *The Formation of Christian Understanding*. Wood – rightly, in my judgment – argues against the domination of the Christian theory of interpretation by general hermeneutical principles, suggesting that Christian under-standing is 'an understanding whose criteria are informed by the particular aims and interests that motivate it'.[19] The crucial question for Wood is thus not 'What kind of text?' but 'What is the character of Christian understanding?' The effect of recasting the hermeneutical question in this way is, clearly, to shift the centre of gravity away from the text as a discrete entity,

---

[19] C. Wood, *The Formation of Christian Understanding. An Essay in Theological Hermeneutics* (Philadelphia: Westminister, 1981), p. 21.

and instead to draw attention to community *use*. 'Theological hermeneutics begins by asking what sorts of abilities constitute the possibility of the distinctively Christian use or uses of these texts, and then goes on to ask how these abilities are gained and strengthened.'[20] The real issue, therefore, is 'the connection between the text and its user or users'. Thus:

> It is crucial to identify the particular use or uses with which one is concerned, and then – recognising that 'understanding' always refers to the acquisition or possession of determinate, or at least determinable, abilities with regard to its object – to specify the sort of understanding at issue.'[21]

What is immediately striking in such an account is the lack of reference to divine action – to God's use of the text, or, perhaps, God's use of the church's use. None of what Wood says excludes the possibility of such reference. But a worry on this score may be sharpened when Wood goes on to note that Scripture only functions to disclose God 'when it is activated to do so', and that this activation 'depends to a large extent upon the interpreter's readiness to use scripture to that end'.[22] Wood's general proposal is, of course, well taken as a critique of the kind of transcendental hermeneutics in which interpretation is a function of abstractly conceived mentalist subjectivity, rather than an ability in a context. Nevertheless, it leaves relatively unexplored the question of the relation of the text to God, and precisely thereby it opens up a free space which can be filled by 'community'.

This last problem is especially acute in the strongly function-alist account of the canon offered by David Kelsey in his (aptly titled) *The Uses of Scripture in Recent Theology*, where he proposes that 'to call a set of writings "Christian canon" is an analytic judgment: To say "These writings are the Christian canon" is analytic in "This community is a Christian church"'.[23]

---

[20] Ibid.
[21] Ibid., pp. 22f.
[22] Ibid., p. 38.
[23] D. Kelsey, *The Uses of Scripture in Recent Theology* (London: SCM Press, 1975), p. 105.

Accordingly, for Kelsey the primary criterion for canonicity is *use*:

> In declaring just these writings 'canon' the church was giving part of a self-description of her identity: we are a community such that certain uses of scripture are necessary for nurturing and shaping our self-identity, and the use of 'just these,' i.e. 'canonical,' writings is *sufficient* for that purpose".[24]

On this basis, it is quite natural that the canon be seen as a function of community identity.

> To call [the biblical writings] 'canon' is to say that the writings, taken together, no matter what their diversity from one another, function *ensemble* when used in the common life of the church and serve as the sufficient occasion for that presence of God which preserves the church's identity as a single, integral, living reality. No matter how great its inner diversity, this set of writings is to be taken as mirroring in a wholeness of its own the unity of the church's own identity.[25]

Not only does this mean that canonicity is an attribute of Scripture derived from its ecclesial deployment rather than from its relation to the revelatory action of God. It also leads to the prioritizing of a particular understanding of canonicity. To speak of the canon on this account is to speak of the unity and integrity ascribed to a set of texts by a community engaged in the process of self-identification rather than of the normativity ascribed to those texts by their relation to an activity of God. 'Canon' advertises ascribed wholeness; and such an ascription is best understood, therefore, as 'a *policy* decision'.[26]

A third example is Rowan Williams's sophisticated restatement of a 'catholic' understanding of the inseparability of church and Scripture in 'The Discipline of Scripture'. The essay proposes that – over against 'closed' accounts of the interpretation of Scripture in which reading is merely a matter

[24] Ibid.
[25] Ibid., p. 106.
[26] Ibid., p. 177.

of passive reception of already constituted meaning – reading is properly 'dramatic' or 'diachronic'.

> The meanings in our reading, [he writes] are like the meanings in the rest of our experience, they are to be discovered, unfolded ... So long as our humanity remains unintelligible except as a life of material change, irreversible movement, it is unlikely – to say the least – that we could establish non-diachronic modes of reading as primary.[27]

Or again: 'Christian language takes it for granted ... that meanings are learned and produced, not given in iconic, ahistorical form. It grows out of a particular set of communal and individual histories, and its images and idioms are fundamentally shaped by this fact.'[28] And so:

> Christian interpretation is unavoidably engaged in 'dramatic' modes of reading: we are invited to identify ourselves in the story being contemplated, to re-appropriate who we are now, and who we shall or can be, in terms of the story. *Its* movements, transactions, transformation, become *ours* ... [A] dramatic reading means that our appropriation of the story is not a static relation of confrontation with images of virtue or vice, finished pictures of a quality once and for all achieved and so no longer taking time, but an active working through of the story's movement in our own time.[29]

'Dramatic' or 'diachronic' reading thus highlights both the *temporal* and the *active* character of our interpretation of texts; it is a matter of 'a complex of interwoven processes: a production of meaning in the only mode available for material and temporal creatures'.[30] The effect on the notion of 'canon' is twofold: first, (as with Kelsey) to construe canonicity as unity, and, second, to make it largely a function of community.

'Scripture' (Jewish as well as Christian) comes to exist as such in a

---

[27] R. Williams, 'The Discipline of Scripture', *On Christian Theology* (Oxford: Blackwell, 2000), p. 49.

[28] Ibid.

[29] Ibid., p. 50.

[30] Ibid., p. 55: a statement whose commitment to a certain ontology of history cannot be discussed here.

> community that says and does identifiable and distinctive things;
> that has some means of articulating a particular identity. The unity
> of Scripture has to do with how it becomes part of this articulation,
> how it establishes itself as a point of reference (a *canon*) for a
> community with a definite and perceptible historical unity. Its
> unifying themes are established according to what is understood as
> unifying the community.[31]

Williams is quick to point out that '[t]his is *not* to reduce its
unity to something decided upon by the community to suit
whatever happen to be its priorities';[32] but the grounds for this
assertion are opaque, and remain so without any extensive
discussion of – for example – the communicative presence of
the risen Christ or the activity of the Holy Spirit.[33]

What are we to make of these several attempts at re-stating
the canon, taken together? There is, doubtless, an immediate
attractiveness in giving a large role to ecclesiology – or, more
fitting, perhaps, ecclesiality – namely, that it is over questions of
the nature and activities of Christian communal life that
dogmatics would appear to have the greatest prospects of
rapprochement with the human historical sciences which have
done so much to erode the theological notion of the canon.
Deployed in a certain way – as an ontological *substratum* to
everything else which theology wants to say[34] – ecclesiality can
function as the point at which history, socio-cultural and
political theory, and theology can intersect. Church construed
as human community is patent of both historically immanent
and theological explanation. In terms of our present concern,
it appears to offer an idiom through which to rearticulate

---

[31] Ibid., pp. 55f.

[32] Ibid., p. 56.

[33] Some hints in this direction can be found in another essay in the same volume,
'Trinity and Revelation', pp. 131–47. And one should note the Christological
ramifications of Williams's remark: 'Christ is "produced" by the history of the
covenant people' (p. 58). Incarnation or immanence?

[34] On this see the very suggestive essay of C. Ernst, 'The Significance for
Ecclesiology of the Declaration on non-Christian Religions and the Decree on
Missions of Vatican II', *Multiple Echo* (London: Darton, Longman & Todd,
1979), pp. 137–48.

Christian claims about the canon without calling into question what have become established depictions of the canon as natural history.

And other advantages suggest themselves. Paying attention to the canon as an ecclesial concept may help extract a theological account of Scripture from the danger of giving too formal or juridical an account of the relation of the canon to the church by stressing that canonicity is best understood in terms of its function in 'establishing and governing certain networks of relationships'.[35] Moreover, such an emphasis is fittingly linked to a concern for 'regional' hermeneutics, that is, for an account of interpretation oriented, not to common human experience or universal theories of consciousness, but to the local practices of specific social-historical traditions.[36] And this is, in turn, companionable with recent application of the theory of virtue to interpretative activity, with its concern to identify the appropriate dispositions which the Christian reader of the canon finds exemplified in the public practices of the church.[37]

Yet problems remain. In dogmatic terms, the major deficiency is not that of setting the canon in relation to the life-practices of the church; there are, as I hope to show, strong doctrinal warrants for making this move (though only as a consequence of prior dogmatic commitments). The deficiency lies rather in the (largely implicit) notion of 'church' at work here. That notion is characteristically severely underdetermined by other features of the dogmatic corpus: Trinity, soteriology, pneumatology, sanctification. As a result, it often threatens to acquire a generic cast, especially when some of its force is derived from general observations about the functioning of texts in communities rather than from the

---

[35] S. E. Fowl, *Engaging Scripture. A Model for Theological Interpretation* (Oxford: Blackwell, 1998), p. 3.

[36] See the essay 'Hermeneutics in Modern Theology. Some Doctrinal Reflections' in the present volume.

[37] See here S. E. Fowl and L. G. Jones, *Reading in Communion. Scripture and Ethics in Christian Life* (Grand Rapids: Eerdmans, 1991).

internal content of Christian self-description. And, furthermore, the implicit notion of church tends to be remarkably modest in its appeal to language about divine action in describing the production, authorization and interpretation of the canon, and heavily freighted towards talk of the church's agency in deciding, ascribing, construing, using and the like. The question which hangs over all such language is whether it is more appropriate to speak of the people of the book or the book of the people.[38]

It is the presence of these problems which, in the end, distinguishes 'ecclesial' accounts of Scripture and the canon from those in mainstream Roman Catholic theology, despite their apparent similarity in correlating 'canon' and 'church'. In classical Roman Catholic theology, 'church' is a potently dogmatic concept, explicated in terms of the union of Christ as head to the church as his body. To talk of the canon as an 'ecclesial' concept or decision is, on this view, not to identify a feature of texts in communities, but a consequence of the 'pneumatic self-understanding of the church':

> In the unity of its life with that of Christ, the church participates in his showing of the saving work of God. The church's self-consciousness is in the end *the self-consciousness of the whole Christ*, head and body. Jesus Christ is the Lord of the church and therefore the Lord of Scripture ... Holy Scripture always refers to this pneumatic unity ... the church's growing consciousness of the

---

[38] There are many similarities between these ecclesial accounts of the canon and that exemplified in the nineteenth century by Martensen, who argues that 'the notion of a canon in Christianity, be it found in the Bible or in the church, points to a conscious mind *for* which it is a canon. The external canon points to an internal canon, by whose aid alone it can be correctly understood; and that internal canon is the *regenerated* Christian mind, in which the Spirit of God bears witness to the Spirit of man': H. Martensen, *Christian Dogmatics* (Edinburgh: T&T Clark, 1898), p. 41. Ecclesial accounts of canon are less individualist and more corporate: the regenerated Christian mind is the common mind of the church expressed in its practices; but the question remains as to whether such accounts are no less subjective (maybe more so, if they fail to deploy Martensen's language about the Spirit).

canon in the course of its history is growth in its *autopistia* led by the Holy Spirit.[39]

Roman Catholic rejection of *sola scriptura* in favour of Scripture *and* tradition is thus a corollary of a rejection of the ecclesiological implications of *solus Christus*, not a theory of how groups use texts in the course of forming and sustaining their identity. It is, in other words, a dogmatic, not a sociological, proposal.

The rest of this paper is given over to making an – *evangelisch* – dogmatic proposal about the canon. Dogmatic portrayal of the canon, I suggest, involves a good deal more than offering an ecclesial gloss to a sociology of texts and their uses. It involves an account of the communicative character of the saving economy of the triune God; it involves an account of the sanctification of texts in the complex processes of their history; it involves careful theological specification of the church's act of canonization; and it involves an account of the work of God in shaping the reader of the canon. Like the dogmatic notion of Scripture of which it is a corollary, canon is a plausible notion only within the setting of a range of doctrinal material, each part of which is needed if distortions or misapprehensions are not to creep in. As William Abraham puts it, the notion of canon presupposes 'a complex theological vision of creation and redemption'.[40] We turn to exhibit some aspects of that vision.

IV

An account of the canon begins with an account of revelation. Fruitful exposition of this doctrine[41] depends upon successful

---

[39] N. Appel, *Kanon und Kirche. Die Kanonkrise im heutigen Protestantismus als Kontroverstheologisches Problem* (Paderborn: Verlag Bonifacius-Drückerei, 1964), pp. 376f.

[40] W. Abraham, *Canon and Criterion in Christian Theology. From the Fathers to Feminism* (Oxford: Clarendon Press, 1998), p. 1.

[41] Properly speaking, revelation is not a 'doctrine', and certainly not a separate dogmatic *locus* (its separation is, in fact, part of the pathology of modern theology). Appeal to revelation is more like a *modus operandi* which pervades the entire dogmatic corpus, and which is a corollary of other primary doctrines (notably, the doctrines of Trinity and salvation).

coordination of a number of concepts and practices. The plausibility of the doctrine of revelation, that is, is a function not only of (for example) a coherent conception of divine action, but also of other factors which furnish the criteria, both intellectual and practical, of such coherence. Hence, an effective doctrine of revelation will be one which is fittingly integrated with more primary Christian doctrines. It will also be one which requires the existence of social traditions – the church – within which appeal to such a doctrine is operative and in which it is expected to carry some weight. And it will be one not unconnected to a certain temper on the part of the theologian, an intellectual and spiritual disposition to the utility of such appeal. Only when all these factors – dogmas, communal context, dispositions – are successfully brought together will the doctrine achieve fruitfulness, plausibility and effectiveness. And the absence of any one factor will in some measure disable the doctrine and its use.[42]

For the purposes of the present argument, our concern is with the fitting integration of the doctrine of revelation with other doctrines as a backcloth to an account of the canon. Theological talk of divine revelation is a corollary of other pieces of Christian teaching; it seeks to identify the consequences for our knowledge of God of the fact that, as Father, Son and Spirit, God freely discloses his being and ways to his creatures as part of the saving economy of divine mercy. At the outset this means that a Christian understanding of revelation will be concerned with the *identity* of the self-manifesting God. Only on the basis of an apprehension of God's identity can questions of the mode of revelation be answered with the right kind of specificity; inattention to the identity of the revealer, and especially inattention to the triune character of that identity, leads quickly to the woodenly deistic language of

---

[42] This is why certain kinds of philosophical defence of the doctrine of revelation, however sophisticated and even incontrovertible their argumentation, strike the dogmatician as theologically crude, even beside the point; they prove the wrong thing, or, perhaps, the right thing in the wrong way, and so misshape the doctrine.

causality which has so afflicted accounts of revelation, biblical inspiration and the canon.

What is required, therefore, is a trinitarian and soteriological account of revelation as the context for talk of the canon. At the heart of such an account is the proposal that revelation is that differentiated action of Father, Son and Spirit in which God establishes saving fellowship with humanity and so makes himself known to us. Revelation is the free work of God in which the mystery of God's will is made manifest and generates the knowledge and obedience of faith. As divine *self*-manifestation, revelation is not merely the communication of arcane information, as if God were lifting the veil on some reality other than himself and indicating it to us. Revelation is an event or mode of relation;[43] it is God's self-presentation to us. As such, its agent is the triune God himself. In revelation, God is outgoing and communicative; revelation is God's eloquence, God's 'speaking out'. The location of this eloquent self-presentation is the history of God with us. That history is the history of the acts in which God establishes saving fellowship with his creatures. It is a history of *fellowship* because at the centre of the history is 'God with us'; it is a history of *saving* fellowship because it is a history which triumphs over the opposition to fellowship with God which is sin. Revelation is therefore reconciliation; indeed, reconciliation is the more comprehensive concept for what is being talked of by revelation.[44] Saving fellowship is communicative fellowship, in which we come to know the agent of revelation who is also the content of revelation: Father, Son and Spirit. As Father, God is the root or origin of revelation as saving self-manifestation: in him is grounded revelation's sheer gratuity and sovereign freedom. As the incarnate, crucified and glorified Son, God is the agent

---

[43] Over against Francis Watson's argument in 'Is Revelation an "Event"?', *Modern Theology* 10 (1994), pp. 383–99, I am unconvinced that 'event' is 'a non-relational term with no particular application to the sphere of human relations' (p. 385). Relations are a history; history is event.

[44] See S. Williams, *Revelation and Reconciliation. A Window on Modernity* (Cambridge: Cambridge University Press, 1995).

through whom the saving history of God with us is upheld against all opposition and denial. As Spirit, God is the agent of revelation's perfection, its being made real and effective in the community of the church as the reconciled assembly of the saints. In its entire sweep, from its generation to its fulfilment, revelation is a work of grace.

Scripture, and therefore the canon, are a function of *Deus dixit*, trinitarianly construed as that complex economy of salvation which originates in God's self-knowledge and has its *telos* in the reconciliation of all things. Scripture and therefore the canon are ordered towards this economy; they are elements in a dynamic and purposive field of relations between the triune God and his creatures.[45] This means, accordingly, that Scripture and its properties, including canonicity, can only be rightly apprehended as an item in this economy. Separated from that context, it becomes reified into an independent entity whose nature and operations can be grasped apart from the network of relations in which it is properly located. And like other historical realities within that economy – temple, cult, kingship, sacraments, order – reification means distortion, for, like those other realities, Scripture has its being in its reference to the activity of God. If that reference is damaged or distorted, its true character is obscured. Such damaging of the reference of Scripture to the divine economy of salvation was one of the chief results of the gradual assimilation of Scripture into theological epistemology in the post-Reformation period; and it has been brought to its conclusion in the steady drive towards nominalist accounts of Scripture implicit within both the use of historical-critical methods and postmodern dissolution of the metaphysics of divine discourse.

There are particular implications here for doctrinal reflection on the canon. Unless it is set in the larger structure of divine action and its creation of human response which we call revelation, 'canon' can become *simply* 'rule'; its normative

---

[45] For what follows, see T. F. Torrance, 'The Deposit of Faith', *Scottish Journal of Theology* 36 (1983), pp. 1–28.

status becomes its own property, rather than a consequence of its place in the divine economy. Above all, reference to divine action falls away, the canon becomes the textualization of revelation, and the substance of revelation is resolved into 'a system of truths or a set of normative doctrines and formulated beliefs'.[46] But as a function of revelation, the canon is not merely list or code; it is a specification of those instruments where the church may reliably expect to encounter God's communicative presence, God's self-attestation. It is normative because of what it presents or, better, indicates (this is part of what it means to have 'apostolicity' as the criterion for inclusion in the canon). Neither revelation nor the canon abolish the mystery of God's freedom, which remains beyond codification. *Because* it is a function of *deus revelatus*, the canon is also a function of *deus absconditus*.[47] Because in revelation God remains hidden – that is, because God's self-communication is his making present of the sheer incomprehensible gratuity of his being and act – a theological understanding of the canon must always be demarcated from an account of non-referential cultural norms. Thus the centre of a theology of the canon must be an account of the action of Father, Son and Spirit, 'the waving hand which imperiously waves the rod, the canon'.[48]

V

The canon is a list of texts. Texts are always, as they say, 'dirty', never ideal; they are produced and authorized by human agents; they are read, and therefore misread. A dogmatic account of the canon, however, may rather easily forget the sheer humanity of the canonical texts and the processes of which they form part. The transcendentalist accounts of the biblical writings associated with certain theologies of divine

[46] Ibid., p. 3.
[47] Cf. G. Siegwalt, 'Le canon biblique et la révélation', *Le christianisme, est-t-il une religion du livre?* (Strasbourg: Faculté de théologie protestante, 1984), p. 46.
[48] K. Barth, *The Göttingen Dogmatics. Instruction in the Christian Religion*, vol. 1 (Grand Rapids: Eerdmans, 1991), p. 57.

inspiration are a case in point, in that they struggle to retain a sense that the texts of which they speak are just that: *texts*, authored, embedded in the murky traditions and practices of religious groups, inescapably tied to the history of books and their making and reception, and (in the case of the canon in its later history) of the making of knowledge through books.[49]

In dogmatic terms, the danger of failing to reckon with the naturalness of the canonical texts is close to hand whenever it is thought that the only way to safeguard those texts' relation to revelation is by denying their naturalness, and instead proposing an immediate relation between God and the texts. Used in this way, θεόπνευστια as it were short-circuits all historical processes. What is problematic in such accounts is not that the notion of inspiration requires appeal to concepts of divine agency no longer available to us: their purported unavailability is not to be attributed to their rational indefensibility but to a coarsened and cramped notion of rationality.[50] The problem is more a metaphysical problem, a problem about the ontology of texts which perform a function in the divine communicative economy. Post-Reformation accounts of inspiration often fell into the trap of materialism, making the texts of the canon into a single quasi-divine entity which – despite all appearances – does not have a natural history worth speaking of. These kinds of accounts of the texts of the canon are similar to crude notions of eucharistic transubstantiation, in that both assume that material, historical realities can only reliably mediate God if they somehow take on divine properties or even participate in the divine being.

---

[49] For general historical materials here, see B. M. Benedict, *Making the Modern Reader. Cultural Mediation in Early Modern Literary Anthologies* (Princeton: Princeton University Press, 1996); R. Chartier, *The Culture of Print. Power and the Uses of Print in Early Modern Europe* (Princeton: Princeton University Press, 1989); idem, *The Order of Books. Readers, Authors and Libraries in Europe between the Fourteenth and the Eighteenth Centuries* (Cambridge: Polity Press, 1993); A. Johns, *The Nature of the Book. Print and Knowledge in the Making* (Chicago: University of Chicago Press, 1998). On Christian texts, see, for example, H. Y. Gamble, *Books and Readers in the Early Church* (New Haven: Yale University Press, 1995).

[50] And besides, we routinely use such language to talk about sacraments, without too much embarrassment or scruple.

This sort of false ontology of canonical texts can be overcome by spelling out the ontological implications of talk of the canon as a 'witness' or 'means of grace'. At the core of both these notions is an assertion that the texts of the canon are human realities annexed by divine use. By emphasizing that the function of the texts is the clue to their ontology, these notions shift out of the quasi-materialist idiom of those accounts which are dominated by the concept of inspiration. Crucially, however, it is divine, not human or churchly, use which has priority in determining the ontology of the canonical texts. In short: the texts of the canon are human communicative acts which are assumed into the economy of revelation and reconciliation.

On this basis, we may return to Wilfred Cantwell Smith's assertion that 'there is no ontology of scripture',[51] with its implication that the term 'canon' does not draw attention to any properties of the texts so listed. It is true that there are not natural properties possessed by these texts and no others which in and of themselves lead to canonization. But this does not mean that the term 'canon' is purely adverbial, a way of advertising community usage. Rather, recognition of canonicity is recognition of those properties which the texts have acquired as a result of their annexation into the communicative activity of Father, Son and Spirit. The texts *are* that which they are appointed to become, namely instrumental means of gracious divine action. The being of the canonical texts is determined by their divine use.[52]

Alongside talking of the canonical texts as 'means of grace', we might also make use of the language of 'sanctification' to indicate that the texts are segregated by a divine decision to play a role in the divine self-manifestation. To speak of

---

[51] W. Cantwell Smith, *What Is Scripture?*, p. 237.

[52] Because of this, the category of 'canon' might be said to function analogously to the category of 'genre' (see here K. Vanhoozer, *Is There a Meaning in This Text? The Bible, the Reader, and the Morality of Literary Knowledge* [Leicester: Apollos, 1998], p. 349). To say that a text is of a certain genre is, in part, to say that it is to be read in such-and-such a way because it *requires* so to be read. Genre is, of

canonicity as sanctification is to affirm both that these texts are natural human historical entities and that they occupy a distinctive place and perform a distinctive role in the economy of salvation. Holiness is properly an incommunicable divine attribute; no created reality, whether person or material object, is intrinsically holy, because God alone, not the creature, is holy. The holiness of any creaturely reality is thus acquired *ab extra*, imputed to that reality by the election of God through which it is separated for a particular divine purpose. The holiness of people, objects and institutions is always therefore *sanctitas aliena*, a fruit of God's own *sanctitas positiva* in its external orientation. Accordingly, the holiness of the biblical canon is acquired, and indicates the use of the canonical texts by God as an instrument of self-attestation. 'Sanctification' here is used to cover the entire range of processes of which the text is the centre: processes of production (including tradition and redaction history); processes of canonization; and processes of interpretation. Sanctified in this way, the canonical texts are, then, a field of divine activity.

As a confession of a sanctifying work of God, the canonization of certain texts means that those texts are not of the same order as other speech-acts of the church. A confession of canonicity is an acknowledgment that – unlike homiletic, liturgical or theological speech, for example – these texts are not merely immanent to the culture of the Christian community. They have, as we shall come to see, a certain 'over- againstness'.

---

course, not simply an intrinsic characteristic of a text, but also a function of the construal of the text by readers. But those construals (if they are *construals* and not simply the rewriting of the text) are not wholly independent of texts, which contain features which shape the readers' reading. Canonical status, likewise, is not merely a textual property. This is especially the case because one of the features to which the category of canon draws attention, namely, the unity of disparate texts, is by definition not something which can be a property of any one of the texts so collected. Canonical status is partly a construal. But, crucially, as we shall see in the next section, 'construal' in the case of the Christian canon is best understood as recognition of divine use rather than as a proposal for readerly deployment. To view a text as an instance of the 'genre' of canonical writings is therefore to affirm that text's place in a wider soteriological framework which offers the key to its being.

Canonized texts have authority. A canon is thus more than a list or repertoire; talk of the canon is not only enumeration but also subjugation under and responsibility towards a norm. The norm is not, of course, merely statutory or legislative; its force is ultimately a function of the canon as means of grace. And its effect is, therefore, to indicate that all other speech of the church is not arbitrary or sheerly creative, but *normed*. As Barth put it:

> With its acknowledgment of the presence of the Canon the Church expresses the fact that it is not left to itself in its proclamation, that the commission on the ground of which it proclaims, the object which it proclaims, the judgment under which its proclamation stands and the event of real proclamation must all come from elsewhere, from without, and very concretely from without, in all the externality of the concrete Canon as a categorical imperative which is also historical, which speaks in time.[53]

VI

We may sum up the argument so far with some words from a magisterial essay by T. F. Torrance:

> Jesus Christ is God's self-address to man, but this self-address in order to achieve its end had to penetrate, take form and domicile itself within the address of man to man, as the Word of Christ abiding among men. The reciprocity established between God and man in Jesus Christ had to create room for itself within the reciprocities of human society, and the Word of God which had come 'plumb down from above' had to deploy itself in the horizontal dimensions of human existence in order to continue its speaking and acting throughout history. This involved the formation of a nucleus within the speaker-hearer relations of men, corresponding to and grounded in the communion between God and man embodied in Jesus Christ, as the controlling basis among believers for the extended communication of the Word of God, and the translation of the self-witness of Christ into witness to Christ,

---

[53] K. Barth, *Church Dogmatics* I/1 (Edinburgh: T&T Clark, 1975), p. 101.

answering the normative pattern of His obedient humanity, as the specific form for the proclamation of God's Word to all men.[54]

What kind of dogmatic depiction is required of those 'reciprocities of human society' which we call the act of canonization? What doctrine of the church is entailed by what has been indicated so far?

The Reformed theologian G. C. Berkouwer is quite correct, I believe, to state that the central issue in this matter (forced upon theology with fresh energy by historical accounts of the canon) is 'the relationship between the canon as both norm and authority and the human considerations that can be discerned in the history of the canon'.[55] There can be no recourse to denials of the element of human decision-making in the process of canonization. To make such a move would not only idealize or spiritualize the canon in the way that older theories of inspiration often threatened to do, but also deny what was proposed in the previous section: that it really is human texts and human textual activity which are sanctified by God, that human activity includes those processes to which we refer in shorthand terms as 'canonization'.[56] What is needed, by contrast, is a theological account of the church's action at this point; we need to give a dogmatic answer to the question of 'the nature of the human activity which can be denoted as the "accepting," the *recipere* of the canon'.[57] Such an answer will provide both a general dogmatic picture of the landscape within which that decision takes place, and a more precise, focussed depiction of the act itself.

In portraying the larger field which encompasses this decision of the church, it is very important not to begin with the church or with the texts of the Bible. Taking up a hint

[54] T. F. Torrance, 'The Word of God and the Response of Man', *God and Rationality* (Oxford: Oxford University Press, 1971), pp. 151f.

[55] G. C. Berkouwer, *Holy Scripture* (Grand Rapids: Eerdmans, 1975), p. 70.

[56] It is, of course, important, not to be beguiled into thinking of canonization as a single event or decision: it is more a muddled set of interwoven processes.

[57] Berkouwer, *Holy Scripture*, p. 72.

of Schmaus', Siegwalt properly argues that in the canon we are not dealing with a 'material principle' (*Sachprinzip*) but a 'personal principle' (*Personprinzip*), such that the crucial issue to be addressed is: 'How does God constitute himself . . . that is to say, pose or impose himself (reveal himself) to human awareness in a way which creates faith?'[58] The direction in which theology must move here is thus 'From God to the canon . . . put differently: *from the principium essendi to the principium cognoscendi.*'[59] Moving in this direction will involve depicting the church's act out of Christology and pneumatology.

Canonization, first, is to be understood in terms of the church's character as assembly around the self-bestowing presence of the risen Christ. In particular, this act of the church is enclosed within the prophetic presence and activity of Jesus Christ. The primary speech-act which takes place within the church and from which all other churchly speech-acts derive is Jesus Christ's own self-utterance. That self-utterance is mediated through the language of prophetic testimony to which Scripture bears witness and which then forms the basis and norm of the church's public speech. But it is all-important to emphasize that this mediation does not mean that Jesus Christ is replaced as speaker by some human text or official, or that he is mute until the church speaks – any more than the mediation of the *beneficia Christi* through sacraments means that Jesus Christ's saving work is inert until sacramentally realised, or that it is the church's sacramental action which renders Christ present and effective.

> [I]n the apostles as the receiving end of His revealing and recon-ciling activity, Jesus Christ laid the foundation of the Church which He incorporated into Himself as His own Body, and permitted the Word which He put into their mouth to take the form of procla-mation answering to and extending His own in such a way that it became the controlled unfolding of His own revelation within the mind and language of the apostolic foundation.[60]

[58] Siegwalt, 'Le canon biblique', p. 42.
[59] Ibid., p. 44.
[60] Torrance, 'The Word of God and the Response of Man', p. 152.

An account of the canon and canonization is therefore an account of the extension of Christ's active, communicative presence through the commissioned apostolic testimony. And, moreover, an account of the church's canonizing acts has to be rooted in the facts that the church is properly a hearing church before it is a speaking church, and that even its speech, when it is properly apostolic, is always contingent upon and indicative of a prior speech-act. Its speech is generated and controlled by Christ's self-utterance.

> [T]here exists prior to and above and after every *ego dico* and *ecclesia dicit* a *haec dixit Dominus*; and the aim of Church proclamation is that this *haec dixit Dominus* should prevail and triumph, not only before, above and after, but also *in* every *ego dico* and *ecclesia dicit*.[61]

Second, therefore, if the church's speech is governed by the self-communication of Christ, the church's acts of judgment (its 'decisions') are governed by the Holy Spirit who animates the church and enables its perception of the truth. The role of pneumatology is primary to 'de-centring' the church's act of canonization, in two ways. Talk of the Spirit is a means of identifying the providential activity of God in the history of the Christian community, including the history of its relation to and treatment of the biblical texts.

> We should [wrote Schleiermacher] conceive of the Spirit as ruling and guiding in the thought-world of the whole Christian body just as each individual does in his own ... [T]he faithful preservation of the apostolic writings is the work of the Spirit of God acknowledging his own products.[62]

And talk of the Spirit is also a means of identifying that the perception of canonicity derives not simply from the natural *sensus communis* of the church but from the charismatic gift of

---

[61] K. Barth, *Church Dogmatics* I/2 (Edinburgh: T&T Clark, 1956), p. 801. Cf. O. Weber, *Foundations of Dogmatics*, vol. 1 (Grand Rapids: Eerdmans, 1981), p. 249.

[62] F. Schleiermacher, *The Christian Faith* (Edinburgh: T&T Clark, 1928), p. 602; cf. I. Dorner, *A System of Christian Doctrine*, vol. 4 (Edinburgh: T&T Clark, 1882), p. 247.

'the sense for the truly apostolic'.[63] In this light, what description is to be offered of the 'great and meritorious act' of canonization?

> I wittingly pass over what they teach on the power to approve Scripture. For to subject the oracles of God in this way to men's judgment, making their validity depend upon human whim, is a blasphemy unfit to be mentioned.[64]

> [A] most pernicious error widely prevails that Scripture has only so much weight as is conceded to it by the consent of the church. As if the eternal and inviolable truth of God depended upon the decision of men![65]

> That it is the proper office of the Church to distinguish genuine from spurious Scripture, I deny not, and for this reason, that the Church obediently embraces whatever is of God. The sheep hear the voice of the shepherd, and will not listen to the voice of strangers. But to submit the sound oracles of God to the Church, that they may obtain a kind of precarious authority among men, is blasphemous impiety. The Church is, as Paul declares, founded on the doctrine of Apostles and Prophets; but these men speak as if they imagined that the mother owed her birth to the daughter.[66]

Calvin's well-known objection to one interpretation of Augustine's dictum that 'I should not believe the gospel except as moved by the authority of the catholic church'[67] is partly, of course, an objection to a certain construal of the authority of the church. But there is something deeper here: what Calvin fears is that to assert that Scripture takes its approbation from the church is radically to misinterpret the character of the church's act with respect to the canon. It is not that he denies that the church does, indeed, 'approve' Scripture, but more

---

[63] Schleiermacher, *The Christian Faith*, p. 603.

[64] J. Calvin, *Institutes of the Christian Religion*, IV.9.xiv, J. T. McNeill, ed. (Philadelphia: Westminister Press, 1960), p. 1178.

[65] Ibid., I.7.i (p. 75).

[66] J. Calvin, 'The True Method of Giving Peace to Christendom and of Reforming the Church', *Tracts and Treatises in Defence of the Reformed Faith*, vol. 3 (Edinburgh: Oliver & Boyd, 1958), p. 267.

[67] Augustine, *Contra epistolam Manichaei quam vocant fundamenti* v.

that such an act of approval is, properly understood, a receptive rather than an authorizing act. Hence two features of the church's act of approval are of critical importance for Calvin. First, it is derived from the Spirit's presence in the church, and therefore by no means autonomous. 'They mock the Holy Spirit,' Calvin says, 'when they ask: ... Who can persuade us to receive one book in reverence but to exclude another, unless the church prescribe a sure rule for all these matters?'[68] Hence his development of the doctrine of the *testimonium internum Spiritus Sancti* as a pneumatological replacement for the idea of ecclesial approbation. But, second, the church's act with respect to the canon is an act of faithful *assent* rather than a self-derived judgment. The language of discipleship is not incidental here: affirming the canon is a matter of the church 'obediently embracing' what comes from God, or of the sheep hearing the shepherd's voice; that is, it is an act of humble affirmation of and orientation towards what is already indisputably the case in the sphere of salvation and its communication in human speech.

> [W]hile the church receives and gives its seal of approval to the Scriptures, it does not thereby render authentic what is otherwise doubtful or controversial. But because the church recognizes Scripture to be the truth of its own God, as a pious duty it unhesitatingly venerates Scripture.[69]

Once again: none of this is a denial that canonization is the church's act; it is simply an attempt to specify what *kind* of act. The problem with naturalistic accounts of canonization is not that they show that establishing the canon is a matter of policy, but that – like Calvin's opponents – policy becomes arbitrary *poiesis*: whim, judgment, decision, rather than normed compliance. How may this act of compliant judgment be more closely described? Four characteristics can be identified.

First, the church's judgment is an act of confession of that

---

[68] Calvin, *Institutes of the Christian Religion*, I.vii.1 (p. 75).
[69] Ibid., I.vii.2 (p. 76).

which precedes and imposes itself on the church (that is, the *viva vox Jesu Christi* mediated through the apostolic testimony) and which evokes a Spirit-guided assent. The church's 'decision' with respect to the canon is thus 'simultaneously its acknowledgement of something which it is receiving from an authority over it'.[70] Only in a secondary sense is canonization an act of selection, authorization or commendation on the church's part, for

> it is not for us or for any man to constitute this or that writing as Holy Writ, as the witness to God's revelation, to choose it as such out of many others, but ... if there is such a witness and the acceptance of such a witness, it can only mean that it has already been constituted and chosen, and that its acceptance is only the discovery and acknowledgment of this fact.[71]

The 'decision' of the church is not a matter of pure *arbitrium*, but of *arbitrium liberatum*. Put differently: this decision has noetic but not ontological force, acknowledging what Scripture is but not making it so.[72]

Second, this act of confession, the church's judgment with respect to the canon, is an act of submission before it is an act of authority. This is because the authority of the church is nothing other than its acknowledgment of the norm under which it stands. 'The Church has exactly as much authority as it exercises obedience.'[73] Robert Jenson's recent and rather startling account of the canon falls at just this point: it fails to give sufficient theological specificity to the notion of 'decision'.

> The canon of Scripture ... is ... a dogmatic decision of the church. If we will allow no final authority to churchly dogma, or to the organs by which the church can enunciate dogma, there can be no canon of Scripture. The slogan *sola scriptura, if* by that is meant 'apart from creed, teaching office, or authoritative liturgy', is an oxymoron.[74]

---

[70] Weber, *Foundations of Dogmatics*, vol. 1, p. 251.
[71] Barth, *Church Dogmatics* I/2, p. 473.
[72] For this distinction, see Berkouwer, *Holy Scripture*, p. 78.
[73] Weber, *Foundations of Dogmatics*, vol. 1, p. 251.
[74] R. Jenson, *Systematic Theology*, vol. 1 (Oxford: Oxford University Press, 1997), pp. 27f.

But does not this subvert the very affirmation it seeks to make, by construing the church's act of judgment as 'a historically achieved commendation by the church as community to the church as association of persons',[75] and not as an act of deference to that which moves the judgment of the church from without? And how may the church resist its persistent desire to be in monologue with itself unless its 'authoritative' decision with respect to the canon is its avowal of a norm beneath which it already stands and beneath which it can only stand if it is to perceive the truth?

Third, as an act of confession and submission, the act of canonization has a *backward* reference. Through it, the church affirms that all truthful speech in the church can proceed only from the prior apostolic testimony. Canonization is recognition of apostolicity, not simply in the sense of the recognition that certain texts are of apostolic authorship or provenance, but, more deeply, in the sense of the confession that these texts are annexed to the self-utterance of Jesus Christ. The canon and the apostolicity (and so the apostolic succession) of the church are inseparable here. 'The apostolic succession of the Church must mean that it is guided by the Canon.'[76] The wider ecclesiological point – so easily obscured in ecclesiologies which take their cues from socio-historical depictions of the immanent dynamics of communities – is that the church and all its acts are *ostensive*, pointing beyond and behind themselves to that which transcends and precedes them. Thus

> [t]he canonic decision of the Church is essentially its confession of the norm already given it, the standard by which it was prepared to let itself be measured ... The canon is an expression of the fact that the Church is only in reference backward actually the Church.[77]

Fourth, as an act of confession, submission and retrospection, the church's judgment with respect to the canon is its pledging of itself to be carried by this norm in all its actions.

[75] Ibid., p. 28.
[76] Barth, *Church Dogmatics* I/1, p. 104.
[77] Weber, *Foundations of Dogmatics*, vol. 1, p. 252.

Canonization is commitment to operate by a given norm, and thereby to have speech and action mastered by that norm. In a very real sense, the canon spells the end of free speech in the church, if by free speech we mean mere *Willkür*. The canon means obligation to appeal to the canon and be ruled by it in such a way that the freedom of the norm is not transgressed but kept in view at every moment as the norm is applied and operated. One consequence here is that the church's *use* of the canon has a distinctively passive character (not usually stated with any clarity in much talk of the 'uses of Scripture'). In an influential essay, Kendall Folkert drew a distinction between a canon of texts which is carried by other religious activity, 'present in a tradition principally by the force of a vector or vectors', and a canon of texts which is the carrier of other religious activities, that is, 'normative texts that are more independently and distinctively present within a tradition ... and which themselves often function as vectors'.[78] A Christian account of the canon is of the latter variety, because canonicity is not a function of use but use a function of canonicity (which is itself a function of divine approbation and use). Affirmation of the canon is thus a commitment to allow all the activities of the church (most of all, its acts of worship, proclamation and ruling) to be as it were enclosed by the canon. Worship, proclamation and ruling do not *make use* of the canon, as if it were a catalogue of resources through which the church could browse and from which it could select what it considered fitting or tasteful for some particular occasion; rather, they are acts which are at all points shaped by the canon and what it sets before the church.

Taken together, these four considerations suggest that, theologically construed – construed, that is, with an eye to its place in the history of the saving self-communication of the triune God – the church's act of canonization is properly passive, a set of human activities, attitudes and relations that refer beyond themselves to prevenient divine acts of speaking

---

[78] Folkert, 'The "Canons" of "Scripture"', p. 173.

and sanctifying. For all the historical, human character of the church's judgment and its emergence from within the common life of Christian communities, there can be no question of the 'mutually constitutive reciprocity' of church and canon,[79] but only of the former's acknowledgment that the latter mediates the apostolic gospel. Like any other element in the church – oversight, service, proclamation, prayer, sacraments, fellowship, witness – the canon is a matter of grace, of a divine promise attached to a creaturely reality. And like all those elements, the canon, too, is ' a playground of human self-will'; but it is also 'the sphere of the lordship of Christ', and so

> If we believe that the Lord is mightier than the sin which indis-
> putably reigns in the Church, if we believe that He is the victor
> in the struggle against grace which is indisputably widespread even
> in the Church, then we can count on it that a genuine knowledge
> and confession in respect of the Canon, and therefore a knowledge
> and confession of the genuine Canon, is not at least impossible in
> the Church, not because we have to believe in men, but because if
> we are not to give up our faith we have to believe in the miracle of
> grace.[80]

VII

So far I have attempted to sketch a dogmatic portrait of the Christian canon as an element in the triune – and especially Christological-pneumatological – reality of God's saving self-communication. To speak of the canon is to speak of that means of grace through which the revelatory self-presence of God in the form of sanctified texts reaches the obedient and attentive community, which responds to that presence by an act of assent and acknowledgement. Such a depiction as this does not command much attention in modern theology, partly because the instinctive nominalism of modern culture tends to

---

[79] G. Lindbeck, 'Scripture, Consensus and Community', in R. J. Neuhaus, ed., *Biblical Interpretation in Crisis* (Grand Rapids: Eerdmans, 1989), p. 78.
[80] Barth, *Church Dogmatics* I/2, p. 598.

doubt the possibility that human products can refer to the divine economy of grace, partly because a proclivity to voluntarism leads us to suppose that the church, like any other society, is a sphere of unchecked invention. The problem of voluntarism extends into the way in which the reader of the canon is often envisaged as somehow co-constituting the text, so that reading and interpreting the canon become what Kenneth Surin calls 'church poetics'.[81]

It is, of course, incontrovertible that the canon may not be neatly extracted from the reading acts of the church. Once again, the canon is a list of texts, and texts are not icons, not merely static locations of fully determinate meaning; they require the activity of readers. Texts are communicative acts, on the part of both authors and recipients; they demand exegesis. At least at this level, textual essentialism does not serve us well, because it assumes that a text is a kind of repository entirely independent of its reception, and thereby extracts the text from the history of the exchanges which it occasions. But if this is so, then – as with the discussion of the church's act of canonization – the crucial task is that of alert theological specification of readerly activity.

Christian reading of the canon is faithful reading, properly exhibiting the fundamental characteristic of all actions of faith, which is self-forgetful reference to the prevenient action and presence of God. Faithful action is *action*; its practitioners are *agents*. But both action and agent are defined by reference to that in the presence of which (of whom) they find themselves and before which (before whom) they are to demonstrate a relinquishment of will. Even in its acts of construing and interpreting, in bringing a communicative interest to bear upon the text, the Christian reading act is a kind of surrender. Above all, faithful reading is an aspect of *mortificatio sui*, a repudiation of the desire to assemble all realities, including texts, including

[81] K. Surin, '"The Weight of Weakness". Intratextuality and Discipleship', *The Turnings of Darkness and Light. Essays in Philosophical and Systematic Theology* (Cambridge: Cambridge University Press, 1989), p. 213.

even the revelation of God, around the steady centre of my will. To read – *really* to read – is to submit to the process of the elimination or correction or conversion of false desire, for it is that false desire – sin – which more than anything else is destructive of the communicative fellowship between God and humanity in which the canon plays its part.

Reading the Christian canon is a matter of *epoche*:

> We have to know the mystery of the substance if we are really to meet it, if we are really to be opened and ready, really to give ourselves to it, when we are told it, that it may really meet us as the substance. And when it is a matter of understanding, the knowledge of this mystery will create in us a peculiar fear and reserve which is not at all usual to us. We will then know that in the face of this subject-matter there can be no question of our achieving, as we do in others, the confident approach which masters and subdues the matter. It is rather a question of our being gripped ... so that it is only as those who are mastered by the subject-matter, who are subdued by it, that we can investigate the humanity of the word by which it is told us. The sovereign freedom of this subject-matter to speak of itself imposes on us in the face of the word as such and its historicity an ἐποχή ... And the knowledge of this mystery will see to it that the work of exposition, which is the goal of all hearing and understanding, at least enters the stage of convalescence from the sickness with which all exposition is almost incurably afflicted, the sickness of an insolent and arbitrary reading in. If the exposition of a human word consists in the relating of this word to what it intends or denotes, and if we know the sovereign freedom, the independent glory of this subject-matter in relation both to the word which is before us and to ourselves, we will be wholesomely restrained, at the very least in our usual self-assured mastery of the relationship, as though we already knew its content and our exposition could give something more than hints in its direction. We shall be at least restrained in our evil domination of the text (even though in this age we can as little rid ourselves of it as we can of our old Adam generally).[82]

The concerns which the reader brings to the canon are never simply innocent; they are (especially when they are theological

---

[82]   Barth, *Church Dogmatics* I/2, pp. 470f.

concerns!) a source of potential distortion, even an assault on the freedom and dignity of the text and its matter; they are judgments which must be judged, and of which we must repent.[83] Contemporary theories of hermeneutical 'virtues' move us in something of the right direction, especially insofar as they insist that fitting reading of a canonical text requires the acquisition of moral and spiritual habits and not simply right critical technology.[84] But it remains doubtful whether virtue theory can successfully break free of the tug towards immanence; these accounts of hermeneutical activity still threaten to leave us within the relatively self-enclosed worlds of readerly psyches and habit-forming communities. If what has been said so far about the place of the canon in a network of soteriological relations between God and humanity is of any value, then it will require a much more vigorously charismatic-eschatological understanding of habits and their acquisition than has been offered in the quasi-Aristotelian accounts so far produced.

VIII

Some modern Christian theologians (especially those with heavy ecclesiological commitments) have been tempted to respond to decanonization – and the corollary process of detra-ditionalization[85] – by pressing the claims of a return to a stable, 'locative' style of church and theology as the only cure to the canonical dyslexia which afflicts us.[86] It is very easy for the

---

[83] On the connections of reading and repentance, see D. L. Jeffrey, *People of the Book. Christian Identity and Literary Culture* (Grand Rapids: Eerdmans, 1996), pp. 167–207 and 353–73; and W. J. Jennings, 'Baptizing a Social Reading. Theology, Hermeneutics, and Postmodernity', in R. Lundin, ed., *Disciplining Hermeneutics. Interpretation in Christian Perspective* (Grand Rapids: Eerdmans, 1997), pp. 117–27.

[84] See again Fowl and Jones, *Reading in Communion*.

[85] See P. Heelas, ed., *Detraditionalization. Critical Reflections on Authority and Identity* (Oxford: Blackwell, 1996).

[86] To put the record straight, it is important not to link such developments to the work of George Lindbeck, as can already be seen from his earlier essay 'The Sectarian Future of the Church', in J. P. Whelan, ed., *The God Experience* (New York: Newman Press, 1971), pp. 226–43.

notion and use of the canon to be caught up in these kinds of dynamics. But the cost is high. Nearly always, such appeals make little use of language about the freedom of God, and tend to take their energy from the fatally attractive mythology of a closed social and intellectual order. But, more than that, they turn the canon into an inviolable possession, even a weapon. The 'canon syndrome'[87] all too quickly lifts the church's life out of temporality and becomes a means of giving material form to the sanctity and safety of the church's mind. It makes indefectibility into something other than a *promise*.

The complicity of the canon in moral evil is undeniable. But one may adopt one of two postures to this state of affairs. The first, dominant in the modern history of freedom, has been genealogical: trace the history, observe the corruptions of producers and their products, and so cast down the mighty from their thrones. No serious Christian theology can afford to be anything other than grateful for some of the fruits of this posture. The other, minority, response, has been to talk of the canon dogmatically as that means of grace through which the judgment of the apostolic gospel is set before the church. If the canon is a function of God's communicative fellowship with an unruly church, if it is part of the history of judgement and mercy, then it cannot simply be a stabilizing factor, a legiti-mating authority. Rather, as the place where divine speech may be heard, it is – or ought to be – a knife at the church's heart.

---

[87] See Adriaanse, 'Canonicity and the Problem of the Golden Mean'.

2

HERMENEUTICS IN MODERN THEOLOGY: SOME DOCTRINAL REFLECTIONS

The territory indicated by my title is impossibly vast, and some delimitations are in order at the beginning. What follows does not attempt any kind of thorough or nuanced historical analysis of the great tangle of issues to which the terms of the title refer. 'Hermeneutics' and 'modern theology' don't exist as simple entities; the terms are shorthand ways of identifying very complex traditions of thought and cultural practices, and a serious attempt to trace those traditions and the variations in their relationship would be little short of a history of Western Christian thought since the rise of nominalism. What is offered here is more restricted and precise, chiefly an essay in Christian dogmatics. At its simplest, my proposal is that the Christian activity of reading the Bible is most properly (that is, Christianly) understood as a spiritual affair, and accordingly as a matter for theological description. That is to say, a Christian description of the Christian reading of the Bible will be the kind of description which talks of God and therefore talks of all other realities *sub specie divinitatis.* There is certainly a historical corollary to this proposal – namely, the need for some account of why the dominant traditions of Western Protestantism (and more recently of Western Catholicism) have largely laid aside, or at least lost confidence in, this kind of dogmatic depiction of the church's reading of the Bible, replacing it with, or annexing it to, hermeneutical theory of greater or lesser degrees of sophistication and greater or lesser degrees of theological content. Why, for example, is Augustine's untroubled appeal to the grammatical and rhetorical tools of ancient interpretative practice so different from modern theology's heavily theorized – and often anxious – investment in a philosophical view of 'interpretation' or 'understanding'? I shall try to sketch the outlines of one possible answer towards the beginning of what I have to say, but the main body of my remarks is given over to constructing a dogmatic argument, though along the way I converse with some important recent texts in theological hermeneutics.

At a number of key points, the argument is cross-grained: it resists the quasi-axiomatic status accorded to an anthropology of the interpreting subject (or community); it does not attempt to establish a theory of 'understanding' as a prior condition for making intelligible the church's reading of the Bible; it insists on the primacy of the church's dogmatic depictions of encounter with the Bible, depictions which invoke the language of God, Christ, Spirit, faith, church without seeking to coordinate such language with that of one or other general theories of religion, textuality, reading or reception. Above all, the argument is contrary insofar as it suggests that fruitful theological work on these issues requires us to give sustained attention to a figure who has virtually disappeared from theological hermeneutics in the modern era, namely Jesus, of whose risen and self-communicative presence in the Holy Spirit the Bible and its reading are a function. Pursuing the issues in the way the essay does inevitably calls into question the self-evident authority which we are sometimes disposed to find in both terms in our title. Is not 'modern' as a qualifier of 'theology' often deployed in such a way as to suggest that it is the predicate which is granted priority over the substantive – that the context of 'modernity' has a given, almost fatal, character, such that it entirely conditions theological work? And does not 'hermeneutics' (as in the frequently urged shift 'from dogmatics to hermeneutics')[1] bear something of the

---

[1] See C. Geffré, *The Risk of Interpretation. On Being Faithful to the Christian Tradition in a Non-Christian Age* (New York: Paulist Press, 1987).

same freight, as a sine qua non of responsible intellectual culture in a historically self-conscious age? The point is not to belabour the terms themselves, which may be used in entirely innocent ways, but rather to point out how the terms can rather easily come to represent spiritual and moral ideas in our culture, ideals which – like the nineteenth- century ideal of 'history' – Christian theology may have good reason to regard as quite other than self-evident. We are, of course, where we are: but *only* there, not in some privileged position in which we are entitled or required to describe ourselves and our acts in other than Christian ways. 'If all truth has an historical dimension, then the truth about history is itself historical, and we must be prepared to accept that further reflection may judge the past differently from the way we do.'[2] No less than modern theology, the culture of interpretation needs to remind itself of this.

1. The Decline of Theology

Strict governance by Christian doctrine is largely absent from much contemporary Christian writing in hermeneutics. Such writing either tends to restrict itself to the task of reporting how certain hermeneutical strategies (reader-response criticism, various strands of deconstructionism, and so forth) might shape an account of the church's reading of the Bible, or – which is more theologically interesting – tends to propose the appropriateness of one or other strategy by appeal to some aspect of Christian teaching (a certain stress on the reading community may be linked to ecclesiology, for example).[3] However, in and of itself, Christian doctrine is rarely regarded as adequate to the task of describing what takes place when the church reads the Bible, and is normally believed to require

---

[2] L. Dupré, *Passage to Modernity. An Essay in the Hermeneutics of Nature and Culture* (New Haven: Yale University Press, 1993), p. 9.

[3] As in F. Fiorenza, *Foundational Theology. Jesus and the Church* (New York: Crossroad, 1985), pp. 118f., and his essay 'The Crisis of Scriptural Authority. Interpretation and Reception', *Interpretation* 44 (1990), pp. 353–68.

either supplementing or (more frequently) *grounding* in general considerations of the ways in which human beings interpret written materials.

Amongst the most sophisticated recent examples of the second sort of text are the two works by Werner Jeanrond, *Text and Interpretation as Categories of Theological Thinking*[4] and *Theological Hermeneutics, Development and Significance*.[5] What is most problematical to the theological reader of these striking works is that the complexity, rigour and subtlety of their development of hermeneutical theology is not matched in their theological content, which by comparison is rather pale and thin. Above all, this is seen in the absence of any deep description of text-acts or reading-acts in *theological* terms. The invocation of theological categories is not seen as furnishing the primary, irreducible language of Christian depiction of the interpretative process, but at best as providing a kind of backcloth or context for the undisturbed use of non-theological theory. Thus the theological character of theological hermeneutics is described only in the most general terms, as deriving from the fact that '[i]t aims at understanding this universe as God's universe'.[6] Or again, the language of 'Spirit' is used to talk of an immanence of God within the human processes of interpretation: 'As long as our discussion of the interpretative conditions is a truly open discussion, one fails to see why God's Spirit should not be able to lead us towards an always deeper appreciation of the truth of the Bible precisely through such discussion.'[7] It is this rather underfed theology which leads to a miscalculated critique of Barth's objection to Bultmann, which Jeanrond believes is driven by an abstract understanding of God's transcendence of the world. What Jeanrond terms 'Barth's passionate vote for the difference between God and human

[4] Dublin: Gill & Macmillan, 1988; German original Tübingen: J. C. B. Mohr, 1986.
[5] London: SCM Press, 1994.
[6] *Theological Hermeneutics*, p. 8.
[7] Ibid., p. 137.

beings',[8] or his view of the 'radical disjunction between God and the world'[9] means that Barth is unable to see hermeneutics as articulating the essentially human conditions for thinking about God. By way of reply, one need only point out that Barth's objection is not a disapproval of study of such conditions and is certainly not driven by a sense of divine otherness or distance. Quite the opposite: it is clear from Barth's writing in the 1950s, especially in *Church Dogmatics* IV, that it is the *presence* of Jesus Christ the risen one which undermines the necessity of large-scale hermeneutical theory as an essential prerequisite for making the gospel meaningful. In effect, Jeanrond's work here is rooted in a conviction of the 'transcendental status of the theory of interpretation',[10] a conviction equally firm in the theological hermeneutics of Jeanrond's mentor Tracy, in, for example, *The Analogical Imagination*[11] and *Plurality and Ambiguity*,[12] which make explicit the way in which modern hermeneutical theory is frequently based upon a transcendental anthropology of the experiencing and interpreting subject whose terms are derived largely from existentialist phenomenology.

Much more fruitful for theological work is the recent study by F. Watson, *Text, Church and World*.[13] No less sophisticated in its engagement with modern theories of interpretation, Watson's work is distinguished above all by its refusal to allow theological language to be relegated to mere background status and by its positive deployment of theology (particularly the doctrines of the Trinity and the church) in both describing

---

[8] Ibid., p. 136.

[9] Ibid., p. 137.

[10] *Text and Interpretation*, p. xvii.

[11] D. Tracy, *The Analogical Imagination. Christian Theology and the Culture of Pluralism* (London: SCM Press, 1981).

[12] D. Tracy, *Plurality and Ambiguity. Hermeneutics, Religion and Hope* (New York: Harper & Row, 1987).

[13] Edinburgh: T&T Clark, 1994. See also Watson's recent insistence on the local character of Christian hermeneutics in his essay 'The Scope of Hermeneutics', in C. Gunton, ed., *The Cambridge Companion to Christian Doctrine* (Cambridge: Cambridge University Press, 1997), pp. 65–80.

and norming the activities of interpretation. Moreover, Watson does not try to offer a universal hermeneutics and is therefore less drawn to lay foundations for what he has to say in a universal anthropology: restricting himself to offering 'a theological hermeneutic for biblical interpretation',[14] he is free to make use of doctrines without having first to justify them by elaborating a larger context of hermeneutical phenomenology.

But, in this connection, mention should above all be made of Charles Wood's earlier work, *The Formation of Christian Understanding*,[15] which, more than any other recent book, restores to doctrine its proper place in the depiction of Christian text- and reading-acts. Even though there are (as we shall see) some criticisms to be made of the way it phrases the centrality of 'use', and in particular of the priority which accrues to the doctrine of the church as a result of the emphasis laid on 'use', Wood's work is of quite fundamental importance for my own account of these matters.[16]

What reasons might be adduced to explain why Christian doctrine has receded into the background in describing the church's reading of the Bible? What has happened? It is, of course, not simply that the church's reading of the Bible itself has completely changed: however much we may decry the woefully inadequate hermeneutics of many of the public self-articulations of mainstream liberal Christianity,[17] devotional and spiritual use of Scripture continues both privately and publicly. Nor is it simply that there have been no attempts at doctrinal construal of the Bible. Conservative Protestantism has produced an entire armoury of materials on just this point –

---

[14] Watson, *Text, Church and World*, p. 1.

[15] Philadelphia: Westminster Press, 1981.

[16] K. Vanhoozer, 'The Spirit of Understanding. Special Revelation and General Hermeneutics', in Lundin, ed., *Disciplining Hermeneutics*, pp. 131–65, is a further notable recent attempt to think dogmatically about issues of hermeneutics.

[17] See, for example, many of the contributions to C. E. Braaten and R. W. Jenson, eds., *Reclaiming the Bible for the Church* (Grand Rapids: Eerdmans, 1995).

though their relative lack of sophistication, their entanglement in polemics and apologetics, their reliance on scholastic or nineteenth-century construals of the nature of the Bible and their generally rationalistic understanding of theological method have all contributed to the marginalization of this strand of Christian thought. But, for better or worse, neither devotional use nor conservative apologetics have had much impact on the high theological culture of the Protestant West; and so we have to ask: why have doctrines declined there?

The history is complex and widely ramified, involving some of the most basic mutations in the rise of modern culture. As an entry-point, however, we might reflect on Ricoeur's synthesis of the history of hermeneutics since Schleiermacher in terms of a twofold process. The first move, which Ricoeur calls 'deregion-alization',[18] is the incorporation of 'special' or 'regional' hermeneutics into one general theory, of which they can be regarded as a particular instance or application. This move, Ricoeur proposes, is initiated by Schleiermacher and completed by Dilthey. A second move, 'radicalization',[19] subordinates the original epistemological concerns of hermeneutics to ontological concerns, so that the centre of gravity shifts from knowing and its acts to the interpreting subject's modes of being in the world – a shift initiated in Heidegger and completed in Gadamer. Though Ricoeur does not address theological issues in his essay, the 'deregionalization-radicalization' motif is a helpful indicator of the trend of modern theological history on at least two fronts.

First, it shows how the diminishment of theological construals of the church's reading of the Bible is an aspect of the steady expansion of general hermeneutics. Minimalizing the self-descriptions of Christian readers and their acts (including doctrinal self-descriptions) and the kind of claims

---

[18] P. Ricoeur, 'The Task of Hermeneutics', *Hermeneutics and the Human Sciences. Essays on Language, Action and Interpretation* (Cambridge: Cambridge University Press, 1981), p. 44.

[19] Ibid.

made by or on behalf of specific texts, and maximalizing the commonalities between different locales of reading-acts or text-acts, hermeneutics presses modern theology to consider those activities which we call the church's reading of the Bible as an instance of a more general phenomenon, whose features are stable and discernible across widely divergent contexts. What it means to read and interpret a text will best be articulated through the elaboration of norms which are unspecific to any one particular text or community.

Second, however, it is important to grasp that the decline of 'special' or 'regional' hermeneutics of the Bible is not simply a matter of recognizing that – like other texts – the Bible also is culture, a product, bound up with historical and social worlds in its inscription, transmission and reception. Nor is it simply a matter of recognizing that reading and interpreting in this particular region are not wholly dissimilar to what goes on in other regions. In and of themselves those recognitions do not disable a Christian theological construal of Christian reading of the Bible, though taking them with the right kind of seriousness may require adjustments to some formal theological accounts of the Bible (for example, concerning the process of divine inspiration). Much more serious in its impact on Christian theology is the fact that the displacement of doctrine is allied with the 'radicalization' of hermeneutics, so that it becomes, in effect, a fundamental, transcendental anthropology. The decline of doctrine in talking of the church's use of the Bible is thus symptomatic of some of the most deeply-rooted spiritual conditions of modernity. De-regionalized and radicalized, hermeneutical theory often proposes that the human activity of interpreting, of mapping out a meaningful world, is a phenomenon which can be isolated, extracted from its context-dependencies and then expounded anthropologically. Understanding or interpreting are thus grasped as part of a cluster of definitions of what it is to be human, at whose centre is something like *inwardness*.

'Inwardness' refers to the way in which selfhood is abstracted from backgrounds or frameworks (social, historical, cultural, linguistic). Externalities of custom and tradition are regarded as just that – external, outside the self, no longer a well-worn track along which we can trace our way through the world, but something other than, alien to and potentially deceptive towards the essential self. What I am is prior to the positivities of culture and tradition; and, if I were to identify the most primitive and proper act of selfhood, it would be consciousness, 'representing' the world to myself by making it an object of experience. In the depth of interiority, I am no longer within a public space; my authenticity and value are demonstrated by detachment 'from particular, historic communities, from the given webs of birth and history'.[20] It is this – the moral and intellectual ideal of spontaneous subjectivity – which is deeply embedded within general hermeneutical theory, and which has as one of its fruits the dislocation of the language of Christian doctrine.

Consider Spinoza's well-known announcement of purpose at the beginning of the *Theologico-political Treatise*, so close in spiritual tone to the opening of Descartes' *Discourse on Method*:

> I determined to examine the Bible afresh in a careful, impartial, and unfettered spirit, making no assumptions concerning it, and attributing to it no doctrines which I do not find clearly therein set down. With these precautions I constructed a method of Scriptural interpretation ...[21]

This is an extraordinarily instructive statement of which a good deal of the subsequent development of Biblical hermeneutics is a nearer or more distant echo. What Spinoza proposes is not simply the abandonment of reading and interpretation as 'practices that make their appearance within traditions',[22] nor simply an idealized picture of the undetermined and utterly

---

[20] C. Taylor, *Sources of the Self. The Making of Modern Identity* (Cambridge: Harvard University Press, 1989), p. 36.

[21] R. H. M. Elwes, ed., *The Chief Works of Benedict de Spinoza*, vol. 1 (London: Bell, 1883), p. 8.

[22] G. L. Bruns, *Inventions. Writing, Textuality and Understanding in Literary History* (New Haven: Yale University Press, 1982), p. xii.

self-transparent reader working with a fresh clean text. It is also that he refuses to consider that theological doctrine has any bearing on the interpretation of the text: indeed, it must be suspended if the mental act of interpretation is to proceed without hindrance. As Spinoza remarks in the previous paragraph, '[s]uch ... doctrine should be reached only after strict scrutiny and thorough comprehension of the Sacred Books ... and not be set up on the threshold, as it were, of inquiry'.[23]

Spinoza offers a classic construal of what in shorthand terms I want to call the 'hermeneutical situation'. Briefly, a construal of the hermeneutical situation is an account of the basic elements which together constitute reading or making sense of texts. Ordinarily, a construal will involve a complex configuration of a number of items: an account of the agents involved (authors, tradents, readers), of their locations (socio-cultural, historical, religious, political) and of their professed or implied goals (having experiences, finding out information, knowing God and so on); an account of objects (texts, in their genetic, traditio-historical, linguistic, semantic and pragmatic dimensions); and an account of acts undertaken by agents with reference to texts (private mental acts, conventional practices and so forth). Undergirding Spinoza's construal are a number of features which prepare us for the insignificance of Christian doctrine for much modern hermeneutics: an idealization of reading the Bible as an instance of general hermeneutical operations (what Spinoza calls 'inquiry'); a construal of the hermeneutical situation in such a way that the judging self is fundamentally important; a conviction that the invocation of theological doctrine is an impediment, since questions of interpretation are pre-doctrinal, to be settled prior to entry into the sphere of the *Credo*; a presupposition that the world of the Bible is a *problem*, since we both pre-exist and transcend that world, entertaining an attitude of distance towards it. Indeed, such is Spinoza's account of the hermeneutical situation that it

---

[23] *Theologico-political Treatise*, p. 8.

can hardly be called a situation at all, at least not in the sense that we are 'situated' within it, for its most fundamental axiom is that of the aseity and transcendence of the interpretative act.

My point here is not to make Spinoza paradigmatic for the entire history of modern theological hermeneutics. Rather, it is to suggest that the self-evident necessity of the hermeneutical talk may conceal from us some of its most essential convictions. Indeed, it is to this deeper level of unearthing basic understandings of what is involved in reading and interpreting that the most profitable lines of inquiry are to be directed. The rest of my remarks, therefore, are given over to a critical theological construal of the hermeneutical situation, by looking first at the situation as a whole, and then in more detail at the elements of a Christian construal of the hermeneutical situation of Christian reading of the Bible, namely Word of God, text, reader and church. To orient the argument, however, I offer some underlying principles on the basis of which I proceed:

1. There is no single thing called 'understanding', and those traditions of modern theology which accept responsibility for articulating or responding to any such phenomenon have in fact usually been recommending a certain anthropology as a transcendental condition for Christian theology. Much greater headway can be made by adopting a low-level approach, in which hermeneutics is as it were 're-regionalized', and the foundational task of elaborating a hermeneutical phenomenology of the interpretive subject is abandoned.

2. The chief task of such a 're-regionalized' theological hermeneutics is not the construction of better theory to *ground* Christian reading of the Bible but the construction of theory which makes sense of that reading by depiction. Its main business, in other words, is making a map of the particular historical, social and spiritual space within which this interpretation occurs, without worrying about inquiring into the (anthropological) conditions of possibility for there being such a space at all.

3. Such a depiction of the 'space' of Christian reading of the Bible is a matter of making a Christian theological construal of the field of reality within which such reading occurs. It is, in effect, a hermeneutical ontology which is required, although the governance of theology requires that this ontology be quite other than a religiously-tinted metaphysic or phenomenology.

4. Accordingly, the language, conceptuality and modes of explanation of a Christian construal of the hermeneutical situation will not be pre-doctrinal. It is a *theological* theory which is required, not an essay in the interpretation of Christian symbols understood as penultimate expressions of something more humanly basic. As theological theory it is enclosed and determined by the *positum* of Christian theology – proximately, the *Credo* of the church, ultimately the Word of God – to which it is responsible and in response to which it is a movement of intellectual self-articulation.

5. Most of all: theological hermeneutics will be confident and well-founded if it says much of the reality which is the axiom of all Christian life and thought: the living, speaking reality of the risen Jesus Christ present in the Spirit to the assembly of God's people.

2. The 'Hermeneutical Situation'

Christian reading and interpreting of the Bible is an instance of itself. The complex configuration of text-acts and reading-acts, the use of this text with those intentions to achieve these ends, is *sui generis*. It is not, of course, wholly dissimilar from other acts of reading undertaken by other readers in other communities with other purposes and self-definitions. But establishing the commonplaces and overlaps between Christian and other acts of reading, however valuable in exposing docetism, often serves the purpose of underwriting a foundational anthropology which eclipses what in fact is most interesting about what happens when Christians read the Bible: that the Bible as text is the *viva vox Dei* addressing the people of God and generating faith and obedience. It is this address which is constitutive of the

Christian hermeneutical situation, and it is this which in the last analysis means that that situation is without analogies.

Starting here means being rather out of step with at least one of the most authoritative strands of modern hermeneutical theory (Ricoeur's 'radicalized' tradition of hermeneutics), which has had as a chief goal the elaboration of an account of the nature of understanding which will be applicable across a wide range of contexts. Insofar as hermeneutics inherits many of the tasks of epistemology, it tends to envisage understanding as a mode of consciousness; theory characterizes such consciousness by identifying primary human phenomena which come into play when understanding occurs. For this tradition, the leading question is thus: 'What is it to understand a text, apart from any specific employment of it?'[24] If this question fails to prove fruitful, however, it is above all because it severs understanding from use. Instead, that is, of thinking of understanding as a term used to clump together a host of different practices, or as a set of abilities employed in particular situations to handle specific texts, it becomes a kind of invariant trans-regional mental or perhaps experiential process. Over against this, a critic like Gerald Bruns argues that much more ground can be gained by considering understanding not as 'a mode of consciousness' but as 'something that goes on in certain situations',[25] as 'a traditional practice that can be studied as one would study, say, a social custom',[26] for meaning exists 'only in its versions, which belong to time, history, and the occasions of use'.[27]

This latter account of understanding as a social practice or skill in context is a much more helpful entrée to theological reflection on the church's reading of the Bible. Partly this is because it loosens up the debate by shifting the area of

---

[24] Wood, *The Formation of Christian Understanding*, p. 16.

[25] Bruns, *Inventions*, p. xi.

[26] Ibid.

[27] Ibid., p. 12; cf. also Wood, *The Formation of Christian Understanding*, pp. 53f.: 'There is no understanding in general, of which every achieved understanding is an instance.' More generally, I am indebted to the emphasis on action theory in interpretation in various works by N. Wolterstorff, notably *Works and Worlds of Art* (Oxford: Clarendon Press, 1980) and *Divine Discourse. Philosophical Reflections on the Claim That God Speaks* (Cambridge: Cambridge University Press, 1995).

discussion away from questions of critical methodologies and towards issues of the context within which interpretation occurs. Simply discussing critical tools in and of themselves does not get us too far, any more than we get very far in identifying a person's action by saying: He is using a knife. To do what? Carve her initials? Sacrifice an ox? Murder his rival? Fix the saucepan handle? Acts, including reading-acts and their strategies, are situated within a province of meaning. And so, for Christian hermeneutics, '[t]he issue ... is not with the tools employed by historical biblical critics ... but the domain of meaning into which the results of such critical study are placed. The real issue is the hermeneutical context'.[28] But more importantly, linking understanding and use encourages Christian theology to shake itself free of its investments in an anthropology focussed on acts of interpretation, and to give much more attention to locality, to the field within which interpreters and their acts have real depth and extension.

As a consequence, what is required is a depiction of the hermeneutical situation through a process of what in another context Barth called 'formed reference'.[29] By this, Barth meant the careful description of the specific shape of the situation in its particularity and perceptibility as ... *this*. Successful description of the hermeneutical situation cannot be accomplished by eliminating all its secondary or contingent characteristics. The self-definitions of the participants, their professed goals, their use of this particular text and not some other, their language of 'listening to the Word of God', and so forth, cannot be eliminated or transcended in describing the situation, for in eliminating them we eliminate the situation, or

---

[28] K. P. Donfried, 'Alien Hermeneutics and the Misappropriation of Scripture', in Braaten and Jenson, eds., *Reclaiming the Bible for the Church*, p. 23.

[29] *Church Dogmatics*, III/4 (Edinburgh: T&T Clark, 1961), pp. 18, 23; in *The Christian Life. Church Dogmatics IV/4, Lecture Fragments* (Edinburgh: T&T Clark, 1981), p. 6, the phrase is 'formed and contoured reference'. The context is Barth's depiction of the moral situation as an encounter between the commanding God and the obedient human covenant partner, a situation which is not a variant upon some primary ethical situation, but simply itself. It is a much less heavily theoretical cousin to Geertz's (and Ryle's) 'thick description'.

at least so distort it by theory that it becomes blurred, losing its contours. When the only purchase we have on the situation is thinking about it critically (in terms of its conditions of possibility) rather than descriptively, then it simply recedes from our grasp. 'Formed reference', by contrast, doesn't screen out the positivities. It lets them stand, since they *are* what is being described.

So far, perhaps, so good: hermeneutics doesn't need 'to be reified into a para-science, as epistemology has, and there are enough general principles in the world already'.[30] But this emphasis on locality can be bought at a theological price. Refusing to transcend the situation or fall into abstraction, it naturally tends to put great emphasis on the specificities of the human agents in the situation. Thus Wood's (entirely proper) stress on 'use' and 'content' to displace a universal notion of 'understanding' goes hand in hand with a prioritizing of ecclesiality. This he shares with a great deal of modern theology which has sought to oppose liberal correlationist or revisionist Christianity and its appeal to a foundational phenomenology of the human, by turning to tradition or sociality as the essential condition for theological knowledge. But however helpful this move may turn out to be in terms of forcing Christian theology back to its locale, its weakness is that it rarely issues in vigorous, extended talk of the action of God. Exchanging one's existentialist-phenomenologist conversation partner for an ethnographical social scientist may certainly make it easier to keep hold of the value of the specifics of the hermeneutical situation and its ecclesial and traditional character. But an anthropology of the uses of the interpreting community is still an anthropology, and more is needed. The ecclesial co-efficient is graspable only within a larger field, a field defined above all not by Christian or church use but by the presence and activity of God. A Christian depiction of the Christian hermeneutical

---

[30] C. Geertz, 'Introduction', *Local Knowledge. Further Essays in Interpretive Anthropology* (New York: Harper, 1983), p. 5.

situation will thus be a depiction determined all along the line by the priority of the Word of God.

A worked example of the limitations of the notion of 'use' as a Christian description of the reading of the Bible can be found in the less than adequate accounts of Barth's theology of Scripture in the work of Lindbeck and Frei.

In 'Barth and Textuality',[31] Lindbeck presents Barth's account of the Bible as a theory of textuality, closely allied to a particular understanding of the task of the church. Lindbeck finds in Barth a continuation of the Reformation insistence on Scripture as self-interpreting in the sense that *as text* it is a coherent and achieved world of meaning; as Barth's thought develops, 'the strange new world becomes ever more intra-textual, firmly located within the biblical text'.[32] Barth's lesson for modern Christianity is thus that the church 'has no future except in its own intratextual world',[33] and that Christian communities must 'relearn the use of their own tongue'.[34] The mistake here is to go no further back than communal practice, stopping short at ecclesiology and not pushing on to the doctrines of Trinity and revelation, which are crucial to Barth's design, but which Lindbeck dismisses rather brusquely. As Ronald Thiemann notes in his 'Response to George Lindbeck',[35]

> Barth is interested in Scripture as self-interpreting text, because he sees Scripture as the vehicle of the self-interpreting triune God ... It is Barth's view of revelation that warrants his intratextual view of theology. Without that doctrine of revelation, or its functional equivalent, textuality, intratextuality and self-interpreting texts have no *theological* force.[36]

[31] *Theology Today* 43 (1986), pp. 361–76.
[32] 'Barth and Textuality', p. 362.
[33] Ibid., p. 374.
[34] Ibid., p. 372.
[35] *Theology Today* 43 (1986), pp. 377–82.
[36] 'Response to George Lindbeck', p. 378. Further, see here the critiques of Lindbeck by George Hunsinger, in *How to Read Karl Barth. The Shape of His Theology* (Oxford: Oxford University Press, 1991), and 'Truth as Self-involving. Barth and Lindbeck on the Cognitive and Performative Aspects of Truth in Theological Discourse', *Journal of the American Academy of Religion* 61 (1993), pp. 41–56.

A similar problem can be found in Hans Frei's – in many respects masterful – sketch of Barth in the posthumous *Types of Christian Theology*.[37] Frei's account of the priority of 'theology as critical Christian self-reflection or self-description'[38] over philosophy, and his perception that 'what makes theology an orderly and systematic procedure ... is for Barth not a set of universal, formal criteria which are certain and all-fields-encompassing and can therefore be stated apart from any context of specific application'[39] are certainly acute. But, as with Lindbeck, Barth's direct language about the action of God is strangely elided in the description of the work of theology. Hence Frei proposes that, for Barth, prolegomena to dogmatics 'attempts insofar as is possible ... to exhibit the rules or fragments of rules implicit in the ruled use of language which is the sign system of the socio-linguistic community called the church'.[40] By way of response we might suggest that for Barth it is not ruled use, semiotic systems or socio-linguistic behaviour which are definitive of the church, but the electing, reconciling and redemptive activity of God in Christ. Whatever else 'use' may do, it can offer no more than a distinctly secondary clue to the being and activity of the church, and thus to its reading of the Bible.[41]

How, then, is the hermeneutical situation to be construed in Christian theological terms? It is not an abstract or unformed situation. It is not a history which remains unmade until we make it, or which we can fill out at liberty by whatever activities and descriptions seem best to us. Nor is it a situation peopled by idealized figures and objects. It is in every respect contingent and particular. As such, it is a situation within which the Christian reader of the Bible already finds herself. She does not

---

[37] New Haven: Yale University Press, 1992.
[38] *Types of Christian Theology*, p. 38.
[39] Ibid., p. 39.
[40] Ibid., p. 45.
[41] For a brief critique of the notion of 'using' the Bible, from the standpoint of divine priority, see C. Gunton, 'Using and Being Used: Scripture and Systematic Theology', *Theology Today* 47 (1990), pp. 248–59.

enter the situation from outside, or escape from it by transcendental theory; she does not occupy a position of superiority or neutrality, from which the situation can be surveyed at a distance and judgments can be made about it. Indeed, it is a situation in which we are those exposed, those who cannot rely on themselves to possess certain competencies or devices (whether of method or experience) in order to find their way around. For it is a situation in which we are addressed by the God and Father of our Lord Jesus Christ. In all this, the hermeneutical situation is, to state matters in the broadest doctrinal categories, an episode in the history of God's relation to humanity in his works of creation, salvation and perfection. That history, and within it the mystery of God's self-manifestation, is a history which is essentially twofold: a history of God's acts, acts which in turn evoke, sustain and bring to their final telos human acts; these human acts are truly human precisely in glad consent to the shapely givenness of reality, including their own human reality. Enclosed within the mystery of God's self-manifestation, an account of the church's reading of the Bible is to be undertaken, first, by strong depiction of God as 'Word'. As Word, God is not absent or mute but present and communicative, not as it were waiting to be 'made sense of' by our cognitive or interpretative activities, but accomplishing in us the knowledge of himself. Second, therefore, the Bible's character as text is only provisionally described by general theory of textuality and text-acts; greater space is to be given over to developing ways of talking of the Bible as means or instrument of divine action. Third, a different anthropology comes into play when talking of the church's reading of the Bible, one in which spiritual dispositions such as faith, hearing and obedience are definitive of the self as primary modes of being human in correspondence to the self-bestowing, evocative presence and action of God. And, fourth, the reading of the Bible will be described as the *church's* reading: as activities undertaken by the community which *is* (and which is not merely ornamentally labelled as) the *creatura Verbi divini*. Described in these very general terms, the church's reading of the Bible will not be conceptualized via an aesthetics of the classic, a critical theory of communicative action, or an archaeology of tradition, but by the doctrines of God, Christ, Spirit, salvation and church. To a fuller account of these themes we now turn.

3. Word of God

A Christian theological construal of the church's reading of the Bible is a theology of the Word of God.

Two initial remarks are in order. (1) If we were to strive for adequacy and completeness here, some development of the doctrine of the Trinity would be required.[42] One of the functions of that doctrine in Christian theology is to conceptualize how self-manifestation is ingredient to the being of God: as Father, Son and Spirit, God is antecedently one who wills, effects and brings to fruition the knowledge of himself on the part of his creatures. The integration of the doctrines of Trinity and revelation is always threatened when revelation, isolated from consideration of the being of God, becomes a theological epistemology and is developed in such a way as to furnish a non-dogmatic prologue to dogmatics proper. This frequently happened in post-Reformation Protestant dogmatic work. The separation of revelation from a trinitarian account of divine prevenience (some of whose aspects are traced by R. F. Thiemann, *Revelation and Theology. The Gospel as Narrated Promise*,[43] and which is thoroughly criticized by Barth in the first volume of the *Dogmatics*) left Christian theologizing about the Bible ill-prepared to think through in any fundamental way the challenges posed by the rise of non-theological construals of the Bible, whether in historico-critical or hermeneutical dress. At least one lesson to be learned from this history is that we ignore the interpenetration of dogmatics and hermeneutics at

---

[42] See Vanhoozer, 'The Spirit of Understanding', for a sketch of such a trinitarian hermeneutic.

[43] Notre Dame: Notre Dame University Press, 1985.

our peril. In the present context, however, this trinitarian setting for doctrine concerning revelation and the Bible can only be presupposed, and only some more proximate description attempted. (2) The phrase 'Word of God' is a good deal preferable to 'revelation', the latter being both too abstract and, in its post-Reformation usage, too tied to epistemological or foundational concerns. Word of God, by contrast, more readily conveys the proper sense that the processes of the knowledge of God are activities stemming from the personal act of divine self-articulation, embodied in Jesus Christ, and thus helps us to focus on the axiom on which all else rests: as this one, God is and speaks.

What features of the Word of God elicit our attention in this particular context? First, God is self-communicative. God's works in creation, salvation and perfection are, as Barth puts it, 'not a dark and dumb event, but perspicuous and vocal'.[44] 'Work' and 'Word' coinhere. God's action is not speechless, a silent force, an opaque causal power; it has as one of its goals the shedding abroad of the knowledge of itself, and so it speaks. As a consequence, when we talk of God's 'revealedness', of the reality of God as something perceptible, we do not do so by supplementing our discussion of God's acts with a second discussion of our own acts as human creators of meaning. God's reality is in and of itself communicative ('radiant', Barth would say), and in one real sense this self-communication is direct. This – as we shall see in the next

---

[44] *Church Dogmatics* IV/3 (Edinburgh: T&T Clark, 1963), p. 8. The context of this is Barth's extensive recovery of the prophetic office of Christ in *Church Dogmatics*, IV/3. It is worth recording that this doctrine offers a fruitful dogmatic context within which to expound a theology of the Bible. The older Protestant dogmatics customarily treated the Bible in two places: first (and primarily) in the locus *de revelatione* and second (with much less intensity) in the treatment of the *munus propheticum Christi*, where the mediating functions of Bible and church proclamation were discussed. When handled in the first locus, the Bible often became associated with the foundational enterprise of seeking indubitable foundations for knowledge, as well as with the rationalistic method of deducing proofs for doctrines from biblical propositions. Handled in the second context, however, the Bible is much more happily related to the living presence and activity of the risen Christ.

section – is not a denial of the way in which divine self-disclosure is mediated through texts and the complex histories of their production and reception. Rather, it is an affirmation that God's self-communication is not merely some ultimate 'whence', a point of reference which lies apart from us at several removes. Construed in such a way, God's self-disclosure may form an ultimate background of the human acts through which we construct meaning, but it is scarcely an operative reality and is factored into the depiction of the hermeneutical situation only in a rather marginal way.

In a compelling essay entitled 'Trinity and Revelation',[45] Rowan Williams argues that revelation is best approached 'from the standpoint of a new form of life and understanding whose roots can be traced to the initiating phenomenon'.[46] Despite much strong language of the absolute creativity and radical generative power to be ascribed to Jesus, the *indirectness* of the notion of revelation as 'initiating phenomenon' is troubling, as in the following passage:

> 'God reveals himself' means that the meaning of the word 'God' establishes itself among us as the loving and nurturing advent of *newness* in human life – grace, forgiveness, empowerment to be the agents of forgiveness and liberation. This advent has its centre, its normative locus, in the record of Jesus; it occurs among us now as the representation of Jesus through the Spirit; and it rests upon and gives content to the fundamental regulative idea of initiative, creative or generative power, potentiality, that is not circumscribed by the conditions of the empirical world – the *arché* of the Father, the ultimate source.[47]

However important and valuable it may be to speak of 'the advent of newness' as the context which establishes the meaning of the word 'God', are we not saying more when we talk of revelation? Are we not saying that here it is a matter of *Dei loquentis persona*?

[45] Williams, *On Christian Theology*, pp. 131–47.
[46] Ibid., p. 134.
[47] Ibid., p. 145.

Second, God's self-communication is free, sovereign and spiritual. It is not called forth by acts undertaken by creatures, but as *self-*communication it is God's freely-willed disclosure. It occurs in the majesty of his sovereignty, according to his own good purposes, with no origin beyond himself and no goal beyond those which he himself wills. Here God is inalienably subject: God's Word is a free act, which itself sets the conditions for its own occurrence and reception, and which utterly transcends any stance we may adopt towards it. And so, it is spiritual, unavailable for systematization, a reality which cannot be degraded into routines, creaturely configurations or conventional practices or habits of speech. In all these respects God is, as Barth puts it in a strange phrase, 'the Lord of the wording of His Word';[48] his communicative action is not restricted to providing an initial stimulus to human historical projects, but maintains its sovereign liberty in the whole sweep of its occurrence. In considering the Word of God, we never step outside the sphere of the divine aseity.

Third, God's self-communication is purposive, having as its *telos* the establishment of knowledge of God in those to whom God manifests himself. The 'anthropological' or 'existential' coordinate is thus not supplied by the human subject considered as a quasi-independent reality, and indeed does not need to be so supplied, since God's act of self-bestowal already achieves its 'realization' in the human realm. At this point, of course, Christian theology will talk of the person and activity of the Holy Spirit. But, in our present context, it is sufficient to note that the purposive character of God's self-revelation means that God is not first of all abstract and indefinite and only subsequently 'made meaningful' when, in some sense, we act on him. Because God is intrinsically and not merely by application *pro nobis*, his eloquence and radiance are *effectual.*

If God as Word is construed in these ways, what effects can be seen in a theological description of the hermeneutical situation? It means that our account of the hermeneutical

<hr />
[48] *Church Dogmatics* I/1, p. 139.

situation is not dominated by the presumption of a historical gap between the Bible and the modern Christian reader, the presumption that 'we do not live in the biblical world, that its features and habits are strange to us'.[49] This sense of distance can produce one of two strategies. On the one hand, it can issue in the exquisite, almost ascetic probing of historical distance (what Gadamer in a fine phrase called 'the noble and slowly perfected art of holding ourselves at a critical distance in dealing with witnesses to past life'),[50] so as to prevent any deadening of historical consciousness. On the other hand, it can push hermeneutics to strive to close the gap in order to appropriate as best it can what is alien. Much of the labour of hermeneutically oriented revisionist theology is expended upon the task of negotiating some kind of correlation between the strange biblical world and the realities of contemporary experience.[51] But both strategies are rendered superfluous if the hermeneutical situation is defined not out of the paradigm of historical remoteness but out of the presence of God as Word. What determines the hermeneutical situation, and thus the acts of human agents in that situation, is the presence and activity of Jesus, the 'revealedness' of God.

What does 'presence' mean here? The history of the notion of *Christus praesens* in modern theology is intricate; at least one strand used the term in an idealist or romantic sense to denote the presence of Jesus *to my self-presence*, thus reducing his over-againstness. As Hans Frei argues, in this tradition

> [t]he endeavour ... to represent the presence of Christ in and to our presence may well mean to the Christian the total diffusion of Jesus into our presence so that he no longer has any presence of his own. The cost of being contemporaneous to him would then be, it

---

[49] R. W. Jenson, 'Hermeneutics and the Life of the Church', in Braaten and Jenson, eds., *Reclaiming the Bible for the Church*, p. 93.

[50] H.-G. Gadamer, *Philosophical Hermeneutics* (Berkeley: University of California Press, 1976), p. 5.

[51] The discussion of theological hermeneutics in P. Hodgson, *Winds of the Spirit. A Constructive Christian Theology* (Louisville: Westminster/John Knox Press, 1994), pp. 10–14, is a standard recent example.

seems, that he no longer *owns* his presence, or, if he does, that we cannot apprehend or comprehend that fact. He cannot *turn* to us; he can only *share* with us what he no longer owns for turning. For his turning to us is accomplished only in *our* imagination or perhaps *our* moral decision.[52]

Or, we might add, in *our* interpretation.

But presence may mean something quite different, at once more gratuitous and disruptive. The presence of Jesus can be construed as his utterly gracious and miraculous gift of himself as the risen one, his 'turning' to us (to use Frei's word), in which he is and speaks with us. His presence encloses us, and as self-communicative presence it is already indefatigably ahead of all our appropriations or 'readings' of it. This is as true for hermeneutics as it is for morals or doctrines. For our present concern, this means that the little fragment of historical action which we call the church's reading of the Bible is what it is because, in the power of the Holy Spirit, Jesus makes it contemporary with himself, commissioning it as a sphere of his presence and speech. The 'time' of the hermeneutical situation does not, as it were, radiate backwards or forwards from the interpreter's self-presence; Jesus' givenness as the risen one constitutes it as the now where he speaks as Word and is to be heard.[53]

To sum up: because God in Jesus Christ speaks, because Jesus is God's living Word, then the 'hermeneutical situation' falls under the rule: 'We do not know God against his will or behind his back, as it were, but in accordance with the way in which he has elected to disclose himself and communicate his truth.'[54] Once this is grasped, then doctrines begin to do the work so frequently undertaken by anthropology or theories of historical

---

[52] H. Frei, *The Identity of Jesus Christ. The Hermeneutical Bases of Dogmatic Theology* (Philadelphia: Fortress Press, 1975), p. 34.

[53] Further on the implications of the notion of *Christus praesens* for hermeneutics, see D. Ritschl, *Memory and Hope. An Inquiry concerning the Presence of Christ* (New York: Macmillan, 1967), esp. pp. 61f.

[54] T. F. Torrance, *Divine Meaning. Studies in Patristic Hermeneutics* (Edinburgh: T&T Clark, 1995), p. 5.

consciousness in determining the nature of the hermeneutical situation, thereby making possible the 'formed reference' which is the basic mode of theological depiction. How this reorients a theological account of the church's reading of the Bible will be seen in greater detail as we look at the topics of text, reader and church.

4. Text

Two initial orientations. (1) Once again, doggedly: we are on the path of a theological construal of the Bible as text. And so it has to be pointed out that theological hermeneutics will properly avoid staking too much on one or other theory of textuality, and certainly will not be too ready to heed a call 'to reflect on the process and assumptions of textual interpretation in a fundamental manner'[55] as part of a requirement 'to search for a *universal* theory of the process of interpretation'.[56] Of course, theology has much to learn from recent work on the nature of texts, especially from those theories which look at texts as fields of action. Such accounts are very profitable in helping break apart conventions of biblical interpretation – whether it be archaeological use of biblical texts as historical sources, or formalist aesthetics, or 'symbolic' readings of the Bible as a kind of textual crystallization of experience. This kind of work is evidently companionable with the kind of theological depiction attempted here. But theological appeal to these theories ought only to be ad hoc and pragmatic, a matter of finding a tool to do a job. Anything more systematic – 'the development of the theory of the understanding of texts in order to ground theological text interpretation to an appropriate foundational theory'[57] – goes well beyond the limits which theology ought to set for itself. (2) Equally, however, a theological account cannot be ahistorical. A theorist of textuality

---

[55] Jeanrond, *Text and Interpretation*, pp. 7f.
[56] Ibid., p. 8.
[57] Ibid., pp. xvif.

like Jeanrond quite properly protests against the incipient docetism in many theological accounts here.[58] Not only do we have to say what our forebears (and some of our living relatives) have been unwilling to say, namely, that the Bible is a contingent collection of texts produced by human agents (authors, redactors, tradents, even perhaps suppressors) and not directly inscribed by God. We also have to say that, as such a contingent textual reality, the Bible in no way eludes the historical and cultural entanglements of all texts. However right we are to want to talk of God's use of the text, we may not do so in a way which makes the text into a pure, timeless *verbum externum*. Certainly the Bible, like any text, is possessed of a measure of determinacy, even given its internal variety and complexity; it is such and not otherwise, it invites certain postures and resists others, and so on. But the Bible is not an absolutely stable entity, a single 'world' which unproblematically draws us into itself in such a way that its meaning is perfectly achieved, constituted with such a degree of finality that it is in principle identical in any context whatsoever. The Bible is within a communication situation; it is a field of interests. And it is this, not only because in some sense it is realized in reading, but also because both text and reading are within material history, parts of the economic, political and ideological conflicts which make up a culture and its institutions.[59] Whatever else is said about God's use of the Bible as 'appropriated human discourse',[60] we need to be clear that it is this kind of text which is appropriated.

What, then, is to be said theologically of the textual artefact in the Christian hermeneutical situation? An initial thesis might run: the text of the Bible is an instrument of divine action, a

---

[58] Though he is rather wide of the mark in including Barth's account among them: *Theological Hermeneutics*, p. 136.

[59] Cf. Williams, 'The Discipline of Scripture'; idem., 'Does It Make Sense to Speak of Pre-Nicene Orthodoxy?', in R. Williams, ed., *The Making of Orthodoxy. Essays in Honour of Henry Chadwick* (Cambridge: Cambridge University Press, 1990), pp. 1–23.

[60] Wolterstorff, *Divine Discourse*, p. 187.

means through which the *viva vox Dei* speaks to the congregation of faithful believers in the course of the history of salvation. If the text be considered thus, then theological hermeneutics is concerned above all with 'the practice of interpreting Scripture for divine discourse'.[61]

The Bible is an instrument of divine action in that, through the text, God's speech is encountered. This affirmation relativizes the Bible, because to talk of the text as an instrument of divine action is primarily to say something about God, not about the text. There is no straight line from the text to the speech or Word of God, and its human language is not something of which divine speech can be unambiguously predicated. Here God speaks in a veiled form, sacramentally.[62] But the affirmation also means that no purely 'natural' account of the Bible will be theologically satisfying. The determining factor in a theological account of the Bible as text will thus be 'the relation of *God* to Scripture', or, in more complex fashion, 'God's "use" of the uses of Scripture'.[63] This affords what Jeanrond calls a 'communicative perspective' on the text, that is, an understanding of what the text is and what practices surround it in the context of a given pattern of reading. Crucial to a theologically articulated 'communication perspective' will be the depiction of the text as mode of divine speech.

> The central communicative perspective of the primary text-acts in the New Testament is the original acknowledgement on the part of humankind that Jesus is the Christ, and that in him God is revealed. This communictive perspective is the decisive inner textual principle of the composition of the canon of the New Covenant. The communicative perspective of the secondary text-acts is the

---

[61] Ibid., p. 18.

[62] Barth's reluctance to talk of the Bible as directly God's Word is set out in Wolterstorff, *Divine Discourse*, pp. 63–74; a somewhat crisper account is found in B. McCormack, 'Historical Criticism and Dogmatic Interest in Karl Barth's Theological Exegesis of the New Testament', *Lutheran Quarterly* 5 (1991), pp. 211–25, esp. p. 220. For a deep analysis of the wider issue, see E. Jüngel, *God's Being Is in Becoming* (Edinburgh: T&T Clark, 2001).

[63] D. H. Kelsey, 'The Bible and Christian Theology', *Journal of the American Academy of Religion* 48 (1980), p. 396.

interpretation – i.e., the understanding, explanation and assessment – of these texts from the standpoint of historical and cultural distance and in the light of the particular existential horizon of the interpreter.[64]

What is missing here? A robust account of divine action as antecedent to either acknowledgment or understanding, explanation and assessment on our part.

How are these two aspects of the Bible – its naturalness and yet its mediation of divine speech – to be related? The immediate temptation is to omit one or other of the characterizations, either by refusing to speak of the text as a field of divine action, or by attributing to the Bible what are in fact properly non-communicable divine attributes (for example, infallibility). The mistake in both these moves is that of supposing that, if divine speaking is to be talked about with reference to the Bible, it can only be by identifying it with the text as text, united (hypostatically?) to the Word of God. A *sacramental* account of the relation is much more plausible. The text is 'sacramental' in that God's agency is real and effective and yet indirect – not in the sense of being pushed to the background, but in the sense that God speaks through the intelligible words of this text and acts in, with and under the acts of the church's reading of it. Provided that we do not fall into the error of thinking of God's 'sacramental' action as automatically called forth by human acts and objects, and provided that the guarantee of God's speaking is purely a matter of his Spirit and promise, then we need not fear magic here.[65]

What are the effects of this stress on divine agency on how the text itself is construed? Two lines of reflection suggest themselves. First, as divine speech and address, the text has

[64] Jeanrond, *Text and Interpretation*, p. 103.
[65] In his comparative study of Frei and Barth on Scripture, David Demson rightly draws attention to the significance for Barth of God's 'appointment, calling and commissioning' of the apostolic testimony (for the description of which the language of divine election is firmly required), and to the lack of such language in Frei: *Hans Frei and Karl Barth. Different Ways of Reading Scripture* (Grand Rapids: Eerdmans, 1997).

authority. Though its genres are widely divergent (and though genre itself is not only a matter of textual form but also of reading-stance), the Bible as a whole is *address*, the *viva vox Dei* which accosts us and requires attention. God's address is interceptive; it does not leave the hearer in neutrality, or merely invite us to adopt a position vis-à-vis itself and entertain it as a possibility. It allows no safe havens; it *judges*. It is an 'elemental interruption of the continuity of the world'.[66] Christian theological doctrine about the authority of the Bible and about the Bible's status as 'Holy Scripture' has its roots here, in the *bouleversement* which God's Word effects. Such doctrine is, crucially, not to be understood abstractly or formally, independent of the events of divine speech and the hearing which it evokes. The 'authority' of the Bible is not some textual quality per se, somehow inherent in this collection of pieces of inscribed discourse. Nor is it something which can be grasped as a purely formal relation between text and reader, or between text and teaching (as the quasi-legal language in which it is phrased can sometimes suggest). The authority of the Bible is real and operative; to speak of this authority is to articulate the relation between God as Word and the actions and dispositions of the church as the text is read. The text's authority, its 'holiness' as 'scripture', is grounded in the fact that the text mediates divine speech in such a way as to command and establish reverence.

Second, the text is self-interpreting and perspicuous. This is not a claim that God's Word can be read off from the text unproblematically, as if the text were entirely transparent, and the act of reading were a matter of pure receptivity, without interests or perspectives. Again, self-interpretation and perspicuity are only intelligible in the context of a portrayal of divine action, not as material conditions of the text. In the context of divine action, a theological construal will affirm that,

---

[66] A favourite phrase of E. Jüngel, here cited from 'The Dogmatic Significance of the Question of the Historical Jesus', *Theological Essays II* (Edinburgh: T&T Clark, 1995), p. 91, where it is being used to talk of the disturbing quality of revelation.

as *sui ipsius interpres*, the text is not simply inert until activated by human readers. 'Texts, like dead men and women, have no rights, no aims, no interests.'[67] Qua texts, of course not; but, as instruments of divine action, texts are prevenient, determining the shape of our reading not only by passive resistance but also by active presentation of the speech of God. In a similar vein, the *claritas* of the Bible is not a material textual attribute but a spiritual event. Clarity is not the same as self-evidentness, and so does not render superfluous the work of 'making' sense through exegesis and interpretation. The Bible is perspicuous as a function of the radiance of God the Word; here God's light is effective in manifesting the gospel and stands in no need of an interpretative élite (clerical or academic) before it can illuminate the people of God.[68] In sum: both the character of the Bible as self-interpreting and its perspicuity are confessions, faith's depictions of the activity of God discerned in the church's activity of reading the Bible. As descriptions of the Christian hermeneutical situation, they guide the church's reading by portraying the field within which particular reading-acts of this particular text take place. This does not necessarily permit their use to prohibit in advance certain kinds of inquiry, but rather shows how they serve to indicate that what counts as a Christian reading of the Bible will include certain expectations of divine action as axiomatic and operative in acts of interpretation.

5. Reader and Church

A Christian theological depiction of the hermeneutical situation will involve the development of a Christian theological anthropology of reading, that is, an account of readers, reading communities and reading-acts which makes extensive appeal to the language and belief structure of Christian faith. The tendency of hermeneutics in modernity to arrange itself

---

[67] R. Morgan, with J. Barton, *Biblical Interpretation* (Oxford: Oxford University Press, 1988), p. 7; cf. pp. 270f.

[68] See here Berkouwer's excellent discussion of perspicuity in *Holy Scripture*, pp. 267–98.

around (usually implicit) anthropology necessitates a particular vigilance at this point, though there is little in the recent theological literature which shows much sophistication either in critique or in construction: by and large, dogmatic issues have not surfaced, and distinctively Christian theological accounts have been rare. This has been particularly true in theological writing on the roles of readers and reading communities which has been stimulated and guided by theories which give high profile to reception or reader response. As we shall see, such theories raise crucial dogmatic questions about human intentionality which are often left unaddressed.[69]

In setting out an anthropology of reading, Christian theology will have to develop what Charles Taylor calls an 'argument from transcendental conditions',[70] that is, an argument which looks at the conditions outside the reading self which make it possible for there to be such a self at all. What will be affirmed in such a theological argument?

First, the reader is to be envisaged as located within the hermeneutical situation as I have been attempting to portray it, not as transcending it, or making it merely an object of will. The reader is an actor within a larger web of events and activities, supreme among which is God's act in which God speaks God's Word through the text of the Bible to the people of God, instructing them in and teaching them the way they should go. As a participant in this historical process, the reader is *spoken to* in the text. This speaking, and the hearing which it promotes, occurs as part of the drama which encloses human life in its totality, including human acts of reading and understanding:

---

[69] This is true even in works of such methodological sophistication as J. Barton's *Reading the Old Testament. Method in Biblical Study* (London: Darton, Longman & Todd, 1984), or E. V. McKnight's *Post-Modern Use of the Bible. The Emergence of Reader-Oriented Criticism* (Nashville: Abingdon Press, 1988). The few recent attempts to articulate the anthropological issues include Kevin Vanhoozer's essay 'The Spirit of Understanding'; W. J. Jennings, 'Baptizing a Social Reading'; E. Rogers, 'How the Virtues of an Interpreter Presuppose and Perfect Hermeneutics. The Case of Thomas Aquinas', *Journal of Religion* 76 (1996), pp. 64–81; and D. L. Jeffrey's very important study *People of the Book*.

[70] C. Taylor, 'Overcoming Epistemology', *Philosophical Arguments* (Cambridge, Mass.: Harvard University Press, 1995), p. 9.

the drama of sin and its overcoming. Reading the Bible is an event in this history. It is, therefore, moral and spiritual and not merely cognitive or representational activity. Readers *read*, of course: figure things out as best they can, construe the text and its genre, try to discern its intentions, whether professed or implied, place it historically and culturally – all this also happens when the Bible is read. But as this happens, there happens the history of salvation; each reading-act is also bound up within the dynamic of idolatry, repentance and resolute turning from sin which takes place when God's Word addresses humanity. And it is this dynamic which is definitive of the Christian reader of the Bible.

For Augustine, this history or dynamic was one of the essential conditions for Christian reading. Certainly he is quite sharp at the beginning of the *De doctrina christiana* with those who despise the proper grammatical and rhetorical methods of interpretation: 'Their excitement must be restrained by the recollection that although they have a perfect right to rejoice in their great gift from God they nevertheless learned even the alphabet with human help.'[71] But he is also very clear that

> [i]t is vital that the reader first learns from the scriptures that he is entangled in a love of this present age, of temporal things, that is, and is far from loving God and his neighbour to the extent that scripture prescribes. It is at this point that the fear which makes him ponder the judgement of God, and the holiness which makes it impossible for him not to admit and submit to the authority of the holy books, compel him to deplore his own condition.'[72]

Calvin, similarly, sets out his account of the Bible, not simply in the context of the need for some kind of warrants for Christian teaching or polemic, but as part of a larger concern to show how God's self-manifestation exposes, chastises and does away with the depraved project of idolatry. 'God, the Artificer of the universe, is made manifest to us in Scripture, and ... what we ought to think of him is set forth there, lest we seek some

---

[71] *On Christian Teaching*, Preface, 7 (Oxford: Oxford University Press, 1997).
[72] Ibid., 2.19.

uncertain deity by devious paths.'[73] Or again, a modern
Reformed theologian, T. F. Torrance, notes the inseparability
of biblical revelation from the larger framework of reconciliation between God and sinners:

> the Word of God comes to us in the Bible not nakedly and directly
> with clear compelling self-demonstration of the kind that we can
> read it off easily without the pain and struggle of self-renunciation
> and decision, but it comes to us in the limitation and imperfection,
> the ambiguities and contradictions of our fallen ways of thought
> and speech, seeking us in the questionable forms of our humanity
> where we have to let ourselves be questioned down to the roots of
> our being in order to hear it as God's Word. It is not a Word that
> we can hear by our clear-sightedness or master by our reason, but
> one that we can hear only through judgment of the very humanity
> in which it is clothed and to which it is addressed and therefore
> only through crucifixion and repentance.[74]

Christian acts of reading Holy Scripture are thus episodes in
the history of God's gracious, communicative encounter with
the redeemed sinner. Christian reading is, therefore, not within
the range of human competence, for the reader's capacities are
distorted by sin – by choice of wrong ends to which to put the
text; by desire to fashion that which the text says into something
which pleases, rather than something which disturbs or judges
or commands or calls to repentance; by dominance of interests.
Reading Scripture is therefore a microcosm of the history of
judgment and salvation, a point at which that history is realized
in the process of God's communication.

> Our polluted cognitive and spiritual environment darkens under-
> standing ... Self-love can pervert the course of interpretation as it
> does every other human activity. It is the Spirit of understanding
> who enables us to transfer attention away from ourselves and our
> interests to the text and its subject matter. Understanding ... is a
> matter of ethics, indeed, of spirituality.[75]

[73] Calvin, *Institutes of the Christian Religion*, I.6.i, p. 71.

[74] Torrance, *Divine Meaning*, p. 8.

[75] Vanhoozer, 'The Spirit of Understanding', p. 161; cf. Jeffrey, *People of the Book*,
p. 203.

Accordingly, a crucial area for theological reflection is the nature of the reader's *will*. If sin renders us unwilling to hear and manipulative in our reading, then properly-ordered reading is characterized by a certain passivity, a respect for and receptivity towards the text, by a readiness to be addressed and confronted. Attention, astonishment and repentance, together with the delight and freedom in which they issue, characterize the reader of Holy Scripture when he or she reads well, that is, with courtesy and humility. Of course, such 'respect for the otherness of the Other as Other'[76] is by no means proper to Christian acts of reading. It animates the account of the reading of literary texts, for example, in H. Bloom's *The Western Canon*,[77] or in many of the writings of George Steiner.[78] What is distinctive about Christian reading is the domain of objects within which it occurs, and the descriptions to be offered of its agents and their ends. In *this* domain, hearing the text is not simply hearing a 'classic' but listening to divine address. As such, it is an incident in the process of mortification and vivification, which is the fundamental pattern of the life of those baptized into Christ. Crucially, this means that to read Scripture well is to undergo a chastening of the will, even, perhaps, 'the death of the subject and of the will'.[79] Anything less would fail to take seriously the eschatological character of Christian life and therefore of Christian reading. It is surely here, in questions of the wilful character of reading-acts, that the most searching questions are to be asked of the cluster of hermeneutical theories which accord prominence to the creative activities of readers and reading communities in constituting or co-constituting the meaning of the text.

---

[76] A. C. Thiselton, *Interpreting God and the Postmodern Self. On Meaning, Manipulation and Promise* (Edinburgh: T&T Clark, 1995), p. 51.

[77] *The Western Canon. The Books and School of the Ages* (New York: Harcourt Brace, 1994).

[78] See, for example, his seminal 1979 essay '"Critic"/"Reader"', reprinted in P. Davies, ed., *Real Voices. On Reading* (London: Macmillan, 1997), pp. 3–37, or *Real Presences* (Chicago: University of Chicago Press, 1989).

[79] Jennings, 'Baptizing a Social Reading', p. 126.

Whatever else it may wish to say, Christian theology will surely be troubled by any account of the reader's intentions which gives such significance to reading decisions that reading the text in effect becomes rewriting it.[80]

But if the will of the Christian reader is always thus 'mortified', it is also 'vivified', that is, reoriented by being made capable of directing itself to true ends, including the end of hearing God's Word. The self-effacement of the reader, born of the reader's eschatological status as a subject of regeneration, issues in the recovery of the will as it is grasped by God, accosted and enabled to direct itself attentively to the place where God elects to speak.[81] In short: the basic structure of a Christian anthropology of reading will be such that the Christian will find herself caught up in the passage from being a 'hard-hearted' to a 'broken-hearted' reader.[82] Or, as Calvin puts it in a passage which neatly sums up both the *ascesis* and the *ethos* of Christian reading:

> If we ... are not our own but the Lord's, it is clear what error we must flee, and whither we must direct all the acts of our life.
>
> We are not our own: let not our reason nor our will, therefore, sway our plans and deeds. We are not our own: let us therefore not set it as our goal to seek what is expedient for us according to the flesh. We are not our own: in so far as we can, let us therefore forget ourselves and all that is ours.
>
> Conversely, we are God's: let us therefore live for him and die for him. We are God's: let his wisdom and will therefore rule all our actions. We are God's: let all the parts of our life accordingly strive toward him as our only lawful goal. O, how much has that man

---

[80] Worries along these lines are expressed by, for example, K. Vanhoozer, 'The Spirit of Understanding'; Jennings, 'Baptizing a Social Reading'; A. C. Thiselton, 'Reader-Response Hermeneutics, Action Models, and the Parables of Jesus', in R. Lundin, et al., *The Responsibility of Hermeneutics* (Grand Rapids: Eerdmans, 1985), pp. 104f., and A. C. Thiselton, *New Horizons in Hermeneutics. The Theory and Practice of Transforming Biblical Study* (London: HarperCollins, 1992), pp. 499–555.

[81] This point is explored with some force in D. L. Jeffrey's account of the hermeneutics of Wyclif in *People of the Book*, pp. 167–207.

[82] Ibid., p. 370.

profited who, having been taught that he is not his own, has taken away dominion and rule from his own reason that he may yield it to God! For, as consulting our self-interest is the pestilence that most effectively leads to our destruction, so the sole haven of salvation is to be wise in nothing and to will nothing through ourselves but to follow the leading of the Lord alone.[83]

This anthropology could be developed along a number of different trajectories. If reading is part of what Calvin calls 'service' of God, which involves a 'departure from self',[84] then a Christian anthropology of reading will give high profile to *faith*, in its broadest sense of the shape which human life takes in response to the prevenient, gracious Word of God. The 'faithful' reader is the reader whose being and acts are grounded *extra se*, and who corresponds, exists in analogy, to God's creative and redemptive action. Faithful reading is not so much constructive or constitutive of what is heard, but *consent* – consent to the text as an instrument for the speaking of God, and therefore the self-presentation of God's will to save. Reading is an exercise in *conscientia*, not in the modern sense of reflexive moral awareness, but in the much larger sense of 'the response of the human consciousness to the divine judgment',[85] in which we are stripped of our efforts to impose a shape on the text and made capable of free and attentive listening. Or again, such reading could be seen as a mode of discipleship, of 'following the Word',[86] or of obedience. What is most important is that any such language be rooted in talk of the presence and activity of Jesus in the Spirit and of the modes of activity which that presence engenders. A Christian anthropology of reading will need to emphasize both the overruling and redirecting activity of the Spirit in the reader (what Calvin calls the 'bidding of God's Spirit'),[87] and also the reader's own

[83] Calvin, *Institutes of the Christian Religion*, III.7.1 (p. 690).
[84] Ibid.
[85] T. F. Torrance's definition of Calvin's use of the term in *The Hermeneutics of John Calvin* (Edinburgh: Scottish Academic Press, 1988), p. 163.
[86] Vanhoozer, 'The Spirit of Understanding', p. 157.
[87] *Institutes of the Christian Religion*, III.7.1 (p. 690).

invocation of the Spirit, which is the basic act of existence in Christ. Christian reading is thus, very simply, a *prayerful* activity.[88] Prayerfulness is not a spiritual embellishment, or even a preliminary recoil or gathering of resources before proceeding to read in an entirely natural manner. Prayer constitutes and accompanies Christian reading, setting willed acts of interpretation in an entirely new context, relativizing them and transforming them, beseeching God to effect the transparency and conformity of reading-acts to acts which God in Christ performs through the Holy Spirit. Far from being a mere vague ambience within which our interpreting wills continue as normal, prayer is the humbling and reorientation of our agency, which now finds its end in hearing God's Word.

This specifically theological account in effect 'de-standardizes' the reader. Reading, on this account, is only at a very basic and rather trivial level a basic human enterprise for which all rational persons are competent. Engaging in the particular activity of reading Holy Scripture as the Word of God requires that I be a particular kind of person, one who through the Spirit is liberated from self-concern and the pursuit of self-defined interests, and formed both to love and seek for the ends which God establishes for human life. This is why a Christian theological hermeneutic will give space to describing the formation of the soul of the reader, so that Christian skills of reading and Christian reader-roles can be learned and practised. Thus:

> [T]o interpret God's discourse more reliably, we must come to know God better. A hermeneutics of divine discourse requires supplementation with discussions of other ways of knowing God, and of ways of knowing God better. And engaging in the practice of interpreting texts so as to discern God's discourse requires engaging simultaneously in whatever practices might yield a better knowledge of God. Those practices will be practices of the heart as well as the head, of devotion as well as reflection.[89]

---

[88] See here E. Charry, *By the Renewing of Your Minds. The Pastoral Function of Christian Doctrine* (Oxford: Oxford University Press, 1997), p. 21.

[89] Wolterstorff, *Divine Discourse*, p. 239.

In some recent writing, this point has been secured by appeal to the language of virtue, character and the acquisition of habits through learning skills and adopting roles.[90] Such language is an entirely proper way of drawing attention to the fact that, if we are to be wise readers of Scripture, we need to become particular kinds of people. Yet used carelessly, such language can threaten to immanentize or psychologize the eschatological character of life in Christ. Mortification and vivification are intrusive, and not simply unproblematic extensions of our existing egos. Moreover, 'skills' and 'roles' are always ambiguous. They do not exist without social frameworks, and such frameworks are notoriously protective against critique, even repressive. Furthermore, skills and roles can rather easily become reliable routines at our disposal. There are no infallible safeguards here. But at least it needs to be said that the internal content of a Christian anthropology of reading – in particular, strong reference to the free, sovereign and spiritual character of God's Word and its self-presence in the event of the giving of the Spirit – ought to serve as a warning that even the best methods or the most sensitive acquired habits can never possess what is only achieved in the promise and gift of God.

What, finally, of the public aspects of Christian attention to the Word, the 'culture' of reading? Christian readers read as part of the company of God's people, who assemble to hear God speak. As with everything else, a basic rule in talking about reading is: 'The really important questions about oneself, about what kind of person one fundamentally is, are not questions which can be settled by introspection.'[91] If this is so, then the intelligibility of a Christian theology of readers and their acts will depend upon the creation and inhabitation of social spaces in which the hearing of Scripture is practised well.

---

[90] See, for example, Vanhoozer, 'The Spirit of Understanding', p. 161; E. Rogers, 'How the Virtues of an Interpreter Presuppose and Perfect Hermeneutics'; Fowl and Jones, *Reading in Communion*, pp. 29–109.

[91] A. Kenny, *The Self* (Milwaukee: Marquette University Press, 1988), p. 31.

The constellation of dispositions and skills which are deployed by the wise Christian reader cannot be grasped apart from the life and practices of the Christian community, for they are drawn from public stores of accumulated knowledge and experience, and they take form as ruled behaviour.[92] They are also reinforced by public activities in the church which both appeal to and draw upon a Christian culture of reading. Corporate reading conventions are best seen in such things as canon, creed and tradition. The Christian convention of the canon shapes reading by construing the Bible as an integrated, purposive whole. The credal convention seeks to ensure that a Christian reading of the canon is governed by appropriate (that is, biblically informed) expectations, and so offers a minimalist map or guide to what a reading of the Bible will yield. The Christian convention of tradition maintains that one important test of the Christianness of a reading will be whether it can be shown to belong to the family of readings which constitute the church's exegetical traditions.

Such examples seek to show that reading, even of the most secluded sort, is a form of *sensus communis* as much as it is a private mental act. Yet one caveat concerning talk of a Christian culture of reading remains: it is of the greatest importance that in talking of the corporate aspects of Christian reading we do not allow theological language about the church to dissolve into generic language about 'forms of life', 'sociality', even 'ecclesiality'. Talk of God's action has to be retained as real and operative. 'Ecclesiality' has enjoyed enormous prestige in modern Protestantism since Schleiermacher, especially in some recent attempts to break up the logjams of liberalism by appeal to social-scientific or philo-sophical theories of language, culture and custom. But 'ecclesiality' and 'church' are not concepts of the same kind; and to talk of the latter we need to say much of God and the

[92] See here A. C. Thiselton, 'Knowledge, Myth and Corporate Memory', in Doctrine Commission of the Church of England, *Believing in the Church. The Corporate Nature of Faith* (London: SPCK, 1981), pp. 45–78.

gospel.[93] This means, therefore, that Christian theology will want to lay emphasis on the sheerly intrusive character of God's Word, which is not tameable by socialization. At least one of the functions of the doctrine of *sola scriptura* is to erect a barrier against the drift of an ecclesial culture of reading into hardness of heart. In short: the church, if it reads well, always reads against itself.

6. In Place of a Conclusion

> It is therefore necessary above all else to be moved the fear of God towards learning his will ... After that it is necessary, through holiness, to become docile, and not contradict holy scripture – whether we understand it ... or fail to understand it (as when we feel that we could by ourselves gain better knowledge or give better instruction) – but rather ponder and believe that what is written there, even if obscure, is better and truer than any insights that we can gain by our own efforts.[94]

> The student who fears God earnestly seeks his will in the holy scriptures.[95]

> And who can ensure that we say what is right and say it in the right way but the one 'in whose hands we, and our sermons, exist'?[96]

---

[93] For two twentieth-century examples from my own Anglican tradition of talk about the church which is rooted very directly in talk of God, see A. M. Ramsey, *The Gospel and the Catholic Church* (London: Longmans, Green, 1936), and D. M. MacKinnon, *The Church of God* (London: Dacre Press, 1940). On the former, see R. Williams, 'Theology and the Churches', in R. Gill and L. Kendall, eds., *Michael Ramsey as Theologian* (London: Darton, Longman & Todd, 1995), pp. 9–28; on the latter, see P. Wignall, 'D. M. MacKinnon. An Introduction to His Early Theological Writings', *New Studies in Theology* 1 (1980), pp. 75–94.

[94] Augustine, *On Christian Teaching*, II.17.

[95] Ibid., III.1.

[96] Ibid., IV.88.

3

READING THE BIBLE:
THE EXAMPLE OF
BARTH AND BONHOEFFER

I

Two things at least are clear about the relationship of Barth and
Bonhoeffer: that disentangling the history of their relation is of
considerable importance for making sense of Bonhoeffer, if
not of Barth; and that the disentangling is a rather delicate
operation which involves some discriminating interpretation of
the writings of two complex theologians.[1] Much, for example,
hangs on what we are to make of Bonhoeffer's scattered
remarks on Barth, revelation and non-religious interpretation
in the prison writings, and of Barth's puzzled response to
them.[2] Bonhoeffer experts will no doubt put me straight, but
my own – highly corrigible – judgment is that the prison texts
do not contain the most important or interesting things which
Bonhoeffer had to say: there is much more theological good
sense on questions of the presentation of the gospel to be
found in the Finkenwalde homiletics lectures, for example.[3]
The common attempt to display the coherence of these
writings from the end of Bonhoeffer's life with more developed
aspects of his thought – his appropriation of Barth's early

---

[1] The best recent account is A. Pangritz, *Karl Barth in the Theology of Dietrich
   Bonhoeffer* (Grand Rapids: Eerdmans, 2000).
[2] See Barth's letter to Eberhard Bethge in *Fragments Grave and Gay* (London:
   Collins, 1971), pp. 119–22.
[3] D. Bonhoeffer, 'Finkenwalder Homiletik', in *Gesammelte Schriften*, IV (Munich:
   Kaiser, 1961), pp. 237–89.

critique of religion,[4] Bonhoeffer's fondness for the Old Testament and his concern with the gospel as moral and social reality – are only partially successful, and the fragmentary state of the remarks leave them perilously exposed to abuse by interpreters invoking Bonhoeffer's shade for modish theological or ecclesiastical projects. Again, a good deal in clarifying Bonhoeffer's relation to Barth hangs on pondering Bonhoeffer's worry that Barth gave insufficient weight to the ethical. Barth was, I believe, quite right when he pointed out in his letter to Bethge that Bonhoeffer's emphasis on the ethical was in fact 'just the outlook which I presupposed';[5] indeed, Barth was from the beginning no less a moral theologian than Bonhoeffer, and his *Ethics* deserves at least the same kind of serious study that has been devoted to Bonhoeffer's work of the same title.[6]

My suggestion here, however, is that rather than pursuing questions about positivism of revelation or about the worldly and ethical, light can be shed on the relation of Bonhoeffer and Barth by looking at the place of the interpretation of Scripture in their respective theologies. Both give a thoroughly theological depiction of reading Scripture, that is, a depiction in which language about God is direct and operative; both, therefore, define the human act of interpretation as radical attentiveness and self-relinquishment to God's saving self-communication through the instrumentality of Holy Scripture. This, I suggest, is one of the points at which these two church

---

[4] Whilst the prison writings are in continuity with Barth's criticism of religion as a discrete cultural magnitude, they extend the critique in a way which goes well beyond Barth, and I remain uneasy with interpretations of the *Letters and Papers* which see Bonhoeffer as simply protesting against the restriction of God to a supposed sacral sphere (for this interpretation, see, for example, D. M. MacKinnon, 'Parable and Sacrament', *Explorations in Theology* (London: SCM Press, 1979), pp. 166–81, and, more recently, Williams, *On Christian Theology*, pp. 40f., 84f., 104 n. 20).

[5] Barth, *Fragments Grave and Gay*, p. 120.

[6] On the presence of ethical concerns in the early Barth, see now D. Clough, 'Ethics in *Krisis*. The Significance of the *Römerbrief* for Karl Barth's Ethics', Ph.D. diss., Yale, 2000.

theologians come very close to each other, and offer much food for thought to church and theology now.

Curiously, the significance of Scripture and its interpretation for understanding both Barth and Bonhoeffer has often been passed over rather quickly, and both have frequently been subjected to heavily conceptual interpretation. In the case of Barth, it is rarely recognized how much of his teaching in the 1920s and beyond took the form of exegetical lectures. Of the fifteen lecture courses Barth offered at Göttingen, for example, seven were exegetical; and, though the amount of time spent on direct exegetical teaching declined as Barth's career progressed, he did lecture on John, Philippians, Colossians and James at Münster, Philippians and James in Bonn, and Colossians and 1 Peter in the late 1930s in Basel. And, of course, even when he was not offering biblical lectures, Barth was constantly at work on the lengthy exegetical sections of the *Church Dogmatics*. Given the fact that of these courses only those on 1 Corinthians and Philippians were published in Barth's lifetime, and only the John course so far published posthumously, the neglect of this aspect of his work is unsurprising; but it continues to promote a rather distorted picture of his theology and its development. At best, Barth's biblical writings are treated as a quarry for theological themes, or as exemplification of his break with theological liberalism, rather than as straightforward attempts to talk about the contents of the Bible. Bonhoeffer himself saw things rather more accurately: in his 1931/2 Berlin lectures on 'The History of Systematic Theology in the Twentieth Century', he remarked that Barth's theology is 'not to be explained in terms of the collapse of the war ... but in terms of a new reading of Scripture, of the Word which God has spoken in God's self-revelation ... This is not war psychosis but listening to God's Word'.[7] What preoccupied Barth in the 1920s was not the so-called 'crisis of representation' in European high culture, but dogmatics and exegesis, and, by derivation, questions of how exegesis ought properly to be

---

[7] Cited by Pangritz, *Karl Barth in the Theology of Dietrich Bonhoeffer*, p. 36.

undertaken, and of what strategies best serve the hearing of the Word.

In the case of Bonhoeffer, again, much of the literature takes little account of the fact that 'the majority of Bonhoeffer's work is biblical exposition'[8] apart from his two dissertations *Sanctorum Communio* and *Act and Being*. The fact that the recent *Cambridge Companion to Dietrich Bonhoeffer*, for example, says virtually nothing on this theme simply confirms that students of Bonhoeffer have often gravitated towards other issues: sociality and the ethical, most of all.[9] One result of this is an over-theorized picture of Bonhoeffer; the practical directness of Bonhoeffer's biblical writings, and his sense that biblical exposition is a task of the theologian in which theory may be a hindrance, have been lost from view.

My suggestion, by contrast, is that an account of both Barth and Bonhoeffer, and equally an account of their relation, needs to give a good deal of attention to their writings on Scripture. In doing so, it is important not to be derailed into too much discussion of methodological issues, especially the stance each adopted towards that cluster of interpretative conventions we call the historical-critical method. Both, of course were schooled to interpret Scripture through this method; both found it a tolerable servant but a bad master; both came to

[8] E. G. Wendel, *Studien zur Homiletik Dietrich Bonhoeffers* (Tübingen: Mohr, 1985), p. 68.

[9] An early important survey of the territory was offered by R. Grunow, 'Dietrich Bonhoeffers Schriftauslegung', *Die Mündige Welt*, vol. 1 (Munich: Kaiser, 1955), pp. 62–76; Grunow did much to shape later accounts, such as that by W. Harrelson, 'Bonhoeffer and the Bible', in M. Marty, ed., *The Place of Bonhoeffer* (London: SCM Press, 1963), pp. 115–42. Other basic accounts of Bonhoeffer's biblical interests can be found in J. W. Woelfel, *Bonhoeffer's Theology. Classical and Revolutionary* (Nashville: Abingdon Press, 1970), pp. 208–38; J. A. Phillips, *The Form of Christ in the World* (London: Collins, 1967), p. 84–105; J. D. Godsey, *The Theology of Dietrich Bonhoeffer* (London: SCM Press, 1960), pp. 119–94. See also the important study by M. Kuske, *The Old Testament as the Book of Christ* (Philadelphia: Westminister, 1976). Despite its declared hermeneutical interests, E. Feil's *The Theology of Dietrich Bonhoeffer* (Philadelphia: Fortress Press, 1985) has little to say about Scripture; F. de Lange, *Waiting on the Word. Dietrich Bonhoeffer on Speaking about God* (Grand Rapids: Eerdmans, 2000), is a highly abstract rendering of the materials which seriously misconstrues what Bonhoeffer is about.

believe that, detached from evangelical convictions about revelation, it quickly became theologically and spiritually unserviceable. But the unease of both with dominant interpretative strategies was theologically, not methodologically, driven. Both attempted not so much to create a method as to offer a theological and spiritual construal of Scripture and its reading by the church. In particular, both offer a consistently theological portrayal of what it means to be a reader of Scripture. Both – emphatically – refused to fall into the trap of psychologizing the act of interpretation, as had happened in both romantic and critical hermeneutics. But both considered it important to depict what is involved in being a holy reader of Holy Scripture, even if both sat light on the language of disposition and virtue so beloved of contemporary accounts of interpretation as church practice. It is, I suggest, in the area of these questions that we may not only discover much in common between Barth and Bonhoeffer, but also some ways of thinking to enable critical reflection on our own theology and church life.

II

One of the most crucial development in Barth's theology in his years as professor at Göttingen was his increasing awareness of and alignment of himself with the Reformed tradition.[10] His exposure to that tradition, both in Calvin and in other theologians and confessional writings of the Reformation period, shaped him in at least three ways. First, it gave him early on in his academic work a dogmatic framework within which his kerygmatic and polemical instincts could be refined and disciplined. Though he was later to repair, adjust or rebuild the framework at many points, its basic shape remained intact, even in the *Church Dogmatics*. Second, it offered Barth a set of

---

[10] On this, see the excellent study by M. Freudenberg, *Karl Barth und die reformierte Theologie* (Neukirchen: Neukirchener Verlag, 1997), and H. Scholl, ed., *Karl Barth und Johannes Calvin. Karl Barths Göttinger Calvin-Vorlesung von 1922* (Neukirchen: Neukirchener Verlag, 1995).

theological categories through which to re-articulate his interest in morals, which he had not entirely abandoned even at the most extreme moments of his repudiation of modern Protestantism. And third, it offered him both an account of the nature of Holy Scripture and its place in church and theology, and – in the work of Calvin above all – a model of theological interpretation which enabled him to focus and extend the exegetical instincts of the *Römerbrief*. It is this third point I wish to take up here.[11]

Already in preparing the commentary on Romans, Barth had found Calvin a model of energetic wrestling with the text,[12] and his lectures on Calvin in 1922 give a revealing early account of Calvin's exegetical practice from which much can be gleaned about Barth's thinking on biblical interpretation in the Göttingen period and beyond. Indeed, it is not too much to claim the 'constitutive significance' of this section of the Calvin lectures for his later development.[13] Throughout the lecture cycle, Barth is at pains to emphasize that the Reformed tradition is characteristically concerned with the sovereignty of divine action which enables and sustains a corresponding human action: Calvin the theologian of grace is Calvin the moralist. This also leads in Calvin's case to a particular construal of the nature of exegetical activity. The basic rule which Barth announces is this: 'Wherever, as in the Reformed, it is a matter of acting *with* God and *for* God, knowledge *of* God has to come first'.[14] This means that interpretation is indeed the reader's act; in reading Scripture, it cannot be that the reader is purely passive, for '[t]he relation to the Bible is a living one. The spring does not flow of itself. It has to be tapped. The waters have to be drawn. The answer is not already

---

[11] Here I concentrate on the lectures now translated as *The Theology of Calvin* (Grand Rapids: Eerdmans, 1995); a full account would also need to look in detail at the material on *das Schriftprinzip* in the 1923 lectures on *Die Theologie der reformierten Bekenntnisschriften* (Zürich: TVZ, 1998), pp. 63–103.

[12] Cf. *The Epistle to the Romans* (London: Oxford University Press, 1933), p. 7.

[13] Freudenberg, *Karl Barth und die reformierte Theologie*, p. 138.

[14] *The Theology of Calvin*, p. 388.

there; we have to ask what it is.'[15] This act of reading is necessarily 'objective': 'The Bible', Barth says, 'calls for objective study.'[16] But Barth is already finding in Calvin a specific construal of the act of 'objective study', one whose 'objectivity' is not studied neutrality but rather a humble orientation towards God's communicative spontaneity. To read 'objectively' is thus to read in awareness of and dependence upon a divine movement. 'God himself must bear witness concerning himself to those who would receive and pass on the witness of the biblical author.'[17]

In effect, what Barth discovers in Calvin is an account of the act of the interpretative situation which sees the reading of Scripture not as a spontaneous human action performed towards a passive and mute textual object, but as an episode in the communicative history of God with us. 'God is not just the theme but also the Lord of biblical truth'[18] – God, we might say, is not only textual content but also the primary agent of the text's realization before us. This is why a 'purely historical understanding of the mind of scripture would be for Calvin no understanding at all. The mind of scripture cannot be merely the object of exposition but has to be its subject as well.'[19] The reading of Holy Scripture is thus a field of divine activity; it is not simply human handling of a textual object. And that divine activity is God's speech to which we are, quite simply, to attend. 'Exegesis has to be a conversation in which one speaks and the other listens. Listening … is the task of the exegete'.[20] Once again: Barth discovers in Calvin what he calls his 'extraordinary objectivity'.

> We can learn from Calvin what it means to stay close to the text, to focus with tense attention on what is actually there. Everything else

[15] Ibid.
[16] Ibid.
[17] Ibid., p. 389.
[18] Ibid.
[19] Ibid.
[20] Ibid.

derives from this. But it has to *derive* from this. If it does not, then the expounding is not real questioning and readiness to listen.[21]

In brief, then, the Calvin lectures offer an account of interpretative activity in which Scripture is understood not simply as a natural entity to be investigated as historical or religious artefact, but as the textual ingredient of a process of divine self-manifestation. As Barth put the matter in a lecture on Schleiermacher's hermeneutics a year later, the text *refers*, that is, it indicates a transaction initiated from outside the reader whose subject is not *me*. And, moreover:

> How remarkable that [Schleiermacher] does not sem to have considered the possibility that the thought which I understand in what is said by someone else ... might be contingently, without any qualitative or quantitative possibilities of misunderstanding, the truth or Word of God, and that I should then have good reason to treat this address more specifically and more seriously than any other as the bearer of *this* content, a reference to *this* subject. What if New Testament hermeneutics ... were to consist quite simply of taking these texts more seriously in this specific sense?[22]

'Taking these texts more seriously' – that is, reading them out of their content as divine speech and resisting appropriation or annexation – places the interpreter under a requirement to be made into a specific kind of person: a listener, one addressed, and not a judge, critic or observer. The real heart of Barth's conception of the exegetical task of theology in the 1920s and beyond is thus not essentially a quarrel with historical methods per se. The polemic against the historicism of Harnack and others is real enough, but ad hoc. What troubles Barth most is not methods but their expansion into a sufficient explanation of Scripture, their failure to envisage Scripture in terms of the relation of revelatory divine speech and obedient human attentiveness, and their promotion of a false anthropology of interpretative activity. Barth's alternative stated propositionally,

---

[21] Ibid.
[22] *The Theology of Schleiermacher* (Grand Rapids: Eerdmans, 1981), p. 183.

is: *Exegesis is an aspect of sanctification.* This does not mean that we should undertake some independent investigation of the human interpreter, still less that the controlling centre of scriptural interpretation is a process of self-conscious self-cultivation. (Barth later worried that Bonhoeffer had allowed himself to stray a bit too far in this direction.) Sanctification is the anthropological correlate of revelation. 'Sanctified' reading – that is, reading the Bible 'objectively' in the sense he finds in Calvin – is a matter of self-effacing subjection to the drastic converting power of the Word and work of God.

These interlocking concerns – for 'objective' interpretation which sees the Scriptural text as divine speech-act, and for a fittingly converted attention on the part of the reader – emerge early in Barth, and stay with him throughout his theological development. Fairly early on in the *Dogmatics*, near the end of I/2, they find expression in the treatment of 'Scripture as a witness to divine revelation'. Here Barth is concerned to clarify, on the one hand, the nature of Scripture as 'sign'[23] indicating divine revelation, and, on the other hand, what he calls 'a right and necessary attitude of obedience to the witness of revelation'.[24]

What in the Calvin lectures Barth identified as 'objective' interpretation, he now refers to – a little coyly, perhaps – as 'historical' interpretation. Scripture is to be interpreted 'historically', that is, with an eye to what it does as human text, which is to bear witness to divine revelation. Skeletally expressed, Barth's argument is this. Scripture is witness: it is not identical with revelation, but that instrument through which the testimony of the prophets and apostles is set before us. Our thinking about the nature of Scripture is thus determined, on the one hand, by the 'limitation' of Scripture (it is only a human word), and, on the other hand, by the 'positive' element, namely that Scripture is 'revelation as it comes to us'.[25] The relation of the limitation and

[23] *Church Dogmatics* I/2, p. 458.
[24] Ibid., p. 460.
[25] Ibid., p. 463.

the positive element is conceptualized by Barth on analogy to the hypostatic union: 'there is', he writes, 'no point in ignoring the writtenness of Holy Writ for the sake of its holiness, its humanity for the sake of its divinity. We must not ignore it any more than we do the humanity of Jesus Christ Himself.'[26] Hence 'historical' exposition is a non-negotiable requirement: what we must interpret is this human word, but we must interpret this human word for what it is. And interpreting the Bible for what it is, that is, historically, means interpreting these texts in terms of their 'specific intention'.[27] That is, 'when we do take the humanity of the Bible quite seriously, we must also take quite definitely the fact that as a human word it points away from itself, that as a word it points towards a fact, an object'.[28] In short: 'historical' interpretation means 'that we have to listen to what [the Bible] says to us as a human word. We have to understand it as a human word in the light of what it says.'[29] As in the Calvin lectures, so here: encountering the text of Scripture is encountering a human word which is caught up into revelation, though in such a way that it does not surrender its humanity. Not to read the human word as such is not to read it for what it is, and so deny its specific, determinate character as *this* human word which functions in *this* way. 'The Bible cannot be read unbiblically. And in this case it means that it cannot be read with such disregard for its character even as a human word. It cannot be read so unhistorically.'[30] Because the Bible's human task is to refer to and bear the divine speech, any isolation of its humanity (by exclusive focus on 'biblical history' or 'biblical personalities') is in fact *abstract*, out of conformity with its particular human, historical character.

Scripture must therefore be read for what it *is*. But it can only be so read by those in whom a certain change has been

---

[26] Ibid.
[27] Ibid., p. 464.
[28] Ibid.
[29] Ibid., p. 466.
[30] Ibid., pp. 466f.

wrought, on the basis of which we are able properly to attend to 'this historical definiteness of the word'.[31] A reader who does not so attend 'will certainly not be able to understand it, because he has no *locus* from which he can understand it';[32] and so 'there can be no question of a legitimate understanding of the Bible by this reader ... for the time being, i.e., until his relation to what is said in the Bible changes, this reader cannot be regarded as a serious reader and exegete'.[33] For, once again, acts of exegesis have to be governed by and in conformity to what the text is; exegesis is not arbitrary, for 'in exegesis ... there is only one truth'.[34] Barth has a powerful sense of the determinate character of the texts of Scripture:[35] 'the mystery of the sovereign freedom of the substance' must control the way in which Scripture is read.[36] And so Barth goes on:

> We have to know the mystery of the substance if we are really to meet it, if we are really to be opened ready, really to give ourselves to it, when we are told it, that it may really meet us as the substance. And when it is a matter of understanding, the knowledge of this mystery will create in us a peculiar fear and reserve which is not at all usual to us. We will then know that in the face of this subject-matter there can be no question of our achieving, as we do in others, the confident approach which masters and subdues the matter. It is rather a question of our being gripped ... so that it is only as those who are mastered by the subject-matter, who are subdued by it, that we can investigate the humanity of the word by which it is told us. The sovereign freedom of this subject-matter to speak of itself imposes on us in the face of the word as such and its historicity an ἐποχή ... And the knowledge of this mystery will see to it that the work of exposition, which is the goal of all hearing and understanding, at least enters the stage of convalescence from the sickness with which all exposition is almost incurably afflicted, the sickness of an insolent and arbitrary reading in. If the exposition of

[31] Ibid., p. 468.
[32] Ibid., p. 469.
[33] Ibid.
[34] Ibid., p. 470.
[35] Attempts to align Barth and Derrida often founder at this point.
[36] *Church Dogmatics* I/2, p. 470.

a human word consists in the relating of this word to what it intends or denotes, and if we know the sovereign freedom, the independent glory of this subject-matter in relation both to the word which is before us and to ourselves, we will be wholesomely restrained, at the very least in our usual self-assured mastery of the relationship, as though we already knew its content and our exposition could give something more than hints in its direction. We shall be at least restrained in our evil domination of the text (even though in this age we can as little rid ourselves of it as we can of our old Adam generally).[37]

What Barth is expounding here is a theological anthropology of reading Scripture. The text is *thus*; interpretative acts are acts which are properly convenient or suitable to the given, historically discernible, nature of the text as an instrument of divine action. Another way of making sense of what Barth is doing might be to say that he is recommending a practical hermeneutics, one oriented to the text as a communicative event, and one which does not reduce the text either to raw material for historical reconstruction of what is anterior to the text, or to narrative icon. The really important questions in grappling with the nature of Scriptural interpretation concern the identity of the divine revealer, the content of the divine speech, and the fittingly attentive obedience of the hearer. Or, as Barth put it in his swansong lectures: 'The question *about the Word* and this question alone fulfills and does justice to the intention of the biblical authors in their writings'.[38] What, then, of Bonhoeffer?

III

After writing *Sanctorum Communio* and *Act and Being*, Bonhoeffer's interest in systematic and philosophical theology declined. As he became increasingly preoccupied with direct interpretation of Scripture, the genre of his writing shifts to

---

[37] Ibid., pp. 470f.
[38] *Evangelical Theology* (London: Weidenfeld & Nicolson, 1963), p. 35.

become a good deal less formal and conceptual. He becomes, in effect, a practical, biblical theologian, writing with what is often drastic simplicity and force. The determined plainness and resistance to intellectual sophistication is to be taken at face value: to read the biblical writings from the 1930s is not to be invited to reflect, but to be summoned by evangelical address. This is why (*contra*, for example, Charles Marsh) it seems to me entirely proper to read writings like *Life Together* or *Discipleship* as 'pietistic and naive',[39] provided that we use such terms to advertise the fact that Bonhoeffer is concerned to unleash the critical power of the Scriptural word without the mediation of conceptual sophistication. To find in these homiletic writings 'important sub-textual discussions with Bonhoeffer's philosophical conversation partners' or 'an elaborate texture of biblical, philosophical and political thematics'[40] is to miss the point. Again, it is important not to interpret these writings as simply concerned with 'the ethical' or 'the worldly', and thus to see them only as staging-posts on the way to Bonhoeffer's last writings. Such a reading is too abstract, and fails to take into account the crucial factor that, at this stage, Scripture is irreducible for Bonhoeffer; it is not a means of attaining moral concreteness, but, quite simply, the concrete point at which Christian thought and action begin and end.

The character of the biblical writings of the mid- and late 1930s can be seen by setting them alongside Bonhoeffer's well-known published lectures on Genesis in *Creation and Fall*. These lectures are in many respects a transitional document. They clearly stand in the line of Barth's biblical expositions from the 1920s on at least two counts. First, they seek to undertake self-consciously theological exegesis. Bonhoeffer explains at the start of the lecture cycle,

> Theological exposition takes the Bible as the book of the church and interprets it as such. This is its presupposition and this

---

[39] C. Marsh, *Reclaiming Dietrich Bonhoeffer. The Promise of His Theology* (Oxford: Oxford University Press, 1994), p. x.

[40] Ibid., pp. xf.

presupposition constitutes its method; its method is a continual returning from the text (as determined by all the methods of philological and historical research) to this presupposition. That is the objectivity [*Sachlichkeit*] in the method of theological exposition. And on this objectivity alone does it base its claim to have the nature of a science.'[41]

Like Barth, in other words, Bonhoeffer refuses to identify objectivity with method: the *Wissenschaftlichkeit* of exegesis is its orientation to Scripture as the church's book, that is, a text which has its place in that sphere of human life and history which is generated by God's revelation. To read it otherwise is not to read *it*, but to misread it by mislocating and therefore misconstruing the text. Second, theological exegesis construes Scripture as a unified whole, and defines that coherence Christologically. The church, and therefore the theologian of the church,

> reads the whole of Holy Scripture as the book of the end, of the new, of Christ. Where Holy Scripture, upon which the church of Christ stands, speaks of creation, of the beginning, what else can it say other than that it is only from Christ that we can know what the beginning is?[42]

And for this reason, Bonhoeffer's exposition is thematic: within the text, read Christologically, there can be discerned certain key themes which it is the task of the interpreter to draw out.

Yet *Creation and Fall* is of a quite different order from writings such as *Discipleship* or the various meditations on the psalter. Partly it is a matter of context (professional university lecture rather than homily in the context of theological and pastoral formation). But there is also in *Creation and Fall* a residual interest in philosophical matters which often surfaces in a way of interpreting the text through conceptual paraphrase. Barth himself did something similar, notably in *Romans* and *The Resurrection of the Dead*. But in his case, the texture of the

[41] *Creation and Fall. A Theological Exposition of Genesis 1–3* (Minneapolis: Fortress Press, 1997), pp. 22f.

[42] Ibid., p. 22.

concepts was usually (not always, of course) more densely theological, whereas in *Creation and Fall* Bonhoeffer is still in many respects preoccupied with some of the metaphysical questions of *Sanctorum Communio* or *Act and Being*. And so for all its genuinely theological character, *Creation and Fall* does not simply restrict itself to repeating or applying the text.

With the slightly later biblical writings, we are in a different world. The direct, homiletical rhetoric, the deliberate avoidance of technicality or complexity, the prose stripped to the basics, are all tokens of the fact that Bonhoeffer has come round to an understanding of the task of interpreting Scripture which is governed by two convictions: that Holy Scripture is the *viva vox Dei*, and that this living voice demands an attitude of ready submission and active compliance. These two convictions are remarkably similar to what Barth himself discovered in the heritage of Reformed Christianity, and they can now be traced in Bonhoeffer.

The presupposition of the biblical writings of Bonhoeffer's middle period is that in Scripture God makes himself present in a direct way (a point easy to miss in the rather loose moralizing readings of these works, especially *Life Together* and *Discipleship*). Bonhoeffer articulates that presupposition in a remarkable lecture from August 1935 on the 'Making Present of New Testament Texts'.[43] Along with Barth's much more famous riposte to Bultmann from the early 1950s, this lecture is one of the few really serious attempts to call into question on theological grounds the entire project of 'hermeneutical realization' which has exercised such fascination for modern theology and biblical interpretation.

Bonhoeffer distinguishes two senses of *Vergegenwärtigung*. In the first sense, it is a matter of justifying the present before the tribunal of the present; in the second, of justifying the present before the tribunal of the biblical message. Bonhoeffer is decidedly hostile to the former sense, which he believes is

[43] 'Vergegenwärtigung neutestamentlicher Texte', *Gesammelte Schriften*, III (Munich: Kaiser, 1966), pp. 303–24.

trapped in a false relation to Scripture. It assumes that we have in ourselves (whether in reason, or culture, or *Volk*) 'the Archimedean point by which Scripture and proclamation are to be judged'.[44] On this, Bonhoeffer is quite blunt: 'This making present of the Christian message leads directly to paganism.'[45] Bonhoeffer is notably critical of turning the question of 'making present' into a 'methodological question', for lurking within that is a disordered relation to Scripture, indeed, 'a dangerous decadence of faith'.[46]

Such a critique emerges, however, out of a distinctive conception of the nature of Holy Scripture, one which has already moved beyond that presupposed in the exegetical work of *Creation and Fall*, above all by working with a vivid sense of the perspicuity of Scripture. That perspicuity renders redundant the somewhat cumbersome technicalities of the philosophy of existence which burden the exposition of the early chapters of Genesis. What Bonhoeffer contests is the assumption that Holy Scripture is inert until realized by interpretative acts of 'making present'. 'True making present' requires no 'act of making present';[47] rather, it is a matter of 'the question of the *Sache*', of the text itself. The parallel with Barth is striking: issues of interpretation are subservient to issues of the matter of the text, namely, Jesus Christ who here announces his presence. 'When Christ comes to speech in the word of the New Testament, there is "making present". Not where the present puts forward its claim before Christ but where the present stands before Christ's claim, *there is "making present"*.'[48] When projects of *Vergegenwärtigung* absolutize the interpreter's present, summoning the texts before that present review and possible 'realization', Bonhoeffer argues that the human present is not determined by 'a definition of time'[49] but by 'the word of Christ

[44] Ibid., p. 304.
[45] Ibid., p. 305.
[46] Ibid., p. 306.
[47] Ibid.
[48] Ibid., p. 307.
[49] Ibid., p. 304.

as the Word of God'. 'The *concretissimum* of the Christian message and of the exposition of texts is not a human act of "making present", but is always God himself, in the Holy Spirit'.[50]

There is a direct consequence here for the task of interpretation which shapes very profoundly the biblical writings of this period of Bonhoeffer's life. Christian proclamation becomes relevant through *Sachlichkeit*, that is, through being 'bound to Scripture'.[51] The 'matter' of the New Testament is Christ present in the word; he, not I, is the proper logical subject of *Vergegenwärtigung*,[52] and so the making present of the text is nothing other than 'Auslegung des Wortes'.[53] Crucially, this means that the task of establishing relevance is not pre- or post-exegetical; on the contrary, exegesis itself performs this task, and does so because the textual word which is the concern of exegesis is Christ's address of church and world in the potency of the Spirit. That word is not as it were waiting on the fringes of the human present, hoping somehow to be made real; it announces itself in its own proper communicative vigour.

Bonhoeffer's deployment of dogmatic materials in this lecture is quite minimal, restricted to a few Christological and pneumatological hints. But the implied doctrinal framework is remarkably companionable with Barth's use of the doctrines of Christ and Spirit to subvert heavy-duty hermeneutical theory, both in his response to Bultmann and in his treatment of the prophetic office of the risen Christ near the end of *Church Dogmatics* IV. In both, appeal to the place of the text in the fabric of revelation drastically simplifies the questions of hermeneutics. It is worth noting, moreover, that Bonhoeffer's 1935 lecture is in some important ways quite distant from some of the material in the prison writings as they have been interpreted by revisionist theologians. At least in 1935, the answer to

---

[50] Ibid., p. 307.
[51] Ibid.
[52] Cf. ibid., pp. 309f.
[53] Ibid., p. 308. See also 'Finkenwalder Homiletik', pp. 253f.

the question which Bonhoeffer would later ask – the question of '[w]ho Christ really is, for us today'[54] – is very plain: 'HE himself, and HE alone and he in his entirety'.[55]

This account of the utter concreteness of Scripture and its interpretation forms the background to the picture of the true reader of Scripture. The question of the correct attitude which the reader of Scripture is to demonstrate is an important one for Bonhoeffer, who addresses it more expressly than does Barth. Indeed, the 'Introduction to Daily Meditation' written by Bethge under Bonhoeffer's supervision and circulated from Finkenwalde in 1936 caused Barth some unease on precisely this score. In a letter to Bonhoeffer from the Bergli on 14 October of that year, Barth wrote:

> I read it carefully but I can hardly say that I am very happy about it. I cannot go with the distinction in principle between theological work and devotional edification which is evident in this piece of writing and which I can also perceive in your letter. Furthermore, an almost indefinable odour of a monastic ethos and pathos in the former writing disturbs me...[56]

Evidently Bonhoeffer did not share Barth's fear that Finkenwalde might represent a retreat from 'the original Christological-eschatological beginning in favour of some kind of realisation ... in a specifically human sphere'.[57] Barth's fears *might* be appropriate in view of the later prison writings; but in the light of both the lecture of *Vergegenwärtigung* from the previous year, and other things which Bonhoeffer has to say about the proper attitude of the biblical interpreter, Barth's unease was, at least for the moment, misplaced.

More than anything else, it is *listening* or *attention* which is most important to Bonhoeffer,[58] precisely because that self is

---

[54] *Letters and Papers from Prison* (London: SCM Press, 1971), p. 279.

[55] 'Vergegenwärtigung neutestamentlicher Texte', p. 313.

[56] *The Way to Freedom* (London: Collins, 1966), p. 121.

[57] Ibid., p. 120.

[58] It is the 'listening self' rather than the 'worshipping self' which is basic to Bonhoeffer, contra D. Ford, *Self and Salvation* (Cambridge: Cambridge University Press, 1999), p. 250.

not grounded in its own disposing of itself in the world, but grounded in the Word of Christ. Reading the Bible, as Bonhoeffer puts it in *Life Together*, is a matter of finding ourselves *extra nos* in the biblical history:

> We are uprooted from our own existence and are taken back to the holy history of God on earth. There God has dealt with us, with our needs and our sins, by means of the divine wrath and grace. What is important is not that God is a spectator and participant in our life today, but that we are attentive listeners and participants in God's action in the sacred story, the story of Christ on earth. God is with us today only as long as we are there.[59]
>
> Our salvation is 'from outside ourselves' (*extra nos*). I find salvation, not in my life story, but only in the story of Jesus Christ … What we call our life, our troubles, and our guilt is by no means the whole of reality; our life, our need, our guilt, and our deliverance are there in the Scriptures.[60]

This being the case, the proper reader of Scripture is not a technician; to think in such terms would be to adopt a perilously false spiritual posture. 'Proper reading of Scripture is not a technical exercise that can be learned; it is something that grows or diminishes according to my spiritual condition.'[61] We need, Bonhoeffer reminded the recipients of the 1936 circular letter on daily meditation, to 'learn the danger of escaping from meditation to biblical scholarship'.[62] Or, more pointedly:

> The Word of Scripture must never stop sounding in your ears and working in you all day long, just like the words of someone you love. And just as you do not analyse the words of someone you love, but accept them as they are said to you, accept the Word of Scripture

---

[59] *Life Together* (Minneapolis: Fortress Press, 1996), p. 62.

[60] Ibid. I take such remarks from Bonhoeffer as the basis for Marsh's claim that he pits 'revelation's prevenient alterity' against the 'self-constitutive subject' of modernity (C. Marsh, *Reclaiming Dietrich Bonhoeffer*, p. xi) – though it seems an excessively theoretical and laboured way of stating Bonhoeffer's essentially spiritual point.

[61] *Life Together*, p. 64.

[62] *The Way to Freedom*, p. 60.

and ponder it in your heart, as Mary did. That is all. That is meditation.[63]

The point of such remarks is not to subjectivize the Scriptures, making them into simply the occasion for charged feelings. 'Accept' is the key word. '[S]imply go and obey. Do not interpret or apply, but do it and obey it. That is the only way Jesus' word is really heard', Bonhoeffer wrote in *The Cost of Discipleship*.[64] A well-known letter from Bonhoeffer to his brother-in-law Rüdiger Schleicher reinforces the point:

> I want to confess quite simply that I believe the Bible alone is the answer to all our questions, and that we need only to ask persistently and with some humility in order to receive the answer from it. One simply cannot read the Bible the way one reads other books. One must be prepared to really question it. Only then will it open itself up. Only when we await the final answer from the Bible will it be given to us.[65]

The point, again, is not personalizing or immanentizing Scripture, drawing it into the reader's psychic sphere, or perhaps the social sphere of the meditating community. Quite the opposite: 'We will only be happy in our reading of the Bible when we dare to approach it as the means by which God really speaks to us.'[66] And grasping what is involved in that approach involves making a sharp contrast: 'I either know about the God I seek from my own experience and insights, from the meanings which I assign to history or nature – that is, from within myself – or I know about him based on his revelation of his own Word.'[67] Moreover, what we encounter in that revelation is not some satisfying extension of our previous selves, but rather something strange and disagreeable, for 'if it is God who says where he will be, then that will truly be a place which at first sight is not agreeable to me, which does not fit so well with me.

---

[63] Ibid., p. 59.
[64] *Discipleship* (Minneapolis: Fortress Press, 2001), p. 181.
[65] *Meditating on the Word* (Cambridge, Mass.: Cowley, 1986), pp. 43f.
[66] Ibid., p. 44.
[67] Ibid.

That place is the cross of Christ.'[68] In a crucial expansion of the point, Bonhoeffer writes thus:

> Does this perspective somehow make it understandable to you that I do not want to give up the Bible as this strange Word of God at any point, that I intend with all my powers to ask what God wants to say to us here? Any other place outside the Bible has become too uncertain for me. I fear that I will only encounter some divine double of myself there. Does this somehow help you to understand why I am prepared for a *sacrificium intellectus* – just in these matters, and only in these matters, with respect to the one, true God! And who does not bring to some passages his sacrifice of the intellect, in the confession that he does not yet understand this or that passage in Scripture, but is certain that even they will be revealed one day as God's own Word? I would rather make that confession than try to say according to my own opinion: this is divine, that is human.[69]

None of this, it needs to be emphasized, is a matter of abandoning the reading of Scripture to the merely affective, or of promoting ignorant or undisciplined reading. The affections are involved, but they are shaped; and what prevents ignorance and lack of discipline is not methodological rigour, but something infinitely more taxing: what Barth called the *epoché* of the interpreter in favour of the Word of the living Christ.

IV

What, by way of brief conclusion, may be gleaned from what we have seen?

Each in his own way, Barth and Bonhoeffer both found that the events of the early 1930s in Germany required of them a certain focussing, a simplifying and intensifying of the Christian and theological task, in order to avoid betrayal of the church's confession and the office of theologian. In Bonhoeffer's case, this meant a radical reorientation of theology and the life of the Christian community around attention to Holy Scripture. In

---

[68] Ibid., p. 45.
[69] Ibid., p. 46.

Barth's case, it involved carrying on 'theology, and only theology'[70] on the presupposition that 'there is no more urgent demand in the whole world than that which the Word of God makes, viz that the Word be preached and heard'.[71] The response of both to the exigencies which faced them is unthinkable without the evangelical principle of *sola scriptura*. And the centrality of the Scriptural word of Christ for Christian thought and discipleship was for both predicated on and understanding of the instrumentality of Scripture in the communicative economy of God, and led both to a distinctive theological, and therefore spiritual, portrayal of interpretative acts and agents.

Neither Bonhoeffer nor Barth were *wissenschaftlich* theologians; both were practical or pastoral theologians of the church of Jesus Christ. It has been suggested that 'Bonhoeffer was always a more modestly "biblical" theologian than Barth' because

> [t]here is an intensely concrete, non-speculative attitude toward the Bible in Bonhoeffer's thought, a radically 'human' and ethical character, which is lacking in Barth's toweringly brilliant but verbosely 'scholastic' systematization of Christian faith.[72]

I am uneasy with the neatness of that contrast. Barth wrote almost nothing by way of formal *wissenschaftlich* theology – even the Anselm book, the closest Barth ever came to something like Bonhoeffer's dissertation monographs, is a strongly constructive and polemical work. It is undoubtedly true that Bonhoeffer's middle-period biblical writings are intensely concrete in their handling of Scripture. But, equally, Barth – even in the *Dogmatics* – is a biblical theologian, to be understood, as Miskotte put it, 'from below', out of 'the small-print excursuses on biblical interpretation'.[73] Both, in short, were

---

[70] K. Barth, *Theological Existence Today!* (London: Hodder and Stoughton, 1933), p. 9.

[71] Ibid., p. 11.

[72] Woelfel, *Bonhoeffer's Theology*, p. 218.

[73] K. H. Miskotte, 'Die Erlaubnis zum schriftgemässen Denkens', in *Antwort. Karl Barth zum 70. Geburtstag* (Zürich: Evangelischer Verlag, 1956), pp. 33f.

members of the guild, so despised by Kant and most of his heirs, of biblical theologians. Pondering their work may give us cause to reflect on three matters.

First: hermeneutical and methodological questions are at best of secondary importance in the interpretation of Scripture. The real business is elsewhere, and it is spiritual, and therefore dogmatic. Correct interpretation cannot be detached from correct depiction of the situation in which we as readers go to Scripture and encounter God. The task of such a depiction is a dogmatic task, calling for the deployment of the concepts and language through which the church has sought to map out as best it can the astonishing reality of God's saving self-communication. If sophisticated hermeneutical theory fails to persuade, it is largely because, in the end, it addresses the wrong problems, and leaves untouched the real difficulty with reading Scripture. That difficulty – as Bonhoeffer and Barth diagnose it – is spiritual and therefore moral; it is our refusal as sinners to be spoken to, our wicked repudiation of the divine address, our desire to speak the final word to ourselves. From those sicknesses of the soul, no amount of sophistication can heal us.

Second, it is therefore true that a fittingly Christian hermeneutics 'requires the formation and transformation of the character appropriate to Christian disciples'.[74] But Bonhoeffer and Barth counsel real caution here. The required formation and transformation are not natural acts, to be depicted through the vocabulary of virtues and dispositions; nor are they acts which can be described in terms of practices learned from the social realities of ecclesial fellowship. If recent essays in ecclesial hermeneutics have done much to draw discussion of Scripture and its interpretation away from the generic and a-social and steer it towards the Christianly specific, they have nevertheless customarily lacked an eschatology of sufficient strength to resist the naturalizing tendencies of the notions of virtue and social practice. However little it may apply

---

[74] Fowl and Jones, *Reading in Communion*, p. 1.

to Bonhoeffer, Barth's worry about any 'cultivation' of habits of reading – that it may substitute routine for repentance – ought not to go unheeded.

Third: the chief task of Christian theology is exegesis. The reason for that is devastatingly simple: 'Jesus Christ *as he is attested to us in Holy Scripture* is the one Word of God.' Theology is exegesis because its matter is Jesus Christ as he communicates himself through Holy Scripture. And so attention to Holy Scripture is not only a necessary but also – in a real sense – a sufficient condition for theology, because Scripture itself is not only necessary but also sufficient. One way of writing the history of modern theology would be to trace the sad fate of Scripture's sufficiency and its reduction to merely necessary status. The counter to this is: exegesis, exegesis and exegesis. The task of exegesis is far too important to be devolved upon biblical technicians. But if modern theology demonstrates a failure on this score, it does not lie primarily on the part of the guild of biblical scholars, but on the part of dogmatic theologians, who have all too often abdicated responsibility for exegesis, and rested content with genres and modes of argument which have encouraged the conceptual takeover of the biblical gospel. Christian theology is properly evangelical, because it is generated by the gospel. But part of securing that evangelical character will be recovering a rhetoric for theology which simply lets Scripture be. Work on that task – which, in their different ways, Barth and Bonhoeffer also deemed theology's central preoccupation – is scarcely begun.

CHRIST AND THE CHURCH

4

INCARNATION

The doctrine of the incarnation is an attempt at conceptual expansion of the church's confession that Jesus Christ is Lord. It is humble, delighted, repentant and joyful repetition at the level of theological concepts of the primary affirmation of the church: that the church's Lord, Jesus, is the incomparably comprehensive context of all creaturely being, knowing and acting, because in and as him God is with humankind in free, creative and saving love. Theological talk of the incarnation of God in Jesus Christ is thus the orderly intellectual exposition of the divine self-exposition; it is a constructive (and therefore critical) attempt to trace the movement of the being and act of God the Son who takes flesh.

To write in such terms is to invite the reproach that confession and critical inquiry have been fatally confused. But theology would be wise not to rise too swiftly or with too much determination to protest against this reproach. Partly this is because the charge of 'foolishness' is a permanent accompaniment for any authentically Christian theology which is serious about struggling against sin in the intellectual realm: the question of the regeneration of the mind can never be laid aside in the way in which theology responds to its critics. Partly, again, theology's reluctance to make a response of the kind for which its critics might hope is a function of the fact that theology is a positive science, that is, a mode of intellectual activity ordered towards a given reality of a particular character. Theology cannot establish on transcendental grounds the conditions of possibility of its object, neither to itself nor to its critics. To attempt to do so would be to adopt a perverse stance towards the object, one which would, indeed, be almost a wilful rejection of that object and its claim. For that object – God incarnate, the Word made flesh – is not one more matter for the free play of intellectual judgement. Rather, the object is itself judge, wholly and originally; and perhaps *the* test of the authenticity of any theology of incarnation will be whether it emerges from that judgment or prefers, instead, to establish an independent colony of the mind from which to make raids on the church's confession.

This essay proceeds in three stages. First, it gives a more extensive account of the task of a doctrine of the incarnation along the lines just indicated; second, it identifies some characteristic features of modern Christian thought which have impeded unanxious pursuit of that task; and, third, it offers a dogmatic expansion of the Christian confession which tries to display its intellectual and spiritual architecture. We proceed, that is, from orientation to archaeology and thence to exposition.

1. Orientation

Construals of who Jesus Christ is and construals of the nature of the Christological task are mutually reinforcing. Thus, for example, from the end of the eighteenth century the method of Protestant Christology was dominated by deep and sustained engagement with the historical records about Jesus; but the plausibility of the historical methods used to pursue that engagement derived not only from the general prestige of historical science in German and (slightly later) English intellectual culture, but also from the humanist and moralistic interpretations of Jesus which found classic expression in Kant's religious writings. The critical and sometimes apologetic use of historical inquiry both drew upon and confirmed theological convictions about Jesus. However, formal and material concerns rarely exist in equilibrium; much more often, precedence is given to either formal or material. Mainstream modern Christology, especially when it acknowledges an obligation to its wider intellectual environment, characteristically gives a measure of priority to the formal conditions for public speech about Jesus. The reason for this is that the intellectual world in which modern Christology was decisively shaped (Germany at the turn of the nineteenth century) was much preoccupied with the effects upon religious claims of philosophical idealism and the disciplines of historical inquiry to which idealism was closely akin. To put matters very crudely: religious claims about Jesus were subordinate to universally valid processes of intellectual inquiry considered to have greater authority than the merely domestic doctrine of the church. Those universally valid processes of inquiry were, of course, by no means religiously neutral; in the case of Christology, as we shall see, they usually involved an assumption that Jesus is not a presently active figure but simply a figure from the past, available only through historical report. But the effect of their acceptance was that the domestic doctrine of the church was not trusted to have sufficient authority to determine the formal means by which investigation into Jesus Christ might properly be undertaken.

The hegemony of the formal has rarely been overthrown by explicit refutation, which often ends in a methodological tangle. The most persuasive attempts to operate by a different set of rules – amongst Protestants, Barth's Christological metaphysics, amongst Roman Catholics, von Balthasar's Christological dramatics – have not waited upon formal permission to proceed but simply set about the descriptive Christological task, demonstrating in actual use the priority of material claims over formal requirements. Though what follows advocates the priority of substantive doctrine, it nevertheless begins by drawing attention to some of the formal or methodological consequences for Christology of the material content of the church's claim. That material content can be summed up thus: *The doctrine of the incarnation is an attempt at conceptual expansion of the church's confession that Jesus Christ is Lord.*

The doctrine is concerned with *the church's confession that Jesus Christ is Lord.* Because the doctrine of the incarnation is an attempt at a conceptual expansion of the church's confession, it starts from a given. It is neither an arbitrary nor a constructive exercise, but the following of a reality which precedes and encloses its activity. That which is given to Christology is, however, more closely defined not as an intellectual or spiritual *positum*, a received piece of tradition or authoritative Christian experience. What is given is the personal, communicative self-presence of Jesus Christ, in and as whom the creative, redemptive and perfecting works of God, willed by the Father and brought to realization by the Holy Spirit, are enacted. *He* is the given; in his inalienable and unique subjectivity, he is the supreme conditioning factor in all creaturely occurrence and therefore the supreme conditioning factor in all thought and speech about himself. Because he is Lord, he can only be thought of as Lord; if he is not thought of as Lord, and with the rational deference which is due to him as Lord, then he is not thought of at all. As Lord, he is the incomparably comprehensive context of all creaturely being, knowing and acting. The ontological ground of Christology is he himself; similarly, the epistemological ground of Christology – the condition under which true knowledge of this reality is possible – is he himself, for he is the agent through whom knowledge of himself is realized. Because Jesus Christ is Lord, comprehending all other contexts but comprehended by none, thought about him must follow the particular path indicated by his self-presenting reality.

Two images, both taken from Bonhoeffer's Berlin Christology lectures of 1933, reinforce the point. The first is that Christology is the 'centre of its own space'.[1] That is to say, the intellectual activity of theology does not transcend the reality of Jesus Christ but is transcended by it; his reality encloses theology, rather than the other way round. Accordingly, thinking about Jesus Christ cannot be classificatory, a matter of assigning him a place in an existing order of objects, whether material or spiritual. Rather, he is that in terms of which all other reality is to be mapped. The second image

---

[1] D. Bonhoeffer, *Christology* (London: Collins, 1978), p. 28.

reinforces the first by suggesting that Christology is concerned, not with spontaneous human utterance about Jesus Christ but with a divine 'Counter-Logos': 'When the Counter-Logos appears in history, no longer as an idea but as "Word" become flesh, there is no longer any possibility of assimilating him into the existing order of the human logos.'[2] Such a Counter-Logos shapes Christology in a profound way, most of all by repudiating any idea that theological talk about Jesus Christ is a pure initiative: it is, rather, that which *must* be said because the church and its theology have already been *spoken to*, arrested and, in a very important sense, *silenced* by Jesus Christ who is God's Word, the free and lordly utterance of God. 'The incarnation of the Word is the great "Thus saith the Lord" to which theology can only give the assent that it has heard and understood it.'[3] And so: 'Teaching about Christ begins in silence.'[4]

The point of both those images could be stated more formally by saying that for Christian faith and theology, the church's confession of the lordship of Jesus Christ the incarnate Word is analytic not synthetic. That confession indicates a reality which cannot be broken down into more primitive elements or deduced from some higher vantage point, and so it works from an assumption which 'is a genuine and proper assumption, in so far as it cannot be over-topped by any other, and therefore suspended on, and even disputed by, a higher assumption'.[5] Christology deals with that which grounds all things and therefore cannot itself be grounded. 'Christology deals with the revelation of God as a mystery.'[6] Because according to the confession Jesus Christ is divine, he is that than which nothing greater can be conceived; theology, therefore, may not operate as if it were competent or permitted to occupy a position prior to, independent of or outside his reality. The office of theological reason is to follow the

[2] Ibid., p. 30.
[3] K. Barth, *Church Dogmatics* IV/2 (Edinburgh: T&T Clark, 1958), p. 59.
[4] Bonhoeffer, *Christology*, p. 27.
[5] Barth, *Church Dogmatics* I/2, p. 131.
[6] Ibid.

direction in which the divine reality beckons as it sets itself before us; that is theology's discipleship to revelation. And so, the *ratio cognoscendi* for a theological account of the incarnation is the sheer active, self-bestowing majesty of the Word made flesh. A number of consequences follow from this.

First, the doctrine of the incarnation is an exercise of retro-spective rather than constructive or poetic reason. That is, it seeks to draw attention to that which has taken place, that which has already announced itself and made itself a matter for confession; it is not a matter of engaging in a struggle to establish the conditions under which an event of incarnation might be considered a possible object of confession. The rule for theological (indeed, for all) reasoning is: thought follows reality, because possibility follows actuality. The incarnation is thus that *from which* theology moves, rather than that *towards which* it moves. The incarnation is a *perfectum*, an achieved reality which guides theological thinking by ordering thinking towards itself. Such language – guiding, ordering – is inescapably personal, once again reminding us that what generates the theology of the incarnation is the active, self-presenting reality of Jesus Christ who *is*, independent of and inexhaustibly prior to any representation of him that might be made.

Second, therefore, the doctrine of the incarnation is only in a very limited sense a 'valuation' of Jesus Christ. Talk of Jesus Christ as the Word made flesh is not to be thought of as a mythological expression of the religious or moral value which Christians find in him or place upon him as an object of regard or worship. Naturally, of course, all theological language, however objective in orientation and however much it may reach beyond itself, is also an expression of the speaker: to deny this would be docetic. But what is of critical importance is that *in* this self-expressive, 'worldly' character, theological language about Jesus Christ should genuinely *refer*, genuinely – if confusedly and certainly inadequately – point beyond itself to that by which it is confronted. Where such reference fails, and language about Jesus Christ is no longer properly ostensive, then theology becomes merely a nominalist expression of religious feeling, contingently attached to the name of Jesus. But a doctrine of the incarnation must properly operate in a quite different fashion: it must be an acknowledgment of the inherent transcendent goodness, beauty and truth of Jesus Christ the Word made flesh; it cannot be an arbitrary conferral of value or dignity. In the end, this is because of the nature of the reality with which Christology concerns itself. Jesus Christ is Lord; lordship which is conferred is a contradiction in terms. To speak theologically of the Word made flesh is thus not to predicate an honorific title of Christ, or to assign him a place in a Christian world of values, even if it be the highest place. It is to confess him to be the one Lord Jesus Christ, the only-begotten Son of God. Theology is not competent to make any other judgment.

Third, the sphere of the doctrine of the incarnation is the church. Much of the disrepair of the doctrine of the incarnation in modernity stems from the assumption that the doctrine can be transplanted out of its natural habitat – the practices of Christian faith – and nevertheless continue to flourish. This transplanting occurs very often when the doctrine of the incarnation is approached as a matter for apologetics, defended by the deployment of historical evidences, by the reasoning of philosophical theism, or by a theory of religious symbol. All such strategies are characteristically under-determined by the *content* of the doctrine, assuming that it can be defended by showing its compatibility with a generic theory of what is ultimate. The cost, however, is that the 'churchly' character of the theology of the incarnation – its inseparability from the worship, witness and holiness of the church – is laid aside. Crucially, theology thereby loses sight of the all-important word which stands before and brackets the confession of the one Lord Jesus Christ: *Credo*, I believe. The sphere of the *Credo* is the sphere of the church and, as conceptual expansion of the *Credo*, the doctrine of the incarnation cannot aspire to leave behind the domestic culture of the Christian community.

Fourth, however, that 'domestic culture' is not to be envisaged as a happily stable set of ecclesial practices 'containing' Jesus Christ or, perhaps, embodying in its life the same divine reality of which he is the supreme incarnation. (Anglican Christology of the later nineteenth and twentieth centuries sometimes fostered this impression.) To think in such terms is to confuse incarnation and immanence, and thereby radically to misconstrue what it means to say that the church is the sphere in which the doctrine of the incarnation is to be located. The church is not the institutional container of the incarnation; it is, rather, that sphere of human life and fellowship which is besieged by, permanently under attack from, the Word made flesh. One of the most striking features of Bonhoeffer's *Christology* fragments is his insistence that Jesus Christ is a question posed *to* the church, that the church is relentlessly interrogated by the fact that at the heart of its life is the presence of the incarnate one who cannot be assimilated into or clothed by a form of religious life.[7] The consequences of this for theological procedure are immense. It means that – not only for spirituality but for theology, too – 'There are only two ways of possible of encountering Jesus: man must die or he must put Jesus to death.'[8] To speak thus risks seeming indulgent, even histrionic. But it is soberly to draw attention to something close to the heart of an authentic doctrine of the incarnation, namely that the function of any such doctrine is in part to keep the church alert to two realities: the sheer critical force of the one who is confessed, and the pervasive temptation to use concepts for the purposes of idolatrous control.

To sum up so far: the doctrine of the incarnation is oriented to the core element of the church's confession, namely, that Jesus Christ is Lord, the one who as Lord himself sets the conditions under which he comes to be known and acknowledged as such. Theological talk of incarnation is an act of

---

[7] Bonhoeffer, *Christology*, pp. 30f.; cf. T. F. Torrance, 'Questioning in Christ', *Theology in Reconstruction* (London: SCM Press, 1965), pp. 117–27.

[8] Bonhoeffer, *Christology*, p. 35.

retrospection rather than *poiesis*, of acknowledgment rather than valuation, of the church rather than universal reason, of being interrogated by rather than of interrogating the personal reality which is the matter of the church's attestation.

Next, and more briefly, the task of the doctrine of the incarnation is *conceptual expansion* of the church's confession. The expansion takes the form of appeal to and refashioning of a small number of ontological categories, chief among them being *substance, person* and *nature*.

A long and authoritative tradition in modern Christology has held that the conceptual idiom in which the doctrine of the incarnation found classic expression is a declension from authentic Christian engagement with Jesus. That tradition – of which the most authoritative popular example is Harnack's *What Is Christianity?*, but whose presiding genius is Ritschl – was given renewed energy by theological existentialism, and found a more recent voice in liberal Anglican revisionary histories of patristic Christology from the last third of the twentieth century. These diverse figures were in their different ways and for different reasons all agreed on one central point: that the 'metaphysical' conceptuality of the doctrine of the incarnation was an unsuitable vehicle for articulating the ethico-religious concerns which ought to lie at the centre of theological talk about Jesus Christ. This conviction was backed up in a variety of ways: by reading the Christology of the New Testament in 'functional' rather than 'ontological' terms; by critical doctrinal history of the patristic developments, claiming that ontology was an infection caught from the cultural context of Christian faith; by an emphasis upon the saving work of Christ 'for me' over the technicalities of his person; and by a commitment to Christian existence as the foundational reality around which 'objective' doctrines have to be arranged and by which they are to be criticized.

It must readily be admitted that there is a debased form of Christology which is 'abstract' in the sense that it accords such priority to concepts that the personal history of Jesus' life, death and resurrection come to seem almost symbolizations of an idea. No part of Christian theology – least of all theological talk about God in the flesh – should fail to avoid that. Nevertheless, the wholesale rejection of concepts in Christology is untenable on a number of grounds. First, it tends to read the concepts of which the doctrine of the incarnation makes use as belonging more to descriptive than analytical metaphysics, whereas in their Christological employment the concepts are more concerned with the relations between substances than the nature of substances. Description and analysis, obviously, cannot be kept entirely distinct. But when the categories used to give an account of the incarnation are read only descriptively, then they can threaten to become little more than a bizarre piece of metaphysical psychology – as, for example, when the term 'person' is construed as 'personality'.[9]

Second, it is of the utmost importance to emphasize that the *use* of concepts may modify, or even radically transform, their habitual range of reference. As we shall see in looking at some of the basic concepts used in incarnational theology, what is most interesting about them is not their pre-history but their modification when they are bent to serve the purpose of articulating the Christian confession. Liberal Protestant Christology frequently underplayed the element of transformation, in order to maximize the gap between credal Christology and the religion of Jesus, and to minimize the differences between credal Christology and its intellectual environment. But it could only do so by overlooking the intellectually innovative and culturally dislocated character of patristic Christology.

Third, the retention of conceptual language in giving an account of Jesus Christ is a *conditio sine qua non* for the rejection of subjectivism in Christology. Ontological concepts, above all, the concept of 'substance', resist the debasement of Christology to spirituality, and so function as an essential element of theological realism. Christology which does not spell out the ontological dimensions of the person of Jesus Christ in relation

---

[9] Cf. R. Williams, '"Person" and "Personality" in Christology', *Downside Review* 94 (1976), pp. 253–60.

to God finds it very difficult to resist the pull of subjectivism and moralism, and quickly turns Jesus into a mythological condensation of the religious and ethical commitments of the believing self. The use of ontology is thus a way of ensuring that the identity of Jesus is not subject to the vagaries of religious use, and that what faith confesses is who Jesus indissolubly *is*.

Last, the doctrine of the incarnation is an *attempt* at conceptual expansion of the church's confession that Jesus Christ is Lord. Like all Christian doctrine, the doctrine of the incarnation is caught between the necessity of concepts and the fact that they are not naturally fitting. What is required in this situation is not the rejection of concepts but their sanctification. Responsible thought and speech simply could not proceed without some kind of conceptual equipment. What is needed is, therefore, the conversion of concepts. Thought and speech about Jesus Christ are thought and speech annexed by his self-exposition. They are the exercise of 'dethroned and distraught reason'.[10] But though they are not fitting, they are made fitting, sanctified, in service to the communicative presence of Christ, even though they always stand on the threshold of breakdown, in the midst of the crisis of the fact of their own unsuitability for the task they have to perform. That task is to enable rational grasp of the character and scope of the church's confession. The concepts of Christology are not an improvement upon the confession. They do not provide a better warranted, or a more conceptually stable and precise mode of expression – in fact, they are always frail and ill-adapted. Nor are Christological concepts speculative, in the sense of being an attempt to identify transcendental metaphysical conditions from which a doctrine of incarnation might be deduced. Rather, they have the modest task of ordering and arranging the church's thought and speech about Jesus Christ in such a way as to display its shapeliness, coherence and explanatory power. Concepts do not add to the confession, but work both from it and back towards it, starting

---

[10] Bonhoeffer, *Christology*, p. 30.

from that which is well known in the sphere of faith and church, and returning to that sphere having undertaken their task. But concepts can only do this if the theologian deploys them with a sense that they are permanently on the brink of dissolution, always aware of their own impossibility, and never, therefore, any more than an *attempt*.

In such an attempt, it is the task of Christian theology to construct concepts which are *appropriate* to the matter of the incarnation, and to ensure their appropriate use. Concepts and their use are to be judged appropriate, first, if they are sufficiently transparent and delicate to enable apprehension of that which they indicate – the reality of Jesus Christ. Concepts must not obscure, and certainly not dominate, that reality, but should be subservient to it. Second, concepts and their use are to be judged appropriate if they resist the temptation to replace the primary modes of speech in which the church's confession of Christ is expressed: homological, kerygmatic, doxological and aretological language and, above all, the prophetic and apostolic language of Scripture. If it is true that 'the root of dogma is the confession of Christ',[11] then the conceptual matter of dogma needs to be self-effacing, such that dogma will adopt a *rhetoric of indication*. That is, its rhetoric – its language and concepts, its patterns of argument, its 'voice' – will be such that it is a testifying to the matter of incarnation. Its rhetoric will therefore be deliberately minimalist, unelaborate, unfinished, shy of exhaustive explanation, above all, governed by the scriptural witness in which it finds its beginning and end.

2. Archaeology

Modernity is commonly reputed to have laid in ruins the account of Christological reason just outlined. It did not, in fact, do so; it simply installed in the centres of greatest

[11] E. Schlink, 'The Structure of Dogmatic Statements as an Ecumenical Problem', *The Coming Christ and the Coming Church* (Edinburgh: Oliver & Boyd, 1967), p. 34.

intellectual prestige (the research universities) one contingent version of instrumental reason to which most Protestant and, later, some Roman Catholic, theologies found themselves hard put to respond by anything other than concessions. The failure to respond and the readiness to make concessions were rooted in internal failures in Christian theology in the post-Reformation (and possibly the early modern) periods, notably the reluctance to deploy primary Christian doctrine (Trinity, Christology, pneumatology) in criticism of philosophical teaching, and the assumption that methods of inquiry are content-neutral.

One of the chief aspects of the legacy of these failures has been a widespread belief that positive dogmatics is not and cannot be a critical activity. Dominant strands of modern theology have judged that theology can only be a critical undertaking in so far as – unlike the act of confession – its relation to the object of the church's faith is one of inquiry. In conducting its inquiry, it does not presuppose the truth of the Christian confession but tests its viability against independent criteria. The orientation which has been described so far is obviously incompatible with understanding the Christological task as critical in that way. This does not mean that the task is uncritical; on the contrary, Christology is from start to finish a critical activity. But what makes Christology critical is not conformity to certain methodologies, or a generally suspicious attitude towards received tradition, but its object: Jesus Christ who as judge is other than any contingent representation. Christology is critical because of that to which it addresses itself and by which it is addressed. It is internally critical, in that it is sharply aware of the inadequacies of its conceptual apparatus and its capacity for distorting the object to which it turns itself unless it is ceaselessly and repentantly vigilant. It is externally critical in that at crucial points it begs to differ from the intellectual and spiritual conventions of the culture within which the church makes its confession of Christ, including that culture's conventions of criticism. Sufficient has already been said about the internally critical character of Christology, which derives from the impossibility of any comprehensive rendering of its object, the free, personal self-presentation of the Word made flesh. We now turn to look at the externally critical orientation of the doctrine of the incarnation, that is, its polemical or apologetic edge.

There is no 'pure' Christology, no Christology which does not articulate itself with a measure of dependence upon the conventions of its context. But, equally, one test of the adequacy of a Christology will be the vigour with which it prosecutes theological judgments about those conventions, the strength with which it refuses to allow modern challenges to set the terms in which it responds. If on the one hand, Christology allows itself to be transposed into a modern idiom largely without residue, then in some measure its reference to its own object will be obscured. If, on the other hand, it is alert and robust in critical appraisal of the dominant idioms of its culture and refuses their claim to self-evidentness, it may well find itself released from some of the inhibitions under which it has often gone about its work.

A somewhat schematic pathology of modern Christology would identify three such inhibitions: the problem of nominalist treatments of the person and mission of Jesus; the problem of theistic construals of the identity of God; and the problem of the relation of the particularity of Jesus to claims about his universality.

In nominalist Christology, Jesus is illustrative but not constitutive of some reality of ultimate significance.[12] His 'name' (that is, his enacted identity as a particular figure) is relative to some supposed ultimate reality, of which it is a contingent expression. That ultimate reality is available under other (though not necessarily more adequate or comprehensive) descriptions. Whether the ultimate reality be conceived in moral terms (as absolute value) or in religious-theological terms (as divine being) matters little; the consequence for an

---

[12] An important recent example would be R. Haight, *Jesus: Symbol of God* (New York: Orbis, 1999).

account of incarnation is much the same. Jesus Christ is no longer irreducibly identified as an ingredient within the reality of God. He may indicate God's reality, even paradigmatically and supremely so; but he is not identical with it, and so he cannot be the *inconcussum fundamentum veritatis*. As a distinguished representative of this kind of Christology puts it: 'What is central is the transforming event associated with the life and death of Jesus of Nazareth, a transformation that brings about a new way of relating both to God and to other human beings.'[13]

Two particular features of such Christologies deserve comment. First, the incomparability of Jesus Christ is de-emphasized, since his identity is rendered in relative terms. As Hans Frei put it, on this model the description of Jesus' identity

> involves comparative reference to the characteristics, conditions, or destinies of some other persons or of all mankind as they may be viewed from the standpoint of a given cultural or social framework ... [T]he comparative reference is usually to the common qualities of estrangement, self-alienation, or some other basically divisive conflict that may appear within the self, between the self and its society, or between social forces.[14]

The effect of this move is to suggest that Jesus is somehow transcended by some other context, which provides the ultimate ground for understanding him and his actions, in such a way that other persons and actions could be substituted for Jesus without irreparable loss. 'Jesus' names not only a person but qualities enacted by or associated with that person.

Second, accordingly, Jesus becomes 'archetypal', with a couple of consequences. One is that it does not matter very much whether Jesus is a present, operative figure – in effect, it does not matter whether he is risen from the dead. What

[13] S. McFague, 'An Epilogue. The Christian Paradigm', in P. Hodgson and R. King, eds., *Christian Theology. An Introduction to Its Traditions and Tasks* (London: SPCK, 1983), p. 333.

[14] H. Frei, *The Identity of Jesus Christ. The Hermeneutial Bases of Dogmatic Theology* (Philadelphia: Fortress Press, 1975), p. 89.

endures is not necessarily Jesus himself but that which he instantiates or symbolizes. Nominalist Christologies are thus irresistibly drawn to concentrate upon Jesus' moral and religious teaching, or to his enactment of a radically challenging style of human relations, since it is here that his transparency to an ultimate reality can be most clearly discerned. And they are also drawn to exemplarist accounts of the saving significance of Jesus. He saves, not by undertaking a unique mission of which he alone can be the agent, but by acting out and recommending attitudes and commitments which ought to characterize all persons. Within such moralist and exemplarist Christologies, what matters is not that Jesus *is*, but that he *was*. His 'presence' is the persistence of an ideal; it is imperative rather than indicative.

A second consequence is that in Christologies in which Jesus functions as archetype, human action threatens to become the real centre of gravity. The divine act of incarnation quickly becomes mere mythic representation of work which needs to be undertaken by human persons themselves. Kant, for example, argues that

> It is our universal human duty to *elevate* ourselves to this ideal of moral perfection, i.e. to the prototype of moral disposition in its entire purity, and for this the very idea, which is presented to us by reason for emulation, can give us force. But, precisely because we are not its authors but the idea has rather established itself in the human being without our comprehending how human nature could have even been receptive of it, it is better to say that that *prototype* has *come down* to us from heaven, that it has taken up humanity ... This union with us may therefore be regarded as a state of *abasement* of the Son of God if we represent to ourselves this God-like human being, our prototype, in such a way that, though himself holy and hence not bound to submit to sufferings, he nonetheless takes these upon himself in the fullest measure for the sake of promoting the world's greatest good.[15]

---

[15] I. Kant, *Religion within the Boundaries of Mere Reason*, in A. Wood and G. Di Giovanni, eds., *Religion and Rational Theology* (Cambridge: Cambridge University Press, 1996), p. 104.

Faith in Jesus Christ is thus 'practical faith in this Son of God',[16] a mode of conduct stimulated by him rather than an affirmation or acknowledgment of what he is.

Such Christological constructs shatter the logic of incarnation. At best, Jesus is a (the?) symbolic intensification of the divine; at worst, he is merely ornamental. But he is not God enfleshed. He is, perhaps, a mode of the divine self-manifestation, an instrument in the divine pedagogy; but, in the end, he is not the *content* of the divine instruction.

Undergirding this nominalism are two further features of modern Christologies: theism, and a bifurcation of the universal and the particular.

A good deal of theology in modernity has been theistic, in that the specifics of Christian conviction have not generally been considered constitutive of either the process of coming to believe in God or of the content of such belief.[17] In effect, Christian doctrine concerning the Trinity, the incarnation, and the work of the Holy Spirit in the church have been relegated to merely contingent status, interpreted as refinements of or particular positive variants upon more basic theistic belief, into which they can be rendered without loss of anything essential. The authority of theism is the result of the coming together of a number of factors. One is the rise of prolegomena to theology in the early modern period, in which basic belief in 'a god' was considered determinable by philosophical reason without reference to the experience of faith. Another is modernity's unease about revelatory divine action in history, which presses theology to construct its account of the identity of God out of metaphysical resources independent of the religious experience of Israel and the church. A third is modernity's preference for natural over positive religion, largely driven by distaste for the contentious claims of specific traditions and the

---

[16] Ibid.
[17] For two (rather different) accounts of this, see M. Buckley, *At the Origins of Modern Atheism* (New Haven: Yale University Press, 1987), and E. Jüngel, *God as the Mystery of the World* (Grand Rapids: Eerdmans, 1983).

desire to replace them by rational defence of the plausibility of belief in God as the foundation for moral consensus (such sentiments are still the backcloth for a good deal of contemporary Christian theorizing about the relation of Christianity to other world faiths).

In the case of the doctrine of the incarnation, the authority of theism both reinforces and is reinforced by the nominalism of modern theology. Christological nominalism presupposes an ontological separation of Jesus and God, with the result that the content of the term 'God' is filled out by appeal to all manner of resources which are not Christologically shaped: 'theos' and 'Christos' are not mutually determinative. Once this bifurcation is allowed, then the doctrine of the incarnation is immediately unworkable, for that doctrine claims an ontological unity between God and the human career of the man Jesus, a unity not conceivable within the terms of the metaphysics of theism. Divinity, defined *remoto Christo,* cannot exist in union with humanity. And so the claim of the doctrine of the incarnation – that the end of the ways and works of God is to take flesh – comes to be rejected. Within the terms of a theistic understanding of God, there *can be* no hypostatic union, and so Christian theology must restrict itself to a Christology which is non-incarnational (and therefore non-trinitarian) and to a Christology in which Jesus manifests the divine character with singular potency but without ontological entailments.

This is linked, finally, to an antinomy between universal and particular, ultimate and historical. Modern theology was and continues to be deeply shaped by the disappearance of a conviction which shaped Western culture in the pre-modern period, namely the conviction of 'the inextricable tie of all that is ultimately meaningful to Jesus Christ as a particular person'.[18] The conviction was eclipsed by a metaphysical principle which separated the sensible and supra-sensible

[18] B. Marshall, *Christology in Conflict. The Identity of a Saviour in Rahner and Barth* (Oxford: Blackwell, 1987), p. 2.

realms, and which considered that historical accidentals cannot be the bearers of non-contingent truths. This divorce of historical specificity from the absolute had a clearly devastating effect on incarnational doctrine: time, space, the body are other than that which is ultimate, and so Jesus' spatio-temporal and embodied existence cannot be identified with the being of God.

In the face of this legacy, there are at least three ways of reorienting a theological account of the incarnation. One is a form of accommodation, in which Christian theology accepts in some measure the constraints imposed upon it by the forms of its wider cultural environment, and seeks to develop a plausible account of the Christian confession within the limits imposed by those forms. If Christologies of this type are theologically deficient, it is not only because they often produce accounts whose resemblance to the family of Christian orthodoxy is hard to discern, but also because they are intellectually conservative. These Christologies characteristically exhibit considerable deference to external cultural conventions, and a reluctance to make use of Christian resources in the critical evaluation of intellectual traditions. A second response is apologetic: the general theistic framework is presupposed, but room is carved out for Christian theological conviction by demonstrating that Christian beliefs about the incarnation are a necessary corollary of (or at least are not incompatible with) the metaphysics of God. Again, if accounts of this type are deficient, it is because they may underestimate the critical impact of the Christian confession on philosophical conviction. A third option – adopted here – follows a strategy of combining dogmatic criticism with what might be called archaeology. As dogmatic criticism, it evaluates cultural and philosophical customs (including customary teaching about God) in terms of their compatibility with the church's confession, doing so on the basis of the metaphysical and epistemological priority of the church's confession of the gospel over the world's denial of it. As archaeology, it is especially concerned to unearth how contemporary theological conscience may be held to ransom by scruples which properly ought to have no authority over it.

> If we are to understand, we must look, not at the universe, but at one particular; we must not seek first, within the historical series, universal laws of its development in terms of which we can, so to speak, interpret the fact of Christ; we must not seek to bring him within the terms of our thinking, but rather to recast the whole of our intellectual frame of reference by constant recollection of his particularity.[19]

What ought to have authority over the theological conscience is the gospel as confessed by the church. At the heart of gospel is the joyful and awed affirmation that the Word became flesh – that, as the Niceno-Constantinopolitan creed puts it, there is one Lord, Jesus Christ, the only begotten Son, begotten from his Father before all ages, light from light, God from God, true God from true God, begotten not made, of one substance with the Father; that it was through this one that all things were made; that for us and for our salvation he came down from heaven and was incarnate by the Holy Spirit of the Virgin Mary, and was made man. We turn to a more extended exposition of this confession.

3. Exposition

Although the formal Nicene conceptuality may make it initially hard for us to see the point, that confession is an attempt to respond to questions which are lodged in the primitive Christian accounts of Jesus: 'What is this?'; 'Why does this man speak thus? . . . who can forgive sins but God alone?'; 'Who then is this?' (Mk 1.27; 2.7; 4.41). Very little headway can be made in understanding that confession unless we rid ourselves of the lingering suspicion that it is a *suppression* of those primary questions, most of all by offering a definitive and compre-hensive answer to them. In reality, a theological answer to a

---

[19] D. M. MacKinnon, *God the Living and the True* (London: Dacre, 1940), p. 45.

question such as 'Who then is this?' is nothing other than a restatement of the question. The disorientation and wonder which come to expression in the question are permanent; there is no 'solution', and certainly not a conceptual, theological solution. All that theology can do is lay out its concepts in such a way as to attest the identity of that which lies at the heart of the disorientation.

a. The Word became flesh

Word

Christian faith describes what takes place in the life, death, resurrection and glorification of Jesus of Nazareth by saying that 'the Word became flesh'. That is, the one whom we encounter in the history of Jesus, the subject of this sequence of acts and sufferings, is the Word or Son of God. As such, this one participates fully and unreservedly in the divine nature and majesty. He is 'true God from true God': whatever is confessed of the dignity, worth and glory of God is confessed of this one also, who with Father and Spirit is one of the three co-essential and co-eternal persons or modes of the triune being of God. The Christological clause of the Nicene creed establishes this at the beginning by describing the subject of the incarnation as 'one Lord'. To speak of Jesus Christ as 'Lord' is to indicate that he is infinitely superior in majesty to those who confess (or fail to confess) who he is; he *is* (and is not merely considered to be) Lord, for his lordship is antecedent to any evaluation of him or ascription of properties to him. Confession of lordship is therefore properly not a speculative undertaking, but something which the church, and therefore theology, is *forced* to make. Put differently: theology *begins* here; it does not reach this point as a conclusion of a speculative or evaluative process, a process (for example) in which his deity serves as an explanation for certain religious impressions or affects which are generated by consideration of Jesus. Because his divinity is truly *divinity*, it is not contingent but basic. The lordship of the incarnate one is axiomatic rather than derivative, 'in the same factual and self-evident and indisputable way as Yahweh was of old Israel's God'.[20] And as such he can only be 'one' Lord, incomparably greater than and categorically different from all other putative lords. That is, his uniqueness is not relational but absolute. 'Relational' uniqueness is often proposed by those urging the compatibility of Christianity and other faith traditions, since it seems to maintain the status of Jesus Christ in Christian conviction, but in a non-exclusive fashion.[21] The uniqueness of Jesus is his unique status as an object of Christian devotion, but is not such as to exclude other possible objects of devotion. But to talk in such terms is to confuse confession and ascription. Moreover, uniqueness is not predicated of Christian conviction but acknowledged in the object of confession who, as Lord, is absolutely unique. Thus Christian theology speaks of *the* incarnation, of the *one* Lord. We may certainly in some cases speak of comparative uniqueness, uniqueness with reference to other realities. But 'is this uniqueness . . . the uniqueness which according to traditional Christian theology there has been in the Incarnation of the Word of God? . . . [T]he answer is surely *no.*'[22] In short: the uniqueness of Jesus Christ is not an ascription of value but his ontological singularity as the one incarnate Lord. In this respect there is, therefore, a strict equivalence between the first clause of the Nicene definition ('I believe in one God') and the second, Christological, clause ('and in one Lord Jesus Christ'). Belief in the 'one Lord Jesus Christ' is not a supplement to belief in one God but rather a precise statement of the content of such belief, in which it is ingredient.

It is for this reason that the Nicene confession lays considerable emphasis on the fact that Jesus Christ is antecedently the Son of God. He is the 'only-begotten Son, begotten of his Father before all worlds'. The exclusive particle –

[20] Barth, *Church Dogmatics* I/1, p. 405.

[21] See, for example, P. Knitter, *No Other Name?* (London: SCM Press, 1975).

[22] D. M. MacKinnon, 'Prolegomena to Christology', *Themes in Theology. The Three-fold Cord* (Edinburgh: T&T Clark, 1987), p. 172.

'*only* begotten' – is intended to prevent the assimilation of Jesus Christ into the ranks of creatures. The phrase 'begotten of his Father before all worlds' indicates that his coming into being is not after the manner of creatures or within the contingencies of created history, but is an event within God's eternal life ('before all worlds'). 'Begotten' is primarily a negative rather than a positive term, distinguishing the origin of the Son from that of creaturely ('made') reality, so indicating that the Son is a reiteration within the being of God. To be 'begotten' in this sense is to be 'light of light', 'very God of very God', ingredient within the eternal and effulgent completeness of the being of God.

This Word, this one Lord Jesus Christ, is the *subject* of the event of incarnation. He is not its 'object', in that he is not passive or inert but active. The incarnation is therefore not a further instance of a process of becoming, of which the divine life and activity are also part. Nor is the incarnation a creaturely movement; it is free, gratuitous and *ex nihilo*, the exercise of the divine good pleasure and not a necessary consequence of any state of affairs beyond the loving will and purpose of the Father who sends and the free, active obedience of the Son or Word. God is the acting subject; the statement 'the Word became flesh' is in no way reversible, and does not entail any intrinsic creaturely capacity which cooperates or coordinates itself with the action of Father and Word to make the incarnation possible. That action is unilateral and unidirectional, the majestic downward movement of God to the creature.

Became

That movement is the history of Jesus Christ; the history of Jesus Christ is that movement. Most generally described, it is the movement in which the Word *became* flesh, or in which the Son of God came down from heaven and was made man. What is to be said of this 'becoming'?

The becoming to which reference is made is a specific divine action, not a modification of a more general ontology of flux. In formal terms, this means that this 'becoming' is defined by its subject ('the Word'). Ontological categories are strictly subordinate to the unique and irreducible event which they try to depict. 'It is not a matter of a "God who becomes". God's being is not identified with God's becoming; rather, God's being is ontologically located.'[23] In material terms, this means that 'becoming' is not a matter of augmentation or diminution, but rather of that movement in which the being of God in all its fullness is fully achieved:

> The fact that in the incarnation God became man without ceasing to be God, tells us that his nature is characterised by both repose and movement, and that his eternal Being is also a divine *Becoming*. This does not mean that God ever becomes other than he eternally is or that he passes over from becoming into being something else, but rather that he continues unceasingly to be what he always is and ever will be in the living movement of his eternal Being. His Becoming is not a becoming on the way toward being or toward a fullness of being, but is the eternal fullness and the overflowing of his eternal unlimited Being. Becoming expresses the dynamic nature of his Being. His Becoming is, as it were, the other side of his Being, and his Being is the other side of his Becoming. His Becoming is his Being in movement and his Being in movement is his Becoming.[24]

The act of incarnation is a history. Theological talk of the Word made flesh is not a matter of notional arrangement of two static entities (deity and humanity), but a reference to a complex event: it came to pass ... Through the doctrine, we seek to conceptualize the divine dramatics, the movement of the mission of God in condescension. It cannot be emphasized too strongly that the concepts of the doctrine must therefore be governed by the primacy of what Jean Galot calls 'la démarche divine'.[25] However, in its dynamism, the event of the divine procession in the incarnation of the Word is an act of the immutable freedom of God. Some recent incarnational

---

[23] E. Jüngel, *God's Being Is in Becoming* (Edinburgh: T&T Clark, 2001), p. xxv.

[24] T. F. Torrance, *The Christian Doctrine of God* (Edinburgh: T&T Clark, 1996), p. 242.

[25] J. Galot, *Vers une nouvelle christologie* (Paris: Gembloux, 1971), p. 50.

theology has been keen to give great weight to the processive nature of the divine being, and above all to the culmination of that procession at the cross. Sometimes such accounts are made for apologetic reasons, particularly when an incarnational theory of divine passibility is deployed as part of a theodicy. At other times, the motivation may be more strictly dogmatic, in that an incarnational Christology is used as a critical lever against theistic assumptions of the removal of God from historical continency. But in all cases, considerable vigilance is required if the genuine desire to affirm the procession of God in the Word's becoming flesh is not to threaten divine aseity. Whatever else may be said about God's becoming, that becoming must be understood as a mode of his sovereign self-possession, an aspect of his inexhaustible plenitude.

Thus, for a theological construal of the incarnational 'becoming' to succeed, it must not allow itself to be dominated by apologetic concerns but must stick closely to the event of incarnation itself, as it presents itself, without attempting to display any particular 'usefulness' of the doctrine. And it must resist the pressure of a priori generic concepts, exercising maximal creativity in adapting and reordering conceptual materials to suit its particular purpose. Above all, it must offer as full and rich a description as it is able of the incarnation as divine condescension, describing ἐγένετο as free *act* and *free* act. The Word *became* flesh; there is genuine newness here, yet a newness which is rooted in the mysterious freedom of God. 'Becoming flesh' involves no abandonment of deity; the Word does not cease to be entirely himself, but rather takes over, 'assumes', that which is not himself, taking it to his own being. The 'humiliation' of the Word is thus by no means the contradiction of his exaltation; it is, rather, the chosen mode of his exaltation. If the Lord is servant, it is as Lord that he serves.

One way in which the freedom of the Word's becoming flesh can be given conceptual form is by the language of *anhypostasis* and *enhypostasis*. These concepts are a way of stating, first, that the man Jesus has no personal centre of subsistence ('hypostasis') in and of himself, so that he is thus '*an*hypostatic';

and, second, that his hypostasis is 'in' the Word which assumes flesh, so that he is '*en*hypostatic'. The conceptuality has an unfamiliar air, and is liable to promote misunderstanding if taken as a psychological description of Jesus. What it does state is that the Word's assumption of flesh is wholly gratuitous, in no sense the annexation or enlargement of creaturely possibility. The deity of the incarnate one is not natural to his humanity; on the contrary, his humanity is a predicate of the divinity of the Word. His humanity is thus not self-existent, but comes to exist in the event of the Word's 'procession'. In effect, this reinforces what is secured by speaking of the Word's *assumption* of humanity, namely that – against adoptionism – Jesus Christ is not merely a human being who pre-exists the action of the Word and is subsequently exalted to union with him; rather, he is himself the sheerly creative life-act of the Word or Son of God.

In sum, God's 'becoming' is God's determination of himself to be God *in this way*, to take this particular direction which is the fulfilment of his groundless aseity. Self-emptying (*kenosis*) and self-fulfilment (*plerosis*) are not antithetical, but identical. Thus to be what Mark Taylor calls 'thoroughly incarnational'[26] we do not need to posit the disappearance of God, 'the sacrifice of the transcendent Author/Creator/Master who governs from afar'.[27] To speak in such terms is to miss the real force of 'becoming', for that term retains the permanent tension between transcendence and historical presence which Taylor's language of the 'irrevocable erasure' of the transcendent at the incarnation ignores.[28] To be thoroughly incarnational we need a doctrine of the triune God – of God the Father who freely wills this act, of God the Son who is freely obedient and assumes flesh, of God the Spirit through whom God empowers the Son and mediates his incarnate presence. The being of the incarnate God is thus *in* becoming.

[26] Taylor, *Erring,* p. 103.
[27] Ibid.
[28] Ibid.

Flesh

That which the Word becomes is *flesh*. The Word incarnate participates fully and unreservedly in the same human nature (including, but not limited to, embodiment) that we ourselves have. 'Flesh' is not merely an instrument through which an essentially disincarnate Word operates; flesh is that which he is, not that which he merely appears to be.

> Stop your ears, therefore, when anyone speaks to you at variance with Jesus Christ, who was descended from David, and was also of Mary; who was truly born, and did eat and drink. He was truly persecuted under Pontius Pilate; he was truly crucified and [truly] died, in the sight of beings in heaven, and on earth, and under the earth. He was also truly raised from the dead, His Father quickening Him, even as after the same manner His Father will also raise us up who believe in Him by Jesus Christ, apart from whom we do not possess the true life.[29]

He is like us. But he is so in utter liberty, and with no renunciation of the deity of the Word. The fact that the Word is ἔνσαρκος does not abolish or disqualify the fact that the Word is equiprimordially ἄσαρκος. But this same Word is truly enfleshed, and enfleshed, therefore, as a particular human being with an inescapably distinct identity: historical, racial, embodied, gendered.

However, this particular human existence has two specific determinations. First, it is what it is by virtue of the divine self-positing, the mutuality of the mission of the Father and the obedience of the Son in the Spirit's power. Fleshly existence is that which the Word assumes and, in assuming, *creates*. The flesh which he becomes is not a free-standing, pre-existent reality added to the Word, for it has no reality other than that which the Word bestows by the act of assumption. Incarnation is not deification of that which exists apart from God. As Augustine puts it, the incarnation is that in which 'the grace of God is supremely manifest, commended in grand and visible fashion', for

> what had the human nature in the man Christ merited, that it, and no other, should be assumed into the unity of the Person of the

---

[29] Ignatius, *To the Trallians*, ix.

only Son of God? What good will, what zealous strivings, what good works preceded this assumption by which that particular man deserved to become one Person with God? Was he a man before the union, and was this singular grace given to him as to one particularly deserving before God? Of course not! For, from the moment he began to be a man, that man began to be nothing other than God's Son, the only Son, and this because the Word of God assuming him became flesh, yet still assuredly remained God.[30]

Second, this particular human being is of universal scope. That is, what takes place in and as him is definitive of all human persons. His humanity is inclusive, not in the sense that it is not particular, but in the sense that, in the assumption of this particular human identity, a divine determination of all human persons is effected. He assumes 'humanity', that which makes all human persons into human persons; in all his specificity he is the new Adam, that work of God in which created human personhood is reoriented by an inclusive act of divine sovereignty. This universal scope presses for *ontological* definition; it is not mere universal pertinence or applicability or even solidarity, but universal effectiveness in which humanity as a whole is remade.

This remaking takes place as he assumes *sinful* flesh, human existence in repudiation of and rebellion against its ordering by God to find fulfilment in fellowship with God. The Word assumes the full extent of human alienation, taking the place of humanity, existing under the divine condemnation. But his relation to the human alienation which he assumes is not such that he is swallowed up by it. He does not identify with humanity under the curse of sin in such a way that he is himself sinner. He exists at a certain removal from sinful humanity even as he assumes it. It remains utterly foreign, indeed, utterly hateful to him, because it is disoriented, abased, unrighteous, and under God's condemnation. He adopts the condemned human situation without reserve, but with a peculiar distance

---

[30] Augustine, *Enchiridion*, xxxvi.

from our own performance of our humanness. By not following our path, by refusing complicity with the monstrousness of sin, he is and does what we are not and do not do: he is human. In his very estrangement from us as the bearer rather than the perpetrator of sin, he takes our place and heals our corruption. That the Word became *flesh* means that he takes to himself the accursed situation of humanity in sin. But he *takes* it to himself; he does not evacuate himself into our situation. The flesh which the Word becomes is the flesh which *the Word* becomes, and the flesh which the Word *becomes*. In his utter proximity he is utterly distant from the misery of humanity in sin; and only so is he redeemer.

A theological reflection on the fact that 'the Word became flesh' thus tries to bear witness to the identity of Jesus, in and as whom God takes creaturely form, in humble majesty acting for us and for our salvation. In the patristic period, the church's intellectual articulation of the faith took shape through the crafting of two seemingly unkerygmatic but in fact crucial dogmas: that of the 'consubstantiality' of the Father and the one Lord Jesus Christ, and that of the union of the divine and human natures in the person of the incarnate one. These two dogmas provided the key markers of orthodox Christian teaching until the slow process of erosion began in the post-Reformation period. How are we to approach understanding them?

The proper home of the notions of 'substance', 'nature' and 'person' is the church's dogmatic definition of the gospel. In a culture which identifies intellectual authenticity with spontaneity, inwardness and free inquiry, 'dogma' can only be a set of shackles: regressive, authoritarian, ecclesiastical faith. However, dogma is not merely to be seen under its aspect of intellectual governance; dogma governs only by virtue of the fact that it gives access to the Spirit's presentation of the gospel. When the church speaks dogmatically, it does so under the guiding, converting and sanctifying impulse of the Holy Spirit, in a way which is ostensive before it is definitive and obligatory. Dogma exhibits the authority of the truth of the gospel which it states, and only so can it command the free asset of faith. As

'exhibition', dogma is an element in God's self-communication; it is a human statement which offers a normative
reading of the source of the church's life in the revelation to
which Scripture bears testimony.

   Most modern theology disputes such claims. From F. C. Baur
onwards, the dominant strands of historical theology, especially
those with a preference for the priority of natural, 'non-
dogmatic', religion, have been deeply sceptical about the
dogmatic heritage of Christianity, and have offered
'naturalized' accounts of dogma and its development as
contingent (and not always entirely savoury) religious and
political processes. It is undeniable that there is something
permanently valuable in such critical accounts: a protest against
the pathological abstraction of dogma from the life-processes of
the church, and against the entanglement of church teaching
in the politics of suppression. Nevertheless, on theological
grounds we may remain in turn sceptical about whether the
natural history of dogma constitutes a sufficient explanation
(and therefore refutation) of its claims on the Christian mind
and conscience. Rather than historicizing or naturalizing
dogma, a more fruitful counter to its pathology will consist in
careful elaboration of the wider framework within which the
notion of dogma makes sense. Crucial to this will be a pneumatological account of the church and its history (and therefore
of the history of dogma), a depiction of the church as the Spirit-
enlivened community in which human thought and speech are
bent to the manifestation of the gospel. The viability of dogma,
that is, depends upon grasping that – as Westcott put it – 'we
cannot understand the history of Christianity unless
we recognise the action of the Holy Spirit through the Christian
Society'.[31] To say that is – emphatically – *not* to remove dogma
from history or immunize it from criticism; it is simply to
identify that, *in* its historicity and contingency, dogma is a
definitive showing of the gospel's truth and a presentation of

---

[31] B. F. Westcott, *A General Survey of the History of the Canon of the New Testament*
    (London: Macmillan, 1881), p. xlix.

the gospel's claim. With this in mind, we move to some remarks on the two primary Christological dogmas.

b. 'Substance'

The Son or Word, the Nicene creed states, is 'of one substance' ('homoousios') with the Father. The core of what the notion of substance achieves is to alert us, however clumsily, to the fact that the bond between God and Jesus must be ontological and not merely moral. Substance language helps state that what takes place in the history of Jesus is in a direct and immediate way a divine act, and not a mere symbolization of a god whose identity lies elsewhere. 'Substance' thus provides a conceptual blockade against subordinationism, in which the status of Jesus Christ is relegated to that of being first among creatures. Such subordination strikes at the vital nerve of the doctrine of the incarnation by radically recasting the interpretation of Jesus: he is no longer the very actuality of the condescension of God but rather an echo in the sensible realm of the reality of God who remains free only in so far as he is locked in an ultimately abstract and inscrutable transcendence of time and matter. The dogmatic statement that Jesus Christ is 'of one substance with the Father' thus tries to secure the point that 'in Christ we meet that which is *essentially* divine':[32]

> Where Christ is, there is God; and where Christ is active, there God is active also. The self-sacrificing and self-giving love of Christ is the love of God himself, its struggle against evil is God's own struggle, and its victory is God's own victory. In the deed of Christ God realizes his own will and love.[33]

Ritschlian theology in the nineteenth century (and well into the twentieth century, for Ritschl's heirs are many) objected that the language of substance conceives of God's relation to Jesus in naturalistic or quasi-physical rather than suitably moral terms, thereby reducing salvation to an almost magical

---

[32] G. Aulén, *The Faith of the Christian Church* (London: SCM Press, 1954), p. 212.
[33] Ibid., p. 213.

transaction involving special status objects and obscuring the primary idiom of willed moral fellowship between God and his creatures: ontological judgments endanger religious and ethical estimation of Christ. This tradition can justifiably align itself to a long-standing critique of Christological abstraction from Melanchthon to postmodern critics of ontotheology. But, as has already been hinted, the criticism rests on a misapprehension of what ontological language seeks to achieve. In a Christological context, 'substance' is a conceptually minimal attempt to indicate what must be confessed of the relation between God and Jesus. It does not carry with it much by way of descriptive metaphysical content, and does not, for example, commit its users to a type of abstract theism or to a docetic Christology. It is, moreover, properly soteriological in intent, pointing to the place where we might most fittingly begin to answer questions of the identity of the agent of salvation by attesting to his unity with the gracious Lord of the covenant. The home of the notion of substance is thus the church's confession of 'that revelation which creates the redemptive fellowship between God and man'.[34]

This means, therefore, that the notion of substance does not transpose Christology out of a historical register. Quite the opposite: it functions as a key term in a thoroughly historical ontology (the interweaving of mythological and metaphysical language in Christology is inevitable).[35] Accordingly, the familiar antithesis of ontology and function will not bear scrutiny, precisely because the task of ontological language is to point out the identity of the person who is here at work. To dispense with ontological concerns about the person of the saviour is to threaten to collapse the work of salvation into mere moral incitement, and so to separate Jesus' ministry from the grace of God. In contrast, to recover the dogma of the *homoousion* may be to gain purchase on the figure of Jesus by making use of 'an instrument for advancing our understanding

---

[34] Ibid., p. 214.
[35] See MacKinnon, 'Prolegomena to Christology', p. 185.

to enable us to see what it is that is at issue in the simpler, more direct, more immediately moving Christological affirmations of the gospel'.[36]

c. Two Natures, One Person

> Following, then the Holy Fathers, we all with one voice teach that it should be confessed that our Lord Jesus Christ is one and the same Son, the same perfect in Godhead, the same perfect in manhood, truly God and truly man ... One and the same Christ, Son, Lord, Only-begotten, made known in two natures [which exist] without confusion, without change, without division, without separation; the differences of the natures having been in no wise taken away by reason of the union, but rather the properties of each being preserved, and [both] concurring into one Person and one *hypostasis* – not parted or divided into two Persons, but one and the same Son and Only-Begotten, the divine Logos, the Lord Jesus Christ.[37]

Like the notion of substance, the Chalcedonian dogma of the hypostatic union (the union of the divine and human natures of Christ in one person) is not a replacement for Jesus' history, but a means of identifying the unique subject and agent of that history. It is thus all-important to note that the centre of gravity of the definition is not the natures considered in isolation from each other, but rather the event of their union in the one subject Jesus. The definition starts from the union of the natures in the one person and hypostasis of which they are predicated, rather than trying to construct a psychologically credible person by first defining and then uniting two distinct natures. Abstract exposition of the natures is excluded; this subject and agent is irreducibly at the centre.

Starting from the unitary subject in this way prevents an

---

[36] D. M. MacKinnon, 'Substance in Christology', in S. W. Sykes and J. P. Clayton, eds., *Christ, Faith and History* (Cambridge: Cambridge University Press, 1972), p. 291.

[37] I follow the translation in R. V. Sellers, *The Council of Chalcedon* (London: SPCK, 1953), pp. 210f.

account of the incarnation from falling into the trap of proceeding as if humanity and divinity were antithetical. At the very least, such a procedure destabilizes the doctrine, leading, for example, to the idea that certain divine attributes have to be suppressed or jettisoned if the integrity of Christ's humanity is to be maintained. Taken to its extreme, it can issue in highly formal accounts of the natures (especially of the deity), defining them in terms of their mutual opposition and fracturing the doctrine entirely. A long strand of criticism of the doctrine of the incarnation, starting with Spinoza and finding late expression in liberal Anglican Christology has failed at precisely this point: presupposing that God *cannot* be incarnate, and that genuine humanity *must* be violated if assumed by God, it can only see the doctrine of the incarnation as incoherent:

> The doctrines ... such as that God took on himself human nature, I have expressly said that I do not understand; in fact, to speak the truth, they seem to me no less absurd than would a statement that a circle had taken on itself the nature of a square.[38]

Over against this, and on the basis of the particular event of the person of Jesus of Nazareth, the dogma affirms that

> the divinity of Christ cannot be correctly grasped where his temporal and material humanity is denied, and that his humanity cannot be properly understood even in its temporal structure and historical reality, if it is not seen as the self-identification of God in the reality of a human life.[39]

How then is personal union to be understood?

The union is utterly unique, an instance of itself, and in no sense a complement, completion or parallel to any other realities. The hypostatic union is not the most exalted instance

---

[38] B. Spinoza, Letter 36, *Chief Works* (New York: Dover, 1955), vol. 2, p. 353. For a modern example, see A. T. Hanson, *Grace and Truth* (London: SPCK, 1975); idem., *The Image of the Invisible God* (London: SCM Press, 1982).

[39] C. Schwöbel, 'Christology and Trinitarian Thought', in idem., ed., *Trinitarian Theology Today* (Edinburgh: T&T Clark, 1995), p. 128.

of human self-transcendence, of humanity's being 'in God' or of the immanence of God in creation. The incarnation cannot be traced either on the trajectory of humanity's capacity to transcend itself and lose itself in God, or on the trajectory of God's indwelling of creaturely reality. These trajectories may or may not have theological validity; but the hypostatic union is categorically different, neither generalizable nor the condensation of more general realities. Like the relations between the persons of the Trinity, the relation of divinity and humanity in the incarnate one defies analogies. The ground for affirming this uniqueness is the fact that the hypostatic union is an utterly free, uncaused and wholly underiveable act of divine omnipotence, and not merely the culmination of a series or the intensification of an ontological principle of wide application.

> With a strange, one-sided, self-glorious spontaneity, we have to do here with the work and action of the faithfulness and omnipotence and mercy of God Himself, which has no ground of reality except in Himself, or ground of knowledge except in His self-revelation.[40]

The dogma is distinctly a posteriori, a description of an act, not a speculative arrangement of a priori considerations. All along the line, therefore, grasping the dogma is a matter of deploying concepts in such a way that they display a singular reality which precedes and transcends them. Once again: *person* precedes *natures*.

Two particular determinations of this union of divinity and humanity are emphasized by Chalcedon. First, the union of the natures is 'without confusion, without change', for 'the difference of the natures' is 'in no wise taken away by reason of the union, but rather the properties of each [are] preserved'. Though the person, the single ascriptive subject, Jesus is 'one and the same', the natures are not. If they were, then both would be obliterated, and Jesus Christ would be neither divine nor human but some nonsensical third reality. Second, the union of the natures is 'without division, without separation'.

---

[40] Barth, *Church Dogmatics* IV/2, pp. 58f.

That is to say, to talk of divinity and humanity is not to distinguish separate aspects of Christ, as if he were part human and part divine, and as if his properties were divisible between divinity and humanity. Jesus Christ is in his entirety divine and in his entirety human. But this does not entail the conversion of divinity into humanity, or vice-versa, but simply their concurrence in one person.

'Concurrence' is a reticent term, less vigorous than some might wish. In modern Lutheran Christology it has been common to lay great emphasis upon the indivisibility and inseparability of the two natures, and to prioritize the second set of negatives ('without division, without separation') over the first set ('without confusion, without change'). The usual short-term reason for this is that strong talk of the union of the natures is of considerable advantage if one has other grounds for highlighting the identity of God with the suffering Christ. The deeper justification tends to involve a highly negative evaluation of those aspects of patristic Christology which resisted the confusion of the two natures, and a highly positive evaluation of the Lutheran emphasis upon the communication of properties between divinity and humanity – above all, in order to state how God incarnate can be mortal. The kerygmatic cogency of such moves can hardly be doubted. Where they are less secure, however, is in stating the essential presupposition of the union of the natures, namely that divinity *assumed* humanity, that the Word *became* flesh. Unless the dogma of the hypostatic union as a whole is set within the brackets of the *assumptio carnis*, then the union of the natures becomes a *unity*. Over against this, it is vital to retain a firm sense that the hypostatic union is a matter of free grace, and that in an important sense divinity and humanity are asymmetrically related, though without any impugning of the perfection of each nature. Even in union with humanity in Christ, the deity of God remains immutable – directed to the assumption of flesh, by no means a prisoner of its own unchangeableness, but nevertheless unassailably complete in itself.

4. Conclusion

Such, in brief compass and shorn of its many historical modula-
tions, is the Christian doctrine of the incarnation. The viability
of a Christian doctrine of the incarnation rests in part upon its
orderly integration with other tracts of Christian teaching. It
needs to be set in relation to the wider scope of the church's
Christological confession (especially the resurrection of Jesus)
and to its immediately neighbouring doctrines, the doctrines of
the Trinity and salvation. Perhaps one of the major reasons for
the growth of moralistic and non-incarnational Christologies in
the nineteenth century was the dislocation of Christology from
the doctrine of the triune being of God: once the Christian
doctrine of God has fallen into disrepair and is no longer
operative, the doctrine of the incarnation quickly comes to
seem a merely arbitrary bit of speculation, leaving theology free
to expound the humanity of Jesus as if it could be had in
abstraction from his identity as divine agent. Integration into
the right dogmatic context, in contrast, prevents the doctrinal
disarray which results from the hypertrophy or atrophy of
certain doctrines (anthropology waxes, Trinity wanes), or the
deployment of one doctrine to do the job properly assigned to
another (ecclesiology takes over the tasks of pneumatology).
The effects of this kind of misshaping can readily be seen in an
essay by an influential contemporary theologian which suggests
that

> [t]he gospels can be read, not as the story of Jesus, but as the story
> of the (re)foundation of a new city, a new kind of human
> community, Israel-become-the-Church. Jesus figures in this story
> simply as the founder, the beginning, the first of many. There is
> nothing that Jesus does that he will not enable the disciples to do.[41]

The disease which that (baffling) claim purports to diagnose is
Christological and soteriological extrinsicism. But the patient
does not survive the cure; when Christology is absorbed into

---

[41] J. Milbank, 'The Name of Jesus', *The Word Made Strange. Theology, Language,
Culture* (Oxford: Blackwell, 1997), p. 150.

ecclesiology, then Jesus and the event of the incarnation have no shape of their own, no contours and edges, no identity other than that afforded in the repetition of that identity in ecclesial process. We are left with 'an ecclesiological deduction of the Incarnation'.[42] Many of the same features can be traced in other styles of theology, such as those Protestant soteriologies which make Jesus' identity subservient to his being *pro me*, and which expound that *pro me* through a phenomenology of human experience. What is all important, by contrast, is that the shape of the whole should not be distorted by the dysfunction of any one part.

Dysfunction is corrected by attention to the shapely structure of the confession and its biblical foundation. That confession says – with joy and fear and trembling – that the secret of the man Jesus is the majestic, saving self-communication of God. In that act of God Jesus Christ has his basis. And in that act, too, is the basis on which alone Jesus Christ can be known as who he is. He may be seen by all if they care to look; but he may not be recognized without his self-disclosure. And when they have been of sound mind, church and theology have witnessed to that necessity in dogma and prayer. And so: 'Let us grant that God can do something which we confess we cannot fathom. In such matters the whole explanation of the deed is in the power of the Doer.'[43]

---

[42] Ibid., p. 159.
[43] Augustine, Letter 137.2.

5

JESUS IN MODERNITY:
REFLECTIONS ON JÜNGEL'S
CHRISTOLOGY

1. Introduction

Christology in modern Western Protestant divinity often finds itself entangled in two related problems. The first of these is that since the early modern period, the figure of Jesus and doctrine about him has played a diminishing role in determining the substance of Christian convictions about God, humanity and the world. Slowly but inexorably, Jesus has slipped from his place, and is not invoked as the material centre of Christian teaching nor as a heuristic key to other areas, such as the doctrine of the Trinity or theological anthropology. In effect, Jesus has almost receded from view, become so attenuated that he can no longer bear the weight of providing an entire vision of how things are in the world, and can no longer be appealed to as the *fundamentum inconcussum veritatis*. Or if Jesus is still appealed to in this way, it is often no longer as himself, but as symbol of something anterior to himself – God, or experience, or an immanent principle of meaning inherent in all things.

It does not matter too much when the eclipse of the figure of Jesus is thought to have begun. The process of his displacement is commonly considered to have started in the post-Reformation era and to have received a decisive impetus in the theology and philosophy of the Enlightenment. Thus, tracing the history of the reading of the gospel stories, Hans Frei argues

that we can discern how the figure of Jesus is gradually stripped
of his particular narratable identity ('unsubstitutability'),
becoming instead an instance of truths or experiences which
are more properly arrived at and more basically characterized
through general theory (above all, anthropology).[1] However, it
is arguable that the eclipse of the figure of Jesus began much
earlier, with the rise of natural philosophy in the early modern
period. Michael Buckley, for example, argues that, well before
the so-called 'turn to the subject', the delegation of certain
intellectual operations, such as proofs for the existence of God,
onto non-theological sciences, and the development of apologetic strategies in which material Christological convictions
played only a scant role, meant that quite early in the modern
period some Christian thinkers had already ceased to invoke
Jesus in the explication and defence of the gospel.

> [T]he fundamental reality of Jesus as the embodied presence and
> witness of the reality of god [*sic*] within human history was never
> brought into the critical struggle of Christianity ... In the absence
> of a rich and comprehensive Christology and a Pneumatology of
> religious experience Christianity entered into the defense of the
> existence of the Christian god without appeal to anything
> Christian.[2]

But wherever the decline be thought to begin, its result is the
same: the figure of Jesus, and Christian teaching about him, is
no longer considered to be constitutive of the cultural capital
of Christianity, whose investments are accordingly dispersed

[1]   H. Frei, *The Eclipse of Biblical Narrative. A Study in Eighteenth and Nineteenth Century
     Hermeneutics* (New Haven: Yale UP, 1974); idem., *The Identity of Jesus Christ*; idem.,
     Types of Christian Theology; Theology and Narrative. Selected Essays (Oxford: Oxford
     University Press, 1993). For further reflections on these issues (much indebted
     to Frei) see B. Marshall, *Christology in Conflict*. J. M. Creed's earlier classic *The
     Divinity of Jesus Christ. A Study in the History of Christian Doctrine since Kant*
     (Cambridge: Cambridge University Press, 1938) remains a persuasive account of
     the Christological fallout from the replacement of the category of 'revelation' by
     that of 'religion'.
[2]   M. Buckley, *At the Origins of Modern Atheism*, p. 67. For a similar analysis of the interplay
     of formal and doctrinal issues, and of the *theological* roots of the decline of Christian
     culture, see L. Dupré, *Passage to Modernity* (New Haven: Yale University Press, 1993).

elsewhere. Crucially, this nearly always means that Christian doctrine, enjoying only an uneasy relationship to its *proprium* in the person and activity of Jesus confessed as Lord, looks elsewhere for resources to establish both the possibility and the material content of Christian teaching about God and humanity. To talk of God, it looks to philosophical theism; to talk of humanity, it looks to reflective human subjectivity. Thus alienated from the figure of Jesus who is the *positum* of Christian thinking, Christian theology characteristically maximalizes its use of general theory, turning Jesus into a *Gestalt*, a symbolic condensation of matter whose origin lies elsewhere.

The second problem concerns not so much the role played by teaching about Jesus in shaping the content of Christian convictions but rather the substance of Christology itself. The difficulty may be phrased thus: in order to occupy a foundational place in the cultural capital of the Christian religion, the figure of Jesus has to be grasped and presented in a rich, comprehensive and imaginatively compelling way as one whose history, in its sweep from eternity to time and back to eternity, sums up all things in itself. (It was, of course, only because the figure of Jesus was considered to be such a one – alpha and omega, one in whom all things hold together – that it occupied the place it did in Christian thought and culture.) But if his history becomes fragmented, or if it is truncated, or if portions of it are elided for some reason, then it will play its role only with difficulty and eventually cease to play it at all.

Much modern Christology has fallen into difficulty at just this point. Thus the ministry of Jesus (especially his teaching ministry) may be extracted from its larger context in the divine act of incarnation and atonement, and Jesus transformed into prophet or moralist – under pressure, perhaps, from the theory of 'natural religion' (in the eighteenth century), or from liberal dogmatics (as in Harnack), or from sceptical biblical criticism which left only Jesus' eschatological utterances intact (as in twentieth-century existentialist theology). Or again: Jesus' *past* may be so emphasized that his present reality and activity as the one exalted to the side of Father can be lost. Much interest in hermeneutics or in accounts of the historicity of human understanding applied to Christology works from an assumption that Jesus is no longer operative, cannot be considered the agent of his own manifestation in the present, and that the task of theology as theory of interpretation is somehow to 'make him present' to the subjectivity of the believer. Once more: Jesus may be detached from the being of the triune God in such a way that each is defined without reference to the other. And so on. The point is that all such fragmented renderings of Jesus cramp the reach of the whole, from the eternal election of God to the drama of incarnation, death and exaltation and on to Jesus' enthronement and his presence to all things as the risen one who governs and directs all creaturely occurrence. Selected individual scenes may be played, sometimes vividly, but the drama in its entirety somehow falls into disrepair.

In the light of these two clusters of problems, one of the chief tasks for dogmatics is the elaboration of a Christology which will both allow that Jesus is truly and not merely notionally determinative of Christian thought, speech and action in its entirety, and do this out of a 'catholic' Christology, a Christology which expresses the full scope of Jesus as the one who was, and is, and is to come. In Eberhard Jüngel's Christology we can trace both these problems and their attempted resolution. Along with a number of other theologians of the last thirty years or so (and more tellingly than most), Jüngel has expounded a remarkably firm Christocentrism, in his case without sidestepping the task of vigorous debate with the philosophical traditions of modernity. Yet if Jesus is the undisputed centre of his thought, it is only in a surprisingly slender rendering of his identity: Jüngel's perception of the *place* of Christology is uneasily wedded to a restricted presentation of the figure of Jesus.

Jüngel's Christology has evoked very little exposition or critical discussion.[3] He stands at the point of intersection of the

---

[3]   There is a survey in E. Paulus, *Liebe – das Geheimnis der Welt. Formale und materiale Aspekte der Theologie Eberhard Jüngels* (Würzburg: Echter, 1990), pp. 215–314, and

two major strands of German Protestant theology of this century, namely Bultmann and Barth, who are, as he once remarked, 'like two souls in me'.[4] The confluence of these two very different traditions is very marked in his Christological writings. One of the features of Barth's work which most fascinates Jüngel is the mutual grounding of the doctrines of the Trinity and the incarnation – a theme expounded with exquisite care and perceptiveness in his early book *Gottes Sein ist im Werden,*[5] and one which stamps all his writing. Barth's prelapsarian linking of incarnation and the eternal self-election of God as Father, Son and Holy Spirit is for Jüngel a model of how to construct all Christian teaching out of Christology. It also guides him in his critique of theism for its failure to take with full seriousness the revelation of God in Christ. Jüngel is, oddly enough, somewhat less interested in Barth's insistence upon the concreteness of Jesus' life (though he has written on Barth's theme of the 'Royal Man');[6] and Barth's theology of the risen presence and activity of Jesus – explicit throughout the doctrine of reconciliation and receiving especial emphasis in *Church Dogmatics* IV/3 – does not figure large in Jüngel's own Christological thinking. With Bultmann (and Bultmann's pupil Ernst Fuchs, Jüngel's *Doktorvater*) his presentation of Jesus is of an eschatological, erratic, intrusive figure, distant from Israel,

---

more briefly in P. Gamberini, *Nei legami del Vangelo. L'analogia nel pensiero di Eberhard Jüngel* (Rome: Gregorian University Press, 1994), pp. 148–66. See also my earlier survey in *Eberhard Jüngel. An Introduction to His Theology* (Cambridge: Cambridge University Press, 1991[2]), pp. 25–38.

[4] R. Garaventa, 'L'esito del teologia: Dio è altro dall' uomo (intervista a E. Jüngel)', *Il Regno* 2 (1987), p. 38. Further on Jüngel's background in the tensions of German theology of the 1950s, see W. Härle and E. Herms, eds., *Deutschsprächige protestantische Dogmatik seit 1945* II, *Verkündigung und Forschung* 28/1 (1983), pp. 21–5.

[5] *Gottes Sein ist im Werden. Verantwortliche Rede vom Sein Gottes bei Karl Barth. Eine Paraphrase* (Tübingen: Mohr, 1986[4]), newly translated as *God's Being Is in Becoming* (Edinburgh: T&T Clark, 2001).

[6] 'The Royal Man. A Christological Reflection on Human Dignity in Barth's Theology', *Karl Barth. A Theological Legacy* (Philadelphia: Westminster, 1986), pp. 127–38. The theme is also picked up in 'The Dogmatic Significance of the Question of the Historical Jesus' in *Theological Essays II* (Edinburgh: T&T Clark, 1995), pp. 82–119.

cutting across the grain of human time and space, a preacher with whose death God is identified and whose presence now is in the preached word which generates faith. The result of this confluence is Barth without Zinzendorf:[7] the constructive and critical energy of Barth's Christology, but in certain respects without Barth's ceaseless return to the details of the Gospels' central figure and without his idiom in which the *last* word to be said of God and Jesus is: 'It came to pass ...'[8]

We begin with some reflections on Jüngel's early book *Paulus und Jesus*, and then pass to consider themes from his later writings, before concluding with some brief reflections.

2. Paul and Jesus

The main lines of Jüngel's Christology (and, indeed, of some of his thinking in other areas, notably the relation between justification and anthropology) already find expression in his doctoral dissertation *Paulus und Jesus*.[9] It is a flamboyant and provocative work, not at all the stuff of cautious textual or historical analysis, and indebted (in the foreground) to Ernst Fuchs's theory of the New Testament as an eschatological language-event and (in the background) to an amalgam of Heidegger's repudiation of instrumentalism and Barth's theology of the Word. The overall argument of the dissertation – that Jesus' proclamation of the kingdom and Paul's theology of justification cohere as eschatological speech-events in which the law is opposed by faith generated by the Word – is scarcely

---

[7] 'I have become increasingly Zinzendorfian,' Barth wrote to Bultmann in 1952, 'to the extent that in the NT only the one central figure as such has begun to occupy me – or each and everything else only in the light and under the sign of this central figure ... One cannot discuss the fact that "Jesus lives," as we are both convinced. But one can, as a theologian, either refrain or not refrain from thinking to and from this "objective" reality. I myself cannot refrain from doing so, but do it.' K. Barth and R. Bultmann, *Letters 1922–1966* (Edinburgh: T&T Clark, 1982), p. 107.

[8] See K. Barth, *Church Dogmatics* IV/1 (Edinburgh: T&T Clark, 1956), p. 223.

[9] *Paulus und Jesus. Eine Untersuchung zur Präzisierung der Frage nach dem Ursprung der Christologie* (Tübingen: Mohr, 1962, 1986[6]).

sustained: too many exegetical and historical positions are assumed without argument, and then too much allowed to ride on judgments which require far more defence than Jüngel offers. Yet it is a compelling work – in its theory of language, in its presentation of the eschatology of the New Testament as an interception of human temporal self-identity, and in its unashamedly Lutheran reading of Paul. Already we find in the book what most attracts about Jüngel: a sharp eye for the theologically debilitating effect of undisclosed philosophical presuppositions, a passionate one-sidedness, a deep sense that Christian faith and its texts are disturbing. And already, too, we find some of what will give cause for concern. In Christology, above all, there is a certain narrowness, an intense focus on a few aspects of the Christological locus which have to bear the load of the whole.

One of the richest (and, to many readers, one of the most puzzling) aspects of the book is its investment in the idea of language as event.[10] Jesus' proclamation (identified most properly with his parables) is not a sign, the form of some content which is grasped by going through Jesus' speech to something anterior to it. Rather, his proclamation *is* the event of the kingdom of God, so that the basic hermeneutical strategy vis-à-vis the parables is: '*In* the parables the kingdom comes to speech *as* parable.'[11] This rejection of the kind of separation of form and content, *signum* and *res* which is found in Jülicher's classic hermeneutics of the parables, coupled with a potent

---

[10] For background here, see the helpful articles by A. C. Thiselton, 'The Parables as Language-Event. Some Comments on Fuchs' Hermeneutics in the Light of Linguistic Philosophy', *Scottish Journal of Theology* 23 (1970), pp. 437–68; 'The New Hermeneutic', in I. H. Marshall, ed., *New Testament Interpretation. Essays on Principles and Methods* (Exeter: Paternoster, 1977), pp. 308–33, and the two collections edited by J. M. Robinson and J. B. Cobb, *New Frontiers in Theology I: The Later Heidegger and Theology* (New York: Harper and Row, 1963), and *New Frontiers in Theology II: The New Hermeneutic* (New York: Harper and Row, 1964). There is an interesting critical account of the wider history in I. U. Dalferth, 'God and the Mystery of Words', *Journal of the American Academy of Religion* 60 (1992), pp. 79–104.

[11] *Paulus und Jesus*, p. 135.

eschatology, in effect allows Jüngel to treat the parabolic material as revelatory, as 'Word' in the sense of a tradition of language which not only owes its origin to divine action but also is itself the mode of divine action and presence. *Paulus und Jesus* is particularly impressive in pressing the anthropological consequences here: the picture of the encounter of human life with the word of the gospel is radically anti-Cartesian, and catches something of the *bouleversement* brought about by Jesus the judge.

However, it is worth noting that one result of the overwhelming importance attached to the speech of Jesus is that his person and action, his historical mission, enjoy less centrality. It is the event of interruptive speech, and not the agent of the speech-act, which is the locus of revelation. One obvious reason for this is that Jüngel rightly eschews any attempt to reconstruct Jesus as some kind of historical personality. But there are deeper motives at work. For all his severe criticism of historicism, repeated throughout the thesis and especially in the account of the history of interpreting eschatology, Jüngel is very heavily committed to historical-critical methods of reading the New Testament. This is not because he wants to reduce the texts to some supposed state of affairs *behind* them, but because these methodologies help us move towards the core speech-events which set in motion the language-traditions of faith. The almost inevitable result is that the Gospels are read, not as literary wholes with dramatic or narrative structures, but rather as collections of discrete utterances whose place in the overall shape of the story is not of primary significance. Jüngel follows the conventional tradition-historical division of the material into pericopes, and the gospel drama as a whole does not exercise regulative control in interpreting the individual pieces of material. Here, as elsewhere, Jüngel lacks Barth's untroubled confidence in the plain sense of the gospel stories as a sufficient witness to the identity of the saviour – 'sufficient', because put to service by Jesus himself as his elect witness to himself. For that kind of confidence, and its broad, cohesive reading of Scripture, the notion of speech-event – however much its revelatory and eschatological idiom may shift us out of historicizing immanentism – is not a strong replacement.

This rather muted sense of Jesus as personal agent is bound up with two other features of the Christology of *Paulus und Jesus* – the deployment of an eschatology which is overwhelmingly futurist, and the focus upon Jesus' preaching to the relative neglect of his person and activity. The first requires only brief mention. The eschatology of the New Testament (Jüngel tends to think in singular terms) is expounded as a radical rupture of human time, and therefore as a reality which cannot be assimilated within patterns of linear progression or regress from the *nunc stans* of a human subject. 'The measure of time by which measurements are taken here is not oriented to the now of the human subject ... God is the measure of time.'[12] By corollary, Jesus' 'horizontal' time, his presence within the contingent sequences of creation, receives little attention, for, like the kingdom whose coming he proclaims, his coming is the coming of a purely eschatological future which intercepts and overpowers, but is not embedded within, our time. God is, of course, overwhelmingly *near* in Jesus, who proclaims 'the future of the kingdom of God which is near to the present in such a way that thereby humanity comes to be near to God because God has come near to humanity.'[13] But nearness is contrasted not so much with distance as with presence; as the near one, God approaches but does not come within our time. Only as such, Jüngel suggests, is God's coming able to be seen as generative of a new reality beyond the repetitions of temporal identity.[14]

This strictly eschatological rendering of Jesus is, we may believe, infinitely preferable to the immanentism and moralism which still threaten a good many contemporary Protestant

---

[12] Ibid., p. 141; see further 'The Emergence of the New', *Theological Essays II*, pp. 35–58.

[13] *Paulus und Jesus*, p. 181.

[14] See, for example, the various pieces of parable exegesis in *Paulus und Jesus*, pp. 139–74, and the discussion of eschatology and history, pp. 285–9.

Christologies. Yet it indicates a problem which quickly surfaces in reading Jüngel, namely, the question of what sort of positive theological role is assigned to Jesus' sheerly human existence. The problem shows itself with some clarity in what he has to say of the relation of Jesus' preaching to his person. 'The parables', he writes, 'lead us ... not only to the centre of the proclamation of Jesus, but equally point to the person of the proclaimer, to the mystery of Jesus himself.'[15] But the *Sprachbewegung* of Jesus' preaching quickly takes on a life of its own, and comes to appear as something less than a historical transaction. Jesus' parabolic proclamation is his 'self-attestation',[16] and his behaviour a commentary on the parables.[17] But Jesus' behaviour, he goes on to say, is a 'theological, but not a socio-logical or historicising category'.[18] The exclusiveness of the assertion (*either* theological *or* sociological) is troubling, for it may make Jesus such a meteoric figure that his occupancy of a determinate historical and social world seems merely accidental or occasional. Jesus lacks location.

Much the same is true of the communicative context in which the parables occur. Jüngel lays some stress on the form of the parable: the literary *Gattung* (a worldly story becomes the occasion for the word-event of God's eschatological nearness) is taken to be the clue to understanding how God relates to the world in Jesus. The God who comes to speech in the parables comes to the world and distances his hearers from all worldly historical contexts and sets our time free from the past. A flattening-out of the parables follows: the parables all exemplify roughly the same features, and can all be interpreted as instances of the same event of God's coming to speech.[19] But more than this, focussing on the formal features of parable

---

[15] Ibid., p. 87.
[16] Ibid., p. 131; the phrase is from Fuchs.
[17] Ibid., p. 139.
[18] Ibid.
[19] On Jüngel's rather formulaic interpretation of the parables, see W. Brändle, *Rettung des Hoffnungslosen. Die theologische Implikationen der Philosophie Theodor W. Adornos* (Göttingen: Vandenhoeck und Ruprecht, 1984), pp. 292f.

(particularly its mode of reference to eschatological states of affairs) leads to a rather iconic approach, with context of little hermeneutical significance. But speech-acts occur in a public, extra-linguistic world.[20] Part, therefore, of their interpretation will be a pragmatics of eschatological utterance.[21] If Jüngel draws back here, it is because the notion of speech-event, of language as revelatory and disruptive, works against considering language as a form of communal practice. Since parable is the normative form of Christian religious speech, ruled usage is precisely that which is called into question by the word-event of the gospel, for parables work by challenging and subverting semantic convention. The catachrestic nature of eschatological language is certainly – as Jüngel insists – a primary feature of Christian discourse. However, it is at this point that some further consideration of the conventions which eschatological language shatters is necessary, otherwise language comes to be regarded as something other than ruled communal behaviour, as somehow immediately and mysteriously generative of states of awareness.[22] This is not to de-eschatologize or naturalize Jesus. But it is to suggest that the speech-event of Jesus' proclamation is not simply a literary form, a kind of apocalyptic

---

[20] See the discussion in Thiselton, *New Horizons in Hermeneutics*, pp. 283–91.

[21] The theological significance of pragmatic analysis of language has been repeatedly emphasized by E. Arens in a number of publications. See, in the present context, *Kommunikative Handlungen. Die paradigmatische Bedeutung der Gleichnisse Jesu für eine Handlungstheorie* (Düsseldorf: Patmos, 1989), and the application to Christology in 'Leitlinien einer handlungstheoretischen Christologie', in E. Arens, ed., *Gottesrede – Glaubenspraxis. Perspektiven theologischer Handlungstheorie* (Darmstadt: Wissenschaftliches Buchgesellschaft, 1994), pp. 29–48. There is a related critique of formalism in parable exegesis (associated, for example, with Crossan) in L. Poland, *Literary Criticism and Biblical Hermeneutics. A Critique of Formalist Approaches* (Chico: Scholars Press, 1985).

[22] Compare the similar criticism of Ebeling's theory of language by G. Lindbeck in 'Ebeling. Climax of a Great Tradition', *Journal of Religion* 61 (1981), p. 313. In a sophisticated essay co-authored with I. U. Dalferth, 'Sprache als Träger der Sittlichkeit', in A. Hertz, et al., eds, *Handbuch der christlichen Ethik* (Freiburg: Herder, 1978), pp. 454–73, Jüngel makes a good deal of use of socio-pragmatic theories of language and communicative competence; but the theme is almost entirely absent elsewhere (something which Dalferth himself laments in 'God and the Mystery of Words', pp. 89–93).

rhetoric, but a historical transaction in which *this one*, the one who was and acted in this way, also spoke of the coming of God not only in his word but also in his work.[23]

3. Jesus, Word, and Word of God

In moving from Jüngel's early work on the Christology of the New Testament to his work on issues in dogmatic Christology, it is important to bear in mind that he has, so far at least, not published a Christological treatise. Such materials as lie to hand are scattered throughout his writings, in essays, in passages in the course of other arguments, or in sets of theses (these last present particular problems of interpretation since they are published without the lecture texts from which they emerge). At best, all that can be done is piece things together; yet, for all the diversity of occasion of Jüngel's writings, what he has to say has remained remarkably consistent. There are, for example, refinements and elaborations, but no serious retractions or changes of direction, between 'Jesu Wort und Jesus als Wort Gottes', written for the 1966 *Festschrift* for Barth,[24] and 'The Dogmatic Significance of the Question of the Historical Jesus', which appeared in Italian in 1988 and German in 1990. This consistency makes it possible to assemble some of his leading ideas into a systematic shape.

1. One of the pressing issues for German Protestant Christology in the 1950s and 1960s (and especially for one raised as *Neutestamentler* in the shadow of Bultmann) was the relation of faith's assertions about Jesus Christ to the history and self-understanding of Jesus himself. How, on the one hand, can

---

[23] Jüngel's relative inattention to the works of Jesus, and especially his miracles, is noted by, for example, P. A. Rolnick, *Analogical Possibilities. How Words Refer to God* (Atlanta: Scholars Press, 1993), p. 264; G. Rémy, 'L'Analogie selon E. Jüngel. Remarques Critiques. L'Enjeu d'un Débat', *Revue d'Histoire et de Philosophie Religieuses* 66 (1986), p. 156.

[24] 'Jesu Wort und Jesus als Wort Gottes. Ein hermeneutischer Beitrag zum christologischen Problem', in E. Busch et al., eds., *Parrhesia. Karl Barth zum 80. Geburtstag* (Zürich: EVZ, 1966), pp. 82–100, now in *Unterwegs zur Sache. Theologische Bemerkungen* (Munich: Kaiser, 1972), pp. 126–44.

Christology free itself from positivist, historicizing interest in 'facts about Jesus' without falling into docetism? How, on the other hand, can research into the history of Jesus be prevented from lapsing into apologetics, nervously casting around for proofs for Christological affirmations? In Jüngel's terms:

> The historical Jesus proclaimed the kingdom of God, but he did not proclaim himself. The early church, however, proclaimed the proclaimer Jesus as the Christ. Rudolf Bultmann therefore formulated the decisive question which leads from the historical to the dogmatic *formulation of the question* in this way: how are we to understand 'that the proclaimer Jesus becomes the proclaimed Christ'?[25]

Jüngel's approach, about which he has written on a number of occasions, is to propose that, like all theology, Christological thinking 'is essentially realised in the tension between historical knowledge and dogmatic responsibility'.[26] The difference between the two is defined as follows:

> To know something (an event, a person) *historically* means to analyse its having-been, its previous existence, and its effect. To account for something (an event, a person) *dogmatically* means to represent its significance now in the horizon of our current awareness of truth ... Though historical knowledge is the *prerequisite*, the *conditio sine qua non* of dogmatic responsibility to the objects of theology, it can never be the *foundation* of dogmatic responsibility ... Consequently, the knowledge of faith, and that means *dogmatic* responsibility for something (an event or a person), cannot be *grounded* in *historical* knowledge. It is as little possible to do this as it is on the other hand to base historical judgments on dogmatic judgments if the historical judgment is to make a truth claim. And yet all dogmatic judgments in theology are related back to historical knowledge. For God has revealed himself

---

[25] 'The Dogmatic Significance of the Question of the Historical Jesus', p. 84.

[26] Ibid., p. 83. See also 'Das Verhältnis der theologischen Disziplinen untereinander', *Unterwegs zur Sache*, p. 56, thesis 4.2; 'Das Sein Jesu Christi als Ereignis der Versöhnung Gottes mit einer gottlosen Welt. Die Hingabe des Gekreuzigten', *Entsprechungen. Gott–Wahrheit–Mensch. Theologische Erörterungen* (Munich: Kaiser, 1980), pp. 279f., theses 5.2–5.4; 'Thesen zur Grundlegung der Christologie', *Unterwegs zur Sache*, p. 286, theses B 2.22, 2.221.

in the medium of historical events. And *faith* in God is itself always
an historical event and as such accessible to historical knowledge.[27]

It is a characteristically compressed statement, in which three
things at least should be noted. First, it entails a surprisingly
subjective orientation in dogmatics. Dogmatics, Jüngel has
already said in the opening paragraph of the essay, is 'responsible to the possibility of contemporary faith in Jesus Christ',[28]
and so is called 'to represent its significance now in the
horizon of our current awareness of truth'.[29] What is most
striking is that the concern for contemporary faith, for significance, is not articulated by talking of Jesus as a living
contemporary. In effect, this sets up the Christological
question as something like: if Jesus *was* thus and so, what does
it mean now to have faith in that one who once was in that way?
Second, therefore, dogmatic responsibility 'begins where Jesus
is proclaimed and believed as *Christ* . . . Dogmatic responsibility
in the matter of the historical Jesus begins with what I would
like to call this *Christological "as"*'.[30] Its concern is to explicate
the logic of homological predication. Third, however, faith
and confession are not free-floating but 'related back to
historical knowledge'.[31] This backward relation is not a matter
of historical warrants, which would convert the historical
content of belief in Jesus into historical proof of the propriety
of such belief. Much more is it to 'guard [faith] from a docetic
self-misunderstanding'.[32] Hence '*questioning back from the
kerygma* to the historical Jesus is indispensable'.[33]

Jüngel is clearly much influenced by second generation
Protestant existentialist Christology (not only Fuchs, but
Käsemann and Ebeling also), which sought to move beyond
Bultmann's restriction of the historical component of

---

[27] 'The Dogmatic Significance of the Question of the Historical Jesus', pp. 83f.
[28] Ibid., p. 82.
[29] Ibid., p. 83.
[30] Ibid., p. 84.
[31] Ibid., p. 83.
[32] Ibid., p. 87.
[33] Ibid.

Christology to a mere reference to the 'that' of Jesus as the simple occasion of God's eschatological intrusion. There is a proper anterior element in Christology: faith in 'the proclaimed' may not be independent of what can be ascertained about 'the proclaimer'. But however much he may modify the ahistorical character of earlier existentialist readings of Jesus, Jüngel's phrasing of the Christological question still moves within its intellectual structure, and remains tethered to the notion that there are two and only two points of Christological interest: Jesus' proclamation (gen. subj.) and contemporary proclamation of Jesus (gen. obj.). More than Bultmann, Jüngel stresses that Christian theology can, as it were, trace a line between these two points, so that they have a necessary, not merely accidental, connection. And, more than Käsemann and Ebeling, he is conscious of the need for ontological analysis of the person of Jesus, through the language of relation and ultimately through trinitarian doctrine. Yet because the 'proclaimer→proclaimed' schema is still dominant, the development of a more comprehensive Christology is in some measure arrested. There is little, if any, backward reference to Israel and God's covenant with the creation through Israel, for Jesus' proclamation is almost without relief interpreted as interruptive, by definition a wholly new word of judgment and grace. And there is little reference forward into the history of the ascended Christ, the Spirit and the church and on into the consummation of all things, for Jüngel is distinctly reticent about speaking of Jesus as the agent of his own glorification in world-history. There is undoubtedly much more here than is to be found in Bultmann's collapse of Christology into the history of Christian experience secured to Jesus only by the slenderest of threads. Yet when Christology is structured around the question of how Jesus *then* relates to faith *now*, it is not easy to build up an account of Jesus in which the various moments of the Christological material (pre-existence, proclamation, suffering and death, resurrection, exaltation, heavenly session, the Lord's return) together form a total account of God's dealings with creation in which the agent of the whole is Jesus who was, and is, and is to come. Put differently: for Jüngel the relation of the moment of Jesus' earthly history to our present remains a *problem*, in a way which it would not be for a Christology more confident that these different moments can be seen as events within a complex yet unified drama with a plot and a living person as its continuous subject and agent.

Jüngel thus does not quite break free of the tendency of much modern Christology to locate Jesus in the past: within the 'proclaimer→proclaimed' pattern, *Christus praesens* has little place.[34] What constitutes the present is *faith*; the Christological component of the present is not so much Jesus, manifesting himself in the power of the Holy Spirit, but rather faith in Jesus generated by the word of the kerygma. Faith is not, of course, pure subjectivity; it is given as the anthropological correlate of God's word of grace which addresses, 'de-secures' us and grants us a new beginning. Yet Jesus himself remains rather curiously on the sidelines, a past and passive figure mediated through word and faith, one who no longer proclaims but is proclaimed. We now turn to look in more detail at the content of Jesus' proclamation.

2. The main lines of Jüngel's later account of the preaching of Jesus follow what was already presented in *Paulus und Jesus*, notably in regarding eschatology as the clue to understanding the historical Jesus. Jesus 'represents an *elemental interruption* of the continuity of life in his world',[35] for 'the historical Jesus saw the coherence of the reality of the present world as a whole to be called into question by the coming kingdom of God'.[36] God's kingdom is an absolute *novum*, an interstice in time, and therefore not a simple extension of present world history; rather in the coming of the kingdom

---

[34] See here D. Ritschl, *Memory and Hope. An Inquiry into the Presence of Christ* (New York: Macmillan, 1967); G. O'Collins, *Christology. A Biblical, Historical and Systematic Study of Jesus Christ* (Oxford: Oxford University Press, 1995), pp. 306–23.

[35] 'The Dogmatic Significance of the Question of the Historical Jesus', p. 89.

[36] Ibid.

'something comes to the world which absolutely does not belong to it, but which can only be experienced as an *intrusion upon* or *interruption of* the coherence of the world'[37] – hence its expression *in* parable *as* parable, and hence the crisis it brings about in our sense of temporal identity.[38]

How does the one who proclaims this invasive act of God become himself the object of confession and proclamation? For Jüngel, it is crucial to grasp that Jesus' proclamation raises the question of Jesus' person as proclaimer. Proclaimer and proclaimed are not two essentially discrete phenomena held together only by the proper name 'Jesus', for under-standing the proclamation involves understanding that the proclaimer himself is an ingredient within (and not merely a vehicle or occasion for) that proclamation. In terms of the proclamation of Jesus, Jüngel writes: '[he] was present as the great, radical interruption of the continuity of reality and life ordered and ruled in this way or that. Jesus seems to bewilder his contemporaries in the sense that *another* has gained power over them.'[39] But this involves also 'a *singular claim* concerning *the relation of the kingdom of God to his person*',[40] which Jüngel expounds along these lines:

> he understood himself totally in terms of God's kingdom, or, more precisely, in terms of God himself ... God himself, in the event of his kingdom, conditions the existence of Jesus thoroughly and totally. Put more succinctly: *Jesus is not himself apart from God.*[41]

And so we may say of Jesus, caught up by the free coming of God to the world, that 'this human being ek-sists totally and completely from the God who is presently setting forth

[37] Ibid., pp. 89f.
[38] See ibid., p. 91, with 'Jesu Wort und Jesus als Wort Gottes', pp. 130f.
[39] 'The Dogmatic Signifance of the Question of the Historical Jesus', pp. 100f.
[40] Ibid., p. 101.
[41] Ibid., pp. 101f. Elsewhere Jüngel expresses this in terms of the poverty of Jesus, in which he does not possess himself: see '"Theologische Wissenschaft und Glaube" im Blick auf die Armut Jesu', *Unterwegs zur Sache*, p. 28, and *God as the Mystery of the World* (Edinburgh: T&T Clark, 1983), p. 519.

his kingdom.'[42] Jüngel is quick to point out that he is not arguing that we can reconstruct Jesus' self-consciousness and extract a full-blown Christology; his point is more restricted, namely that we are pressed to think of Jesus the proclaimer as generated by God's kingdom and therefore as subsisting in that divine word-act. In Jüngel's terminology, Jesus' being is 'a *being in the act of the word*', or 'a being in the act of the word *of the kingdom of God*',[43] and therefore 'a *being in the act of the Word of God*'.[44] The notion of Jesus' being in the word of the kingdom serves, therefore, to bridge the gap between proclaimer and proclaimed: it is a relatively short step from Jesus' preaching as divine speech-act to Jesus himself as the divine self-articulation.

This step, however, involves Jüngel in going beyond the conventions of existentialist Christology by engaging ontological issues about Jesus' identity. Two clusters of ideas are particularly important: the dual notion of anhypostasia and enhypostasia, and the concept of relation.

> We understand the earthly existence of the man Jesus as a being in the act of the kingdom of God. And we said that in this his being Jesus existed in the anhypostasia of his human being. That Jesus *could* exist in the anhypostasia of his human being, that he was not nothing, is ontologically *grounded* in the enhypostasia of his human being in the mode of being of the Logos, and is to be understood theologically as the *grace* of the turning of God to this man.[45]

---

[42] 'The Dogmatic Signifance of the Question of the Historical Jesus', p. 103. See here also 'Das Sein Jesu Christi als Ereignis der Versöhnung Gottes mit einer gottlosen Welt', pp. 283f., theses 12.5, 12.6.

[43] 'Jesu Wort und Jesus als Wort Gottes', p. 129; cf. pp. 134f.

[44] Ibid., p. 136.

[45] Ibid., p. 140. Jüngel acknowledges his indebtedness to Barth here: see, for example, Barth, *Church Dogmatics* I/2, pp. 163–5, and *Church Dogmatics* IV/2, pp. 49f., 91. For recent criticism of the use of an- and enhypostasia in modern theology, including Barth and Jüngel, see F. L. Shults, 'A Dubious Christological Formula. From Leontius of Byzantium to Karl Barth', *Theological Studies* 57 (1996), pp. 431–46: the critique does not disturb the dogmatic point which the language is intended to express.

Jesus' anhypostatic humanity is manifest in his pre-Easter existence, where he shows himself wholly determined by the proclamation of God's kingdom. That this selflessness of the proclaimer is rooted in his enhypostatic humanity, his being 'in' the Word, is manifest only at Easter.[46] Although Jüngel is troubled by the charge of docetic, ahistorical Christology which the language of an- and enhypostasia raises, his defence is to hand.[47] He recasts the discussion in terms of historical relations, thereby seeking to ensure the primacy of Jesus' historical personhood, of which the ontological terms are analytic but for which they are no replacement. 'The concepts hypostasis, enhypostasia and anhypostasia are to be understood as relational concepts';[48] and we 'have to think of these relations *historically*'.[49] The term 'historical' is used to signal a rejection of the classical Christological language of substance and nature which, on Jüngel's reading, promotes abstract, speculative definitions of the natures of Christ independent of the history of their *unitio* in the personal history of Jesus.[50] Jesus' divinity and humanity are not qualities but 'subsistent relations', to be held together not by some kind of balancing of natures but according to 'the fundamental rule of dogmatic responsibility to the being of Jesus Christ':

---

[46] In *Gott als 'Gott für dich'. Eine Verabscheidung des Heilsegoismus* (Munich: Kaiser, 1983), pp. 152–5, M. Trowitzsch quibbles with Jüngel at this point, arguing that the enhypostatic perspective need not be held over until the post-Easter stage but can already be discerned in Jesus' earthly ministry.

[47] On the loss of Jesus as historical person in the an- and enhypostasia formula, see – besides Bonhoeffer's well-known criticism in *Christology*, pp. 78f., 103 – P. Schoonenberg's summary of the issues in *The Christ* (London: Sheed & Ward, 1972), pp. 58–65. For a counter-proposal, see W. Pannenberg, *Jesus – God and Man* (London: SCM Press, 1968), pp. 337–44.

[48] 'Jesu Wort und Jesus als Wort Gottes', p. 135, n. 27; see also 'The Dogmatic Significance of the Historical Jesus', p. 112, and 'Thesen zur Grundlegung der Christologie', p. 277, theses A 5.2, 5.21. For a wider discussion of the ontology of relation in Christology, see C. Schwöbel, 'Christology and Trinitarian Thought'.

[49] 'Jesu Wort und Jesus als Wort Gottes', p. 137.

[50] See 'The Dogmatic Significance of the Question of the Historical Jesus', pp. 114f., and 'Thesen zur Grundlegung der Christologie', p. 276, thesis A 3.41.

the more consistently and radically Jesus is understood as the
Christ or the more consistently and radically this human person
is understood as the Son of God, the more consistently and
radically his true humanity will thereby be emphasised. And the
more consistently and radically the difference between the
human Jesus and God the Father is emphasised, the more
consistently and radically will his identity with the Son of God be
comprehended.[51]

In thesis form: 'The being of Jesus Christ is, on the one hand,
God's self-relation as relation to the humanity of the man
Jesus and, on the other hand, the self-relation of the man
Jesus as relation to God.'[52]

Does it work, however? Despite the investment in the notion
of historical relation, there remains the question of whether we
do indeed have a human figure here – whether, that is, the
necessary retrospective move from kerygma to proclaimer does
succeed in securing Jesus as more than a kind of historical
marker. If Jüngel fails in some measure to satisfy at this point,
it is not because of his use of the language of hypostasis and its
various extensions, for he shows with some success that
ontological analysis and history need not conflict (however
strongly the lingering mythology of 'functional' Christology
may urge us to judge otherwise). The failure, if such there be,
is a more basic one: a lack of portrayal with any degree of
density, concreteness and depth, of Jesus himself. Jesus is only
in a minimal way a personal agent here, one to whom patterns
of action, development, purpose, will – the whole cluster of
things which make up a perduring human identity – can be
attributed with any degree of naturalness. Here, by contrast,
Jesus is much more narrowly construed as (and almost only as)
speaker. And even as such, his speech is an absolute *novum*,
falling outside the conventions of human communicative

[51] 'The Dogmatic Significance of the Question of the Historical Jesus', pp. 116f.
[52] 'Thesen zur Grundlegung der Christologie', p. 277, thesis A 5.3. In light of this,
S. Greiner's charge of incipient monophysitism (in 'Gott ist Liebe. Ein Beitrag
zum Gespräch mit Eberhard Jüngel', *Theologie und Glaube* 80 (1990),
pp. 432–43) is incorrect, and Gamberini's defence of Jüngel is apt: *Nei legami del
Vangelo*, pp. 155–62.

exchange, and thereby further reinforcing his isolation. Jüngel's appeal to the relational structure of Jesus' being ought to push him to some more extended presentation of Jesus' encounters with his contemporaries; but – as we saw in looking at *Paulus und Jesus* – little space is given over to Jesus as the occupant of a specific historical, social and political locale. There is general reference to Jesus' 'impact on his contemporaries,'[53] and the bewilderment which his proclamation brought about.[54] Yet such is the weight of the eschatology, and such is Jesus' otherness, that contingent circumstance, the stuff of narrative, is rather quickly passed over, and we are left wondering what it means for the Word to be *flesh*.

Moreover, there is need for some more exploration of Jesus' continuing identity between his acts of interruptive speech. His identity is episodic: vivid and intense, certainly, but deficient in depth or extension. Although Jüngel's appeal to the idea of 'Jesus Christ as the event of the Word of God in person'[55] catches the sheer difference and unavailability of Jesus in the Gospels' presentation of him, what it misses is the manner in which this difference is inseparable from the ordinariness of his history. As the enfleshed Word, Jesus is himself in particular circumstances, there and then. And those circumstances are not simply a set of stage props, hastily assembled to furnish a setting for Jesus' announcement of the new; they are the stuff of his identity. At the very least, the category of 'word' could be supplemented by that of 'name', in order to draw attention to Jesus' particular identity and to advertise how that identity occurs in a complex sequence of intentions, actions and interactions, and sufferings. Jüngel, indeed, is not without alertness to the potential of speaking of Jesus as this 'nameable' one. He readily identifies that way in which Barth in the doctrine of reconciliation returns again and again to the specificity of Jesus' history as the concrete *Anfangspunkt* of all theological

---

[53] 'The Dogmatic Significance of the Question of the Historical Jesus', p. 89.
[54] Ibid., pp. 100f.
[55] 'Die Freiheit der Theologie', *Entsprechungen*, p. 16.

reflection.[56] And he finds something of the same in the Christology of Heinrich Vogel (under whom he studied and for whom he retains a permanent respect): the emphatic stress on the *Istigkeit Jesu* in *Gott in Christo* and the *Christologie* has a radically anti-mythological thrust.[57] Yet for all this Jüngel is oddly reluctant to allow the gospel portrayal in its entirety to mould the shape of his Christology, offering instead a sharp presentation of discrete episodes from Jesus' career. The almost inevitably fragmentary effect of tradition-historical interpretation of the narrative, coupled with the hermeneutics of Jesus as speaker, and a massive investment in the *telos* of Jesus' life in the cross, all tend to undermine what Jüngel might otherwise be disposed to attempt: a redescription of the Gospels' rendering of Jesus which – as Barth put it – 'declares a name, binding the history strictly and indissolubly to this name and presenting it as the story of the bearer of this name'.[58]

4. God's Identification with the Crucified

The agenda for Jüngel's theology of the cross is very extensive: not only Christology and soteriology, but also anthropology and the doctrine of the Trinity. Particularly in the writings from the 1960s and 1970s which culminated in *God as the Mystery of the World*, Jüngel pointed out tirelessly that the death of Jesus is to be regarded as *the* definitive divine action which constitutes the ground of a richly theopaschite trinitarianism which expresses faith's confession that God is love, as well as of a soteriology in which salvation consists in liberation from self-realization through works into authentic humanity marked by faith. In short, the Christian gospel, and thus evangelical theology, is concerned with the λόγος τοῦ σταυροῦ. Any kind of comprehensive review of Jüngel's theology of the death of

---

[56] See, besides the essay 'The Royal Man', '"... keine Menschenlosigkeit Gottes ..." Zur Theologie Karl Barths zwischen Theismus und Atheismus', *Barth-Studien* (Gütersloh: Mohn, 1982), p. 336, and 'Karl Barth', ibid., p. 18.

[57] See 'The Mystery of Substitution. A Dogmatic Conversation with Heinrich Vogel', *Theological Essays II*, pp. 151–62.

[58] *Church Dogmatics*, IV/1 p. 16.

Christ would thus involve a treatment of (at the dogmatic level) his doctrines of God, Christ, humanity, salvation and justification, and (at the philosophical level) his critique of the strange affiliation of theism and atheism in modern metaphysics. Here, however, we restrict ourselves, to concentrate on the place of the figure of Jesus in this complex assemblage of doctrinal, metaphysical and historical reflection.

We go straight to the heart of the matter with the concept of the *identification* of God with the crucified Jesus. Jüngel writes that 'in the event of the death of Jesus, and thus at the place where Godforsakenness culminated, God became one with this man. God identified himself with Jesus, with this mortal man.'[59] This identification is manifest at the resurrection, so that Jüngel can speak of the 'identity of God with the crucified, dead and buried Jesus which is revealed in the resurrection of Jesus from the dead'.[60] If we try to define more closely what Jüngel means here, it is certainly true – as Ingolf Dalferth has pointed out – that the cogency of the concept of identification owes more to its proximity to the homological language of faith than to its analytical precision.[61] But Jüngel does offer some pointers to a more precise account. Identification is defined thus:

> Here we understand identification as an event, in which the God who relates himself to himself relates himself to the man Jesus who is distinguished from him, in such a way that, in full unity with this man, he – in the distinction of Father and Son – *opposes* himself, and in this opposition which becomes unsurpassable in the antithesis of divine life and human death, remains *related to himself* – as Spirit.[62]

---

[59] 'Was ist "das unterschiedend Christliche"?', *Unterwegs zur Sache*, p. 298. Similar statements are scattered throughout his writings. See, for example, *Gott – für den ganzen Menschen* (Einsiedeln: Benzinger, 1976), pp. 14f.; or *God as the Mystery of the World*, pp. 190, 193, 329, 363f., 373, 385, 388.

[60] 'Das Sein Jesu Christi als Ereignis der Versöhnung Gottes mit einer gottlosen Welt', p. 276, thesis 1.

[61] See Dalferth, 'God and the Mystery of Words', p. 9; the criticism is somewhat overdrawn.

[62] 'Das Sein Jesu Christi als Ereignis der Versöhnung Gottes mit einer gottlosen Welt', p. 276, thesis 1.11.

What is to be taken from this? First, the trinitarian background of the notion of identification is crucial. It is this which drives the critical history of theism in *God as the Mystery of the World*, and the various attempts to bring together the doctrine of the Trinity, the notion of God as love, and the death of God.[63] Furthermore, it is this which blocks any idea that Jesus is accidental to the being of God, for God's self-relation occurs as his relation to the man Jesus. Second, God's identification with the crucified is an *event*. The point is of some importance. The force of the idea is to ensure that identification is distinguished clearly from immanence. This is the burden of his critique of Hegel in *God as the Mystery of the World* – a critique all the more forceful when set against the backcloth of Jüngel's very great respect for Hegel as the thinker who retained awareness of evangelical insight into the death of God long after its disappearance from Protestant dogmatics. Identification as event, in other words, provides a means of drawing attention to the specificity and uniqueness of God's action in Jesus.

There is, however, a difficulty in Jüngel's presentation at this point. For Jesus' death is expounded in an almost context-less way, in relative isolation from the life which he lived. In the Gospel drama, the death of Jesus has its full weight of meaning as an event which, even in its sheer pointlessness and waste, is the culmination of the life of the one who dies. Calvary 'sums up' the life of Jesus, not as a symbol which allows us to pass over or dispense with all that has gone before, but as that which is the culmination of his life of willed obedience. Though one could expect Jüngel to have an interest in this feature, he shows little sense of its importance, and it may be interesting to speculate why this is so. In part it is that his Christology, oriented to the speech-event of Jesus' proclamation, does not attach much significance

---

[63] See, for example, 'Das Verhältnis von "ökonomischer" und "immanenter" Trinität. Erwägungen über eine biblische Begründung der Trinitätslehre – im Anschluß an und in Auseinandersetzung mit Karl Rahners Lehre vom dreifaltigen Gott als transzendentem Urgrund der Heilsgeschichte', *Entsprechungen*, pp. 276–84; 'Gott ist Liebe. Zur Unterscheidung von Glaube und Liebe', in G. Ebeling et al., eds., *Festschrift für Ernst Fuchs* (Tübingen: Mohr, 1973), pp. 193–202; 'Karfreitag – Das dunkle Wort vom "Tode Gottes"', *Von Zeit zu Zeit. Betrachtungen zu den Festzeiten im Kirchenjahr* (Munich: Kaiser, 1976), pp. 15–62.

to the dramatic features of Jesus' life as the Gospel narratives unfold it: Jesus is less a character with dispositions than an escha-tological voice. Partly it is because, in stressing that the cross is an event in the being of God, Jüngel may run the risk of losing its human specificity. 'Has the Lutheran Christological tradition on which he has drawn made so much of the cross as the act of the crucified *God* that attention is taken away from the *human* Jesus?'[64] None of this is to accuse Jüngel of idealism; but it is to say that the 'unsubstitutable' character of Jesus, his resistance to mythologization, demands that a good deal of attention be paid to the concrete, if his particularity is not to be overwhelmed by interpretative concepts. Donald MacKinnon once suggested that 'a manifest weakness' of some Christology is that

[64] C. Gunton, 'The Being and Attributes of God. Eberhard Jüngel's Dispute with the Classical Philosophical Tradition', in J. Webster, ed., *The Possibilities of Theology. Studies in the Theology of Eberhard Jüngel in his Sixtieth Year* (Edinburgh: T&T Clark, 1994), p. 21. In a provocative comparison of Jüngel and Levinas in the same volume, David Ford notes a related feature: 'There is little about the body in Jüngel in comparison to Levinas. Jüngel's way of giving speech and language priority, while not in competition with doing justice to the physical, can have the effect of ignoring it. This has its consequences with regard to death. The theology of the crucified seems as if it could do without the blood-iness and violence of the passion narratives. Jüngel's notion of identification and differentiation is in somewhat tenuous relation with the contingencies and bodiliness of those tragic events' ('Hosting a Dialogue. Jüngel and Levinas on God, Self and Language', in ibid., p. 44). The Christological question here raises a larger issue about Jüngel's theology which is discussed at some length by R. Spjuth in his important study *Creation, Contingency and Divine Presence in the Theologies of Thomas F. Torrance and Eberhard Jüngel* (Lund: Lund University Press, 1995). Spjuth suggests that Jüngel's account of God's presence to the creation, dominated as it is by eschatological categories (coming, interruption, presence-in-absence, and so forth), lacks a sense of the mediation of divine activity through contingent created acts. This he connects with other features of Jüngel's work: the 'law-gospel' motif (in which 'law' refers to the significations and activities of worldly agents, 'gospel' their eschatological interception); the priority of possibility over actuality; the unease over the sacramental mediation of God's work. Though Spjuth does not expand the argument into a full discussion of Jüngel's Christology, his critique is an instructive indication of some fruitful lines of evaluation. A much less sophisticated treatment of some of the same questions in the area of Christology and the doctrine of creation can be found in J. Richard, 'Théologie évangélique et théologie philosophique. A propos d'Eberhard Jüngel', *Science et Esprit* 38 (1986), pp. 5–30.

it has evacuated the mystery of God's self-incarnation of so much that must take time, that must be endowed with the most pervasive forms of human experience, its successiveness, its fragmentariness, above all its ineluctable choices, fraught equally inevitably with tragic consequence. It is a paradox that in a narrative, in which in the form in which we have received it, the mythological, the typological, even the contrived framework seem to take charge, we have in fact a standing protest against failure to take seriously the sheer concreteness of God's self-incarnating.[65]

Malgré tout, perhaps, Jüngel is not without some difficulties on this score.

However, there is further import in the notion of identification as event. For the language of identification (unlike 'identity' and 'unity', which, somewhat confusingly, Jüngel also uses) serves additionally to highlight the freedom of God in the event of Jesus' death. God is not in any *simple* way *the same as* the crucified; his manifestation of himself does not mean complete disclosure or availability. Once again, the point is worth pausing over.

Identification as a free divine act is closely connected with two other notions which Jüngel deploys: the idea that in Jesus God *comes* to the world, and the idea that in Jesus we encounter the revelation of the hiddenness of God. 'Coming', as we have already seen in Jüngel's treatment of Jesus' proclamation of the kingdom of God, retains a sense of God's non-identity with the world even in the midst of his intimacy with it in the person of Jesus:

> [I]nsofar as it reflects upon the Christian faith, theology has to conceive of God as the one who *came* to the world in Jesus Christ and as such does not cease to *come* to the world. Christian theology may not set aside the task of preserving this tension in its thinking; because of this, it has to insist both that God became unsurpassably worldly in a man and that, as such, he will have us believe in himself as the one who comes to the world. God would be thought of as part, and only part, of the world if his identity with the man Jesus were not understood as the *event* of his identifying, of his coming to the world.[66]

[65] D. M. MacKinnon, 'The Evangelical Imagination', in J. P. Mackey, ed., *Religious Imagination* (Edinburgh: Edinburgh University Press, 1986), p. 181.

[66] 'Metaphorical Truth. Reflections on the Theological Relevance of Metaphor as a Contribution to the Hermeneutics of Narrative Theology', *Theological Essays I* (Edinburgh: T&T Clark, 1989), p. 59.

This notion of 'coming' picks up the threads of a concept to which Jüngel frequently returns, namely the hiddenness of God even in his revelation of himself in Jesus. In some theses from a lecture course of the late 1980s, Jüngel proposes:

> In the event of his revelation God's specific hiddenness is percep-
> tible under its opposite. This secondary mode of the hiddenness of
> God is his earthly hiddenness in the life and death of the man
> Jesus, and to that extent an essential moment in the event of divine
> revelation (in its Christological form). That God is hidden *sub
> contrario* in Jesus' life and death, is revealed through Jesus' resur-
> rection in such a way that the *opposite* under which God is hidden
> does not appear to be a *contradiction* of God's divinity.[67]

Certainly this hiding of God's hiddenness means that in Jesus' humanity God becomes 'accessible ... identifiable ... and experienceable';[68] yet what replaces God's 'absolute hiddenness' is nevertheless properly another *kind* of hiddenness, a 'hidden' hiddenness.[69] Another essay, 'The Revelation of the Hiddenness of God', argues in a closely similar fashion about the Christological ramifications here. 'That God *reveals* himself in Jesus Christ means that the hidden God, who is the God hidden in the light of his own being, has come to the world. However, the *hiddenness* of God ... is not thereby replaced with *absolute disclosure*.'[70] What then of incarnation?

> That the Word became flesh ... that is the revelation of God which
> allows his glory, that is, the hiddenness of God in the light of his
> being, to be present in a part of the world, present in the flesh of a
> human being. The primary hiddenness of God is now identifiable.
> But it is identifiable only in the secondary, worldly hiddenness of a
> quite particular human life. And so it is pertinent to say that this

---

[67] 'Zum Begriff der Offenbarung', in G. Besier, ed., *Glaube, Bekenntnis, Kirchenrecht* (Hannover: Lutherisches Verlaghaus, 1989), p. 218, thesis 5. For an earlier detailed exposition of Luther on this theme, which lies behind what Jüngel has to say here, see 'Quae supra nos, nihil ad nos. Eine Kurzformel der Lehre vom verborgenen Gott – im Anschluß an Luther interpretiert', *Entsprechungen*, pp. 202–51.

[68] 'Zum Begriff der Offenbarung', p. 218, thesis 5.2.

[69] Ibid., thesis 5.3.

[70] 'The Revelation of the Hiddenness of God. A Contribution to the Protestant Understanding of the Hiddenness of Divine Action', *Theological Essays II*, pp. 128f.

secondary hiddenness of God, which is identical with his revelation, is the concealing of the hiddenness of God. By concealing God's primary majestic hiddenness, concealing it indeed in the flesh and blood of Jesus, it reveals God himself.[71]

The language of concealment is uncomfortably docetic, as if Jesus' flesh and blood cloak but do not themselves *manifest* the otherwise unapproachable light of the divine majesty. Jüngel is sharply conscious of the difficulty into which he may be led, and is quick to assert that

> [T]his second mode of the hiddenness of God ... is in no sense a kind of covering or veil which God can put on and then take off again, as if it were a human disguise. The hiddenness of God in the human existence of Jesus of Nazareth is *not externally* related to that which God is in himself ... Even in the greatest of all imaginable contradictions, even in the *contradiction* of eternal life and earthly death, God *corresponds* to himself.[72]

Yet this appeal to the language of correspondence (*Entsprechung*), so central in *Gottes Sein ist im Werden* in stating the coherence of *deus ad intra* and *deus ad extra*, may not be quite enough to dispel the danger. 'Correspondence' and 'hiddenness' obviously pull in contrary directions.[73] Corre-spondence suggests that Jesus' flesh is (with whatever qualifications) directly expressive of God; 'hiding' suggests a more dialectical relation of God to Jesus. Classical Christology located the dialectic within the two natures of Jesus himself, without confusion and without separation. Jüngel, at least when Luther is in the ascendent in his thinking, tends to make the dialectic one between God and the flesh of Jesus, with somewhat unhappy results. If he is prevented from drifting too far in this direction, it is because he has deeply internalized the discipline of Barth's doctrine of the Trinity, and reacts instinctively against any hint that Christian theology can define God *remoto Christo* and still remain Christian.

---

[71] Ibid., p. 129.

[72] Ibid., p. 130. See further 'Zum Begriff der Offenbarung', p. 219, thesis 5.5.

[73] Jüngel tries to sort out some of the tensions in *God as the Mystery of the World*, pp. 344–7.

A final issue which requires comment here is Jüngel's stress that the resurrection is essentially a revelation of the meaning of Jesus' death, with which God identified himself. In trying to avoid a triumphalist account of the resurrection (in which Jesus' death is left behind as not proper to God), Jüngel tends to steer into an opposite difficulty: that of giving insufficient weight to the active contemporaneity of Jesus. 'Jesus Christ can only be thought of as presently active, if his active being is comprehensible as the eschatological unity of the past of the man Jesus (death) and God's eternity.'[74] Where we might expect an account of Jesus' resurrection to move quickly into talk of the presence of Jesus, Jüngel is much more interested in Easter as what might be called the 'making kerygmatic' of the history of Jesus, and above all of his death. In the resurrection, Jesus becomes 'word' – both in the sense of 'kerygma' and in the sense of 'divine manifestation'.[75] The assimilation of resurrection to revelation is indeed striking ('The resurrection of Jesus Christ is revelation κατ᾽ ἐξοχήν'),[76] as is the fact that the *agent* of revelation here is not the risen Jesus but 'God' who '*presents himself* in this event... as being God in definitive unity with the man Jesus'.[77] But it is hard to find here any idea that by virtue of his resurrection Jesus is post-existent: a notoriously difficult concept, but surely an inescapable one if the relation of God to our present is not to be (literally) anonymous. Jüngel speaks readily of God 'with' or 'for' or 'among' us through the resurrection of Jesus; but this language is less humanly specific than that of, for instance, encounter with Jesus in which Jesus himself is the constitutive shape and the agent of God's approach and address to the world.

Jüngel's work in these matters owes a good deal to Ernst Fuchs's interpretation of the resurrection.[78]

---

[74] 'Thesen zur Grundlegung der Christologie', p. 276, thesis A 3.2. See also pp. 276f., theses A 4–4.3.
[75] See ibid., p. 289, theses B 2.275–2.276.
[76] Ibid., p. 290, thesis 3.1.
[77] Ibid., thesis 3.21.
[78] On Fuchs here, see the useful paraphrase in R. Heijne, *Sprache des Glaubens. Systematische Darstellung der Theologie von Ernst Fuchs* (Tübingen: Mohr, 1972), pp. 115f.

> In the resurrection of Jesus his cross becomes word for us ... Whilst Jesus' cross also subsists for itself, word and hearer of the resurrection of Jesus are all along the line integrated ... In the Easter event we are dealing with the *one* miracle of the *revelation* of the nearness of God in grace and forgiveness.[79]

The cross 'becomes word' at the resurrection, both in that the resurrection manifests the significance of Good Friday, and in that the cross is thereby shown to be *pro nobis*. In the resurrection, therefore, the cross is 'realized' as the word which creates faith. All this Jüngel shares, though with one large difference: he is pulled back from the collapse of resurrection into the history of faith by the trinitarian doctrine which undergirds what he has to say. Yet even so, it is hard to spell out the sense we should give to the conviction that *Jesus lives*.[80]

Such worries may be compounded by a reading of a rather elliptical set of reflections on issues in prolegomena to Christology, 'The Effectiveness of Christ Withdrawn', where Jüngel offers reflections on 'a general hermeneutical problem concerning our own relation to the past,' namely:

> There something was – here am I. What does this something have to do with me? What does this piece of the past, this 'once upon a time', have to do with my existence here and now? This general question of historical existence has to be considered even when we ask about *Jesus Christ*. Certainly the question about this person may be a quite unique one, but it nevertheless implies the general

[79] E. Fuchs, 'Glaube und Geschichte im Blick auf die Frage nach dem historischen Jesus', *Zur Frage nach dem historischen Jesus. Gesammelte Aufsätze II* (Tübingen: Mohr, 1960), p. 183. See also 'Das Auferstehung nach 1. Korinthiker 15', *Zum hermeneutischen Problem in der Theologie. Gesammelte Aufsätze I* (Tübingen: Mohr, 1959), pp. 197–210, and 'Muß man an Jesus glauben, wenn man an Gott glauben will?', *Glaube und Erfahrung. Zum christologischen Problem im Neuen Testament. Gesammelte Aufsätze III* (Tübingen: Mohr, 1965), pp. 249–79.

[80] For further exploration of the link of resurrection and revelation in German Protestant Christology of the period, see A. Geense, *Auferstehung und Offenbarung. Über den Ort der Frage nach der Auferstehung Jesu Christi in der heutigen deutschen evangelischen Theologie* (Göttingen: Vandenhoeck und Ruprecht, 1971), and K. Kienzler's study of Ebeling in *Logik der Auferstehung. Eine Untersuchung zu R. Bultmann, G. Ebeling und W. Pannenberg* (Freiburg: Herder, 1976), pp. 63–102 (especially pp. 92–102 on word, faith and resurrection).

question of the relation between our historical existence and that which took place long before we existed.[81]

For Jüngel, the resurrection does not solve the problem (as it does for Barth, in the magisterial discussion of 'The Verdict of the Father'),[82] since the resurrection looks backwards. He writes:

Jesus' effectiveness consists in his *death*, in his *withdrawal*, which faith in his resurrection does not reverse but rather confirm. Perhaps there is no abandonment more creative than that experienced by those whom Jesus had addressed and from whom he was then withdrawn. This fact can be formulated with the thesis that the *death* of Jesus evoked *faith* in Jesus Christ, and that the *absence* of Jesus gave rise to the *New Testament* as a testimony to his presence.[83]

Even the resurrection does not qualify Jesus' withdrawal; and if his absence is 'creative', it is so because it evokes faith and the texts of the New Testament. Jesus is not envisaged as an operative factor in the present history of the world. When resurrection is tied very closely to word and revelation, Jesus' present activity is quite quickly lost. Interpreted as a manifestation of what *has* happened, the resurrection is detached from its wider dogmatic setting in Jesus' *status exaltationis*, and, once disconnected from ascension, heavenly session and the present ministry of Jesus in the distribution of the merits of his saving work as prophet, priest and king (in short: from the *rule* of Christ),[84] the risen one may disappear into the eternity of God.

5. The Humanity of God

God as the Mystery of the World is in many ways an extraordinary book, though one which – whilst it attracted considerable attention on publication and continues to provoke discussion – has not quite

---

[81] 'The Effectiveness of Christ Withdrawn. On the Process of Historical Understanding as an Introduction to Christology', *Theological Essays I*, p. 215.

[82] Barth, *Church Dogmatics* IV/1, pp. 283–357.

[83] 'The Effectiveness of Christ Withdrawn', p. 231.

[84] The concept of 'rule' is so thoroughly chastened by its exclusive definition through the crucified that little is left of the risen Jesus as triumphant (as in Eph. 1.20–23, 4.8–10).

found its audience. Most commentary on the book fastens on what Jüngel has to say about the doctrine of the Trinity in relation to the death of God. Important though this constructive doctrinal material is, it ought not to be isolated from the larger proposal concerning the coinherence of formal issues concerning thought and speech about God and issues in substantive dogmatics. This coinherence, Jüngel argues, has become disturbed in modernity under pressure from theistic metaphysics, and requires a theological dismantling of modern philosophy to prepare the ground for a modern dogmatics. Jüngel's book is offered as an attempt to work on both issues: hence its range and complexity. There is enduring value in the study as testimony to the importance of approaching not only doctrinal issues but also questions of epistemology or semantic theory in terms of the logic of Christian beliefs about Jesus and their entailments for theology proper and anthropology. Much of the intellectual and spiritual resonance of the book derives from the consistency with which Jüngel follows a path 'from the inside towards the outside'.[85] Our concern here, however, is not with the doctrines of God and humanity which Jüngel fashions, nor with his critique of post-Cartesian philosophy, but with the place occupied by Jesus in the book. Given the weighty superstructure which Christology has to support – Trinity, soteriology, anthropology, epistemology, theory of language – what are we to make of the figure of Jesus thus freighted?

Much of the book revisits and expands upon themes we have already discovered elsewhere. Thus Jesus is presented as the one whose parabolic proclamation is the event of God's coming to the world; his death is manifested at the resurrection as that with which God identifies himself, and in which God defines himself as a trinitarian act of love, self-loss in the midst of relation to self and others. The whole is intended as an attempt 'to present both the possibility and the necessity of a narrative theology',[86] and it may seem ungenerous and misplaced to entertain doubts about the success with which Jüngel retains a sense of the concreteness,

[85] *God as the Mystery of the World*, p. viii.
[86] Ibid., p. xi.

'narratability', of Jesus. The book is, after all, an onslaught on idealism, at times even extreme in its insistence that Christian thinking be purged of every trace of theism through facing the scandal of the cross. Yet, as elsewhere, there is a disparity between the robustness of Jüngel's Christologically-derived thought of God and humanity and its rather slender, even at times formal, handling of the figure of Jesus. Two themes provide a sample of questions which could be raised in a reading of this remarkable book.

The first is that of divine presence. Christian theology in modernity, haunted by the atheistic question (taunt?) 'where is God?' faces two options: either 'beyond the alternative of the presence or absence of God only the nonbeing of God can be thought',[87] in which case the question is merely superfluous; or we may seek for 'a positive answer which . . . is beyond the alternative of presence or absence'.[88] Taking the second tack, Jüngel (via Bonhoeffer) offers a Christological reconstruction of the notion of presence in which God's absence on the cross (for atheism a mark of God's non-existence) is an attribute of God's being.

> [I]f God 'lets himself be pushed out of the world' and bears the world on the cross as the world which will not bear him, then the being of God is in fact to be thought of as a being which explodes the alternative of presence or absence. . . . If God existed only in the sense of worldly presence, then he would be conceived of as a massive superlative of worldly presence . . . But if God is present as the one who is absent in the world, if absence is not simply the alternative opposite to the presence of God, then what Bonhoeffer presented as the interpretation of the cross event actually expresses in focused soteriological fashion the ontological characteristics of the divine being.[89]

This concept of a 'Christologically grounded withdrawal of God'[90] allows Jüngel to turn back the atheist question by refusing its presupposition that absence is non-being. Properly phrased, the

[87] Ibid., p. 55.
[88] Ibid.
[89] Ibid., p. 62.
[90] Ibid., p. 63.

question should be: *Wo ist Gott, wenn er so ist?*[91] Very acutely, Jüngel perceives the way in which modern metaphysics of presence swings rather uneasily between, on the one hand, subjective self-presence as that before which all reality has to be validated, and, on the other hand, a notion of God as transcendent, timeless perfection required to sustain the fragmentary moments of the ego. In effect, the metaphysics of presence determines God's existence by his essence – the divine essence is conceived as necessarily static and unaffected by transience, thereby making it impossible to conceive of God's existence as involved with transience at the cross. And, once again, this pushes theology to make a choice: either '[o]ne conceives of the noncontradictory nature of God's being and existence in such a way that one reverts to the metaphysical concept of the being of God and does away with existence',[92] or

> [o]ne thinks of the noncontradictory nature of God's being and existence in such a way that man comprehends the existence of God as the epitome of the divine being. Then, however, the traditional concept of the being of God must be given up because existence demonstrably includes one's being perishable within temporality.[93]

At this point it would have been natural for Jüngel to extend the discussion by turning to a more explicit consideration of Christology: it is, after all, in the doctrines of the incarnate presence of God and the presence of Christ in the Spirit, that Christian theology has developed some of its most characteristically Christian renditions of the nature of divine action in the world. In one sense, this is exactly what Jüngel does: presence has to pass through the needle's eye of Godforsakenness. But the natural pull of his thinking is still towards the category of word, and in *God as the Mystery of the World* this once again provides the master category through which the discussion proceeds. What he has to say is more than usually cryptic, and slides between using 'word' to refer (apparently) to verbal acts of communication and

---

[91] *Gott als Geheimnis der Welt* (Tübingen: Mohr 1977), p. 134; cf. *God as the Mystery of the World*, p. 102.

[92] *God as the Mystery of the World*, p. 187.

[93] Ibid., p. 188.

using it in a highly extended sense to talk of Jesus as the self-presentation of God. What does not readily emerge from these sections of the book is Jesus himself, who figures only fleetingly in the argument as a whole. Certainly Jüngel can write in these terms:

> The decisive thing is that in this word the self-communication of the one who speaks takes place: God speaks out of himself, and as such he addresses us. And here again, the decisive thing is that such addressing self-communication of God takes place under the ontic conditions of historical reality, in indissoluble identity with the particular history of the man Jesus. The word became flesh ...[94]

But the main drift of the argument bypasses this recognition: 'word' is usually the kerygmatic word which provokes faith. Indeed, language is 'the inner ground of history'.[95] This presupposition leaves in its wake a rather flat account of Jesus – a series of rhetorical episodes in which the particularities of time and place and casual incident recede from view.

Something of the same can be found in the handling of a second major theme of the book, that of God's humanity. Biblical texts, Jüngel notes, speak of God 'in that they bring to speech the history of his humanity'.[96] God in revelation is thus one who proceeds:

> God himself proceeds along a pathway ... In his ways, he is God. The ways which God goes cannot be distinguished from the one going, like a pathway from the path-walker. They are rather more like the way of a man's life which in a certain sense is identical with the man's life. Ways of life are ways of the living person to himself ... God's ways are also his ways to himself. They are different from our ways of life in that his 'to himself' is not removed from the divine subject ... But they are like the human ways of life in that the way is inextricably united with the subject.[97]

And so Jesus' history comes to have axiomatic status as the history of God's humanity, for

---

[94] Ibid., pp. 190f.
[95] Ibid., p. 190.
[96] Ibid., p. 157 (translation altered).
[97] Ibid., p. 159.

God has expressed himself, through the event of the identification with the history of Jesus of Nazareth, in the period of time of one man's life, and has ascribed in the event of the resurrection of Jesus from the dead an eternal future to this period of time, so that one must say: God has entered as man into the temporality of human history ('the word has become flesh')....[98]

On the surface this may seem close (perhaps too close) to the easy contemporary use of the notion of story in lush narrative Christologies. Jüngel is far too intelligent a theologian to allow Christology to be overwhelmed by an undifferentiated concept of story, however, and his sharp eye for the eschatology of the New Testament's presentation of Jesus helps him avoid the temptation of thinking of Jesus' (and God's) story as something to be told in a straightforward way, as one more narratable bit of our experience of the world. The word which tells of God's coming is, in Jüngel's favourite phrase from Fuchs, an 'eschatological announcement of time',[99] and so the narrative of Jesus does not simply occupy a place alongside other stories, since it is the story of the coming-to-be of the new creation. Only in this sense does *Denken* always refer itself to *Erzählen*.

So far, perhaps, so good. But when we come to look at the actual shape of the Christological narrative, Jüngel disappoints, as everything is compressed into the *Passionsgeschichte Jesu*. He speaks of the 'fixation ... on the Crucified One' which 'lends the narratives of the story of Jesus as gospel their narrative uniformity'.[100] Hardly objectionable: but 'orientation toward' the passion should not be allowed to issue in a Christology which consists by and large of only one episode. That Jüngel is not free of difficulties here is most apparent in his exposition of trinitarian doctrine in the latter part of the book, where it is the crucified Jesus who is the *vestigium trinitatis*, demonstrating that '[t]he deity of the living God ... is compatible in a very precise sense with the death of this human life'.[101] Certainly, he does

[98] Ibid., p. 301.
[99] Ibid.
[100] Ibid., p. 313.
[101] Ibid. p. 343.

broaden out the base of the doctrine of the Trinity a little to include Jesus' announcement of the kingdom,[102] and the life he lived. 'We see Jesus' violent death on the cross as the external consummation of that which Jesus has lived, which was a life of anticipative, active love which brought the law into conflict with itself and then bore this conflict in itself.'[103] And, further, attention is also given to the personal being of Jesus as 'the human consummation of new fellowship with God'.[104] But the cross remains the centre of gravity, and so, in a much-used formula, the trinitarian God of love is 'the union of death and life in favour of life'.[105] Father, Son and Spirit are, as it were, all placed in and around the event of Calvary, in which the *mission* of the Son is consummated. No theology in which God and incarnation are united will want to subvert these affirmations; but the contraction of Jesus' career to its end and the effect of this on trinitarian concepts remain a problem.

In the opening volume of his *Theodramatik*, von Balthasar remarks that the concentration upon 'event' in some modern theology (he has Bultmann and the early Barth in mind) yields something 'timeless and context-less', something lacking in 'horizontal time'.[106] Whereas in the biblical revelation, he suggests,

> the vertical event has unfolded into a series of times of salvation comparable to the acts of a play. This does not mean that the vertical event-time has been dissolved into a merely horizontal time of successive saving facts, but it *does* mean that the vertical event-time overtakes and refashions horizontal time, using it so that the event may spread itself out in dramatic form.'[107]

---

[102] See ibid., pp. 351–60.

[103] Ibid., p. 361, n. 36.

[104] Ibid., p. 358.

[105] Ibid., p. 299 (translation altered).

[106] H. U. von Balthasar, *Theo-drama. Theological Dramatic Theory. Volume 1: Prolegomena* (San Francisco: Ignatius Press, 1988), p. 27.

[107] Ibid., p. 28. Compare Francis Watson's suggestion that to envisage revelation as absolutely discontinuous is to emphasize 'the initial disruption at the expense of the subsequent integration', in 'Is Revelation an "Event"?', p. 389.

Von Balthasar and Jüngel have a great deal in common: a repudiation of the subjectivism of the German idealist inheritance; a Christocentrism learned from Barth; a rich theology of the divine passion. But von Balthasar, lacking Jüngel's ties to existentialism and its spasmodic Christology, is able to develop notions such as 'mission' or 'role' so that the life of the incarnate one, for all it is the transcendent act of God, has extension, takes place in the historical, public world, and is therefore more than a collection of occurrences or speech-acts.[108] Recasting some of his materials into this kind of idiom might serve Jüngel well in giving expression to his tenacious commitment to undertake Christology as 'thought's pointing to *Jesus Christ, the crucified* – to *himself!*'[109]

6. Conclusion

'It is frightening to stand behind a lectern or sit in a comfortable seminar room and talk about Jesus Christ. It is incongruous.'[110] Reading Jüngel's Christology may serve as a reminder that theology ought to be frightening, perilous – and not only because, properly undertaken, it ought to issue in intellectual, cultural and spiritual non-conformity, but because the one to whom theology gives its attention is unimaginably demanding. It is the jaggedness of Jüngel theology which most commands respect, for his real intellectual virtue is that of relentless critical interrogation of our representations of what he takes to be the heart of Christian faith. A good deal of lesser modern theology pales in comparison: indolent, unimaginative, hidebound by (liberal) convention, too easily familiar with its own subject matter, and far from radical. Not without reason, in a summary of his theology Jüngel notes that 'thinking God himself is a revolutionary event for one's

[108] On this aspect of the *Theodramatik*, see the comments by R. Williams, 'Balthasar and Rahner', in J. Riches, ed., *The Analogy of Beauty. The Theology of Hans Urs von Balthasar* (Edinburgh: T&T Clark, 1986), pp. 26–9.

[109] 'Das Sein Jesu Christi als Ereignis der Versöhnung Gottes mit einer gottlosen Welt', p. 284, thesis 17.

[110] H. Frei, 'The Encounter of Jesus with the German Academy', *Types of Christian Theology*, p. 133.

relation to God, to the world, and to self'.[111] And – again, unlike much lesser academic theology, especially of a generation ago – Jüngel's theology is haunted by the figure of Jesus, for which reason alone he is simply unprepared to consent to the alliance of Christian theology and idealist metaphysics which continues to dominate Western intellectual culture (even in its apparent overthrowing in postmodernity). Yet: the presentation of Jesus himself, at least in the shape in which he is encountered in the Gospels, is strangely uneven – vivid portrayals interspersed with large gaps. Above all, perhaps, Jüngel's Christology communicates only imperfectly how Jesus is absolute presence, the embodiment now of the divine 'I am'. Nevertheless, being grasped by and thinking about that presence requires the kind of intellectual temper – restless, open to astonishment, always ready to start afresh – which we find in Jüngel's best work, but which receives no finer expression than Kierkegaard's invocation at the beginning of *Training in Christianity*:

> It is eighteen hundred years and more since Jesus Christ walked here on earth. But this is not an event like other events which, only when they are bygone, pass over into history, and then as events long bygone, pass over into forgetfulness. No, His presence here on earth never becomes a bygone event, and never becomes more and more bygone – in case faith is to be found on earth. And if not, then indeed at that very instant it is a long, long time since He lived. But so long as there is a believer, such a one must, in order to become such, have been, and as a believer must continue to be, just as contemporary with His presence on earth as were those [first] contemporaries. This contemporaneousness is the condition of faith, and more closely defined it is faith.
> O Lord Jesus Christ, would that we also might be contemporary with Thee, see Thee in Thy true form and in the actual environment in which Thou didst walk here on earth; not in the form in which an empty and meaningless tradition, or a thoughtless and superstitious, or a gossipy historical tradition, has deformed Thee; for it is not in the form of abasement the believer sees Thee, and it cannot possibly be in the form of glory, in which no man has

---

[111] '"My Theology" – a Short Summary', *Theological Essays II*, p. 12.

yet seen Thee. Would that we might see Thee as Thou art and wast and wilt be until Thy return in glory, see Thee as the sign of offence and the object of faith, the lowly man, and yet the Saviour and Redeemer of the race, who out of love came to earth in order to seek the lost, in order to suffer and to die, and yet sorely troubled as Thou wast, alas, at every step Thou didst take upon earth, every time Thou didst stretch out Thy hand to perform signs and wonders, and every time, without moving a hand, Thou didst suffer defencelessly the opposition of men – again and again Thou wast constrained to repeat: Blessed is he whosoever is not offended in Me. Would that we might see Thee thus, and then that for all this we might not be offended in Thee.[112]

---

[112] S. Kierkegaard, *Training in Christianity* (Princeton: Princeton University Press, 1941), p. 9

6

THE SELF-ORGANIZING POWER OF THE GOSPEL OF CHRIST: EPISCOPACY AND COMMUNITY FORMATION

I

In one of the most potent and celebrated Anglican essays on ecclesiology of the last century, Michael Ramsey set himself the following task: 'to study the Church's order not in institutionalist terms but in terms of the Gospel, and to ask ... whether Episcopacy tells us of some aspect of the Gospel which would lack expression if Episcopacy were to be abandoned'.[1] Though its conclusions are rather different from those which Ramsey reached, this paper addresses itself to the same question: 'what truth about the Gospel of God does the Episcopate, by its place in the one Body, declare?'[2] Its concern is to outline an evangelical theology of episcopacy. The word 'evangelical' is not used here as a term of discrimination (over against, for example, 'catholic'), but in a more primary sense. An evangelical theology is one which is evoked, governed and judged by the gospel. In this sense, evangelical is simply equivalent to 'Christian': all Christian theology, whatever its tradition, is properly speaking evangelical in that it is determined by and responsible to the good news of Jesus Christ. (We might, of course, equally say that all Christian theology is catholic, in that it seeks reflectively to trace the universal scope

---

[1] A. M. Ramsey, *The Gospel and the Catholic Church* (London: Longmans, Green, 1936), p. vi.

[2] Ibid., p. 8.

of the truth of the gospel.) Here, however, my particular concern is to indicate how episcopal ministry can be considered an ordered, institutional implication of the gospel. The argument proceeds, first, by articulating the relation of gospel and church, then, second, by outlining an evangelical account of ministerial order, before finally moving to an evangelical theology of episcopacy. The 'case' is made by dogmatic description, not by historical defence. That is, the argument is not that – in the charmingly deceptive phrase beloved of Anglican apologists – 'from the earliest times' the order of the church has been normatively mono-episcopal and that the structure and content of the office has exhibited a high degree of stability: it hasn't. Rather, the argument here is simply that a ministry of oversight is a necessary implication of the church's confession of the gospel. But before turning to that description, some initial indications of the task of an evangelical theology of episcopacy will be useful.

Any case for episcopal order in the church must be evangelical, simply because it is 'by the heart of the gospel message that any ecclesiology ... can and must be measured'.[3] The task of giving an account of episcopal order therefore falls within the realm of dogmatics. Dogmatics aims at the conceptual clarification of the Christian gospel which is set forth in Holy Scripture and confessed in the life and practices of the church. The task of an evangelical dogmatics of church order is to inquire into the entailments of the gospel for the structure of the church as political society; in the matter of episcopacy, such a dogmatics inquires into whether episcopal order is (minimally) fitting or (maximally) necessary to the life of a community at whose centre lies the gospel of Jesus Christ.

An approach from this direction is required for at least two reasons. First, it is vital to trace the connection between gospel and order if we are not to fall prey to the individualism and anticlericalism which have affected a great deal of modern

---

[3] E. Schillebeeckx, *Church. The Human Story of God* (New York: Crossroad, 1990), p. xiii.

Protestant theology and historiography of ministry. The protests of the magisterial reformers against inflated claims for the mediating power of the church and its orders of ministry have in modernity often been translated into assertions of the primacy of private (or perhaps congregational) judgment, and of the merely secondary character of community order in relation to the fundamental reality of unmediated encounter with God in Christian experience. The polemical use made by some modern Lutheran theological and biblical-historical scholarship of the construct 'early catholicism', which serves as a negative contrast to the normative 'charismatic' Pauline communities, is merely one case in point. Such accounts seek to radicalize the contrast between the gospel (typically construed as an eschatological word of deliverance and justification) and order (construed as the routinization of charisma): Paul versus Ignatius. This kind of contrast cannot be overcome by historical considerations alone, by pointing to the existence of some kind of primitive catholic order in the Jerusalem church, for example, because in the last resort the contrast is parasitic on a normative claim that 'charismatic' Pauline Christianity *is* authentic Christianity. Rather, the contrast can be challenged only by drawing attention to the gospel itself and seeking to indicate that order is ingredient within the gospel's logic.

Second, a dogmatic approach is also required if we are to disentangle discussion of episcopacy from the historical apologetics in which a good deal of (especially Anglican) theology of episcopacy has become entangled. This entanglement has been closely tied to the construal of the church's apostolicity through ideas of 'inheritance' or, worse, 'pedigree'. The difficulty into which apologetics of this kind falls is not simply that of the near-impossibility of the task of furnishing incontrovertible historical warrants. Much more is it that the search for origins is always driven by interests, so that doctrinal judgments masquerade as historical observations. Moreover, the pressure of historical apologetics has frequently skewed the content of theological portrayal of episcopal office, turning it into something amenable to historical demonstration. Thereby, crucial theological considerations – the relation of episcopal office to the ministry of all the baptized and, most of all, to the continuing activity of the risen and ascended Christ through the Spirit – are pushed to the margins. Episcopacy migrates to apologetics and polemics, and, detached from dogmatics, apologetics and polemics rather easily strike up alliances with ideology, furnishing retrospective warrants for the adequacy of existing institutional arrangements, and grounds for denying adequacy to other arrangements which fail to conform (a point which even the most generous of the dominant conventions of Anglican ecumenical theology have been reluctant to register). The corrective, once again, is to develop an evangelical dogmatics of the order of the church – as Ramsey put it, 'our view of the ministry had better be evangelical than archaeological'.[4]

In this connection, it is important to lay some emphasis on the *critical* function of a dogmatic theology of ministry. It is not the task of dogmatics to underwrite the practices of the church but to submit them to judgment. Dogmatics does so, of course, as part of the church, and the criterion by which it makes its judgment is none other than that under which the church as a whole has already been placed by its confession: the gospel announced in Holy Scripture. But because it is in this way evangelical, dogmatics is also inescapably critical. In the case of an evangelical dogmatics of order, this may mean, for example, a quite sharp distinction between episcopacy as a given norm for the church's ministry and any particular contingent ordering of the episcopal office in a given context. But the church's capacity to draw such distinctions and critically to evaluate its practices depends in part upon the existence of the instruments of reflection which dogmatics seeks to furnish. In short: because dogmatics is evangelical, it is critical and reformatory.

---

[4] *The Gospel and the Catholic Church*, p. 69.

II

Discussion of the relation of gospel and church must come before discussion of ministerial order, because (as Paul Avis puts it in a remark about Luther) 'the Church precedes the ministry in the logic of grace'.[5] What, then, is the place of the church in the structure of the gospel? We might put the matter thus: the church is ingredient within the divine economy of salvation, which is the mystery of God made manifest in Jesus Christ and now operative in the power of his Spirit. The revealed secret of God not only concerns the unfathomable majesty of God himself; it also concerns that human society which the triune God elects, sustains and perfects 'to the praise of his glorious grace' (Eph. 1.5). From this there emerge two fundamental principles for an evangelical ecclesiology. First, there can be no doctrine of God without a doctrine of the church, for according to the Christian confession God *is* the one who manifests who he is in the economy of his saving work in which he assembles a people for himself. Second, there can be no doctrine of the church which is not wholly referred to the doctrine of God, in whose being and action alone the church has its being and action.

Accordingly, we need to draw a fundamental distinction between the being and act of God and the being and act of the church. This is done in order to secure the vital consideration that the church is not constituted by human intentions, activities and institutional or structural forms, but by the action of the triune God, realized in Son and Spirit. 'The Church is, because Jesus Christ, the Crucified and Risen One, acts upon her ever anew ... She was not before this action; and she is not for an instant without this action.'[6] This is what is meant by speaking, in company with the Reformers, of the church as 'creature of the Word': the church is that human assembly

---

[5] P. Avis, *The Church in the Theology of the Reformers* (London: Marshall, Morgan & Scott, 1981), p. 111.
[6] E. Schlink, 'Christ and the Church', *The Coming Christ and the Coming Church*, p. 116.

generated and kept in life by the continuing, outgoing self-presentation ('Word') of Jesus Christ. 'As the creature of the divine Word the Church is constituted by divine action. And the way in which the Church is constituted by divine action determines the character and scope of human action in the Church.'[7]

An evangelical ecclesiology will thus have a particular concern to emphasize the asymmetry of divine and human action: God's work and the work of the church are fundamentally distinguished. But they are so distinguished, not in order to bifurcate them (which would undermine the fact that the church is indeed ingredient within the economy of God's saving purpose) but in order to accord priority to the gracious action of God, through which the church's action is ordered to its proper end in conformity with the will of God. The *distinction*, in other words, is for the purpose of *right relation*. They are also distinguished in order to specify with the right kind of theological determinacy the respective characters of divine and human, churchly action. Divine action is sheerly creative, uncaused, spontaneous, saving and effectual; human, churchly action is derivative, contingent and indicative. All churchly action – cultic, moral, diaconal – is thus characterized by 'creative passivity', an orientation towards that perfect work which has been done and continues to be done for the church and to the church.[8] That orientation is, of course, what is meant by faith.

There is doubtless a danger of 'spiritualising' the church with such affirmations. It is clearly important that this emphasis on the priority of divine action over the church as an act of human association should not be allowed to eclipse the 'visibility' of the church. The polemical portrayal of Protestant religion as bare subjectivism without objective social form or endurance is

---

[7] C. Schwöbel, 'The Creature of the Word. Recovering the Ecclesiology of the Reformers', in C. Gunton and D. W. Hardy, eds., *On Being the Church. Essays on the Christian Community* (Edinburgh: T&T Clark, 1989), p. 122.

[8] E. Jüngel, 'Der Gottesdienst als Fest der Freiheit. Der theologische Ort des Gottesdienstes nach Friedrich Schleiermacher', in *Indikative der Gnade–Imperative der Freiheit* (Tübingen: Mohr, 2000), pp. 330–50.

doubtless a caricature, but it nevertheless identifies a potentially disruptive element in the dogmatics we have just outlined.
Can a society which is in its essence 'invisible' ever be really
human – that is, historical, material, bodily? In an evangelical
ecclesiology, the gesture – rhetorical and theological – towards
invisibility must certainly be made, and its absence from an
ecclesiology may be symptomatic of other disorders – a lavishly
over-realized eschatology, an eliding of the distinction between
the gospel and its human representations, an atrophied sense
of the church's fallibility, above all, perhaps, a routinization of
the operations of the Spirit. Properly defined, the concept
of the invisibility of the church is a standing denial of any easy
identification of divine and human work. Talk of the church's
invisibility secures the all-important point that '[o]nly as
creatura verbi divini is the Church an object of faith, because
God's action in establishing and disclosing the true relationship
between the creator and his creation that makes faith possible
can be confessed as the content of faith'.[9] Yet when this
necessary gesture takes over, and is allowed to become the only
constitutive moment for ecclesiology, other problems quickly
emerge, and a picture of the church is promoted in which the
human Christian community is unstable, liminal, and so
incapable of sustaining a coherent historical and social
trajectory.

But the community which is constituted by the gospel is,
indeed, an ordered society. The church is the event of the
reconstitution of human fellowship by the saving acts of God
which the gospel rehearses. The 'spirituality' of the church and
its 'visibility' or 'order' are not quite different entities, the
latter, perhaps, clothing the former but bearing no essential or
intrinsic relation to it. Order does not constitute the church
apart from the vivifying and sanctifying grace of the Spirit; but
the life and holiness which the Spirit bestows are ordered
because human, social and continuous. The danger of
collapsing Spirit into structure ought not to frighten us into the

---

[9] Schwöbel, 'The Creature of the Word', p. 131.

equal danger of a purely punctiliar or actualistic ecclesiology. Church order is the social shape of the converting power and activity of Christ present as Spirit. This is not to claim that the Spirit can be formalized, or reduced to a calculable and manipulable element in what is envisaged as an immanent social process. It is simply to say that 'without institutions, the church cannot become "event". This principle is correct, however, only if it is also reversible; unless the church becomes an event, it cannot be the kind of institution it is supposed to be.'[10]

III

We may sum up the preceding with some words from the Heidelberg Catechism, where, in answer to the question: 'What do you believe concerning "the Holy Catholic Church"?', the reply reads:

> I believe that from the beginning to the end of the world, and from among the whole human race, the Son of God, by his Spirit and his Word, gathers, protects and preserves for himself, in the unity of the true faith, a congregation chosen for eternal life.

From this, we may formulate a dogmatic rule for ecclesiology: an adequate doctrine of the church will maximize Christology and pneumatology (for it is Jesus Christ through Word and Spirit who 'gathers, protects and preserves') and relativize (but not minimize or abolish) ecclesial action and its ordered forms. Our next question is: how does this shape an evangelical theology of ministry?

Jesus Christ is himself the minister of the church. He is himself prophet, priest and king; the ministry of revelation, reconciliation and rule by which the church is brought into being, restored to fellowship with God, and kept under God's governance, is the action of Christ himself, the risen and ascended one who is now present and active, outgoing and communicative.

---

[10] M. Volf, *After Our Likeness. The Church as an Image of the Trinity* (Grand Rapids: Eerdmans, 1998), p. 241.

Taking this point with full seriousness will entail wresting ourselves free from the notion (which very deeply affects much ecclesiology and theology of ministry) that at his ascension Jesus Christ as it were resigns his office in favour of human ministers, and that henceforth the church is the real centre of ministerial agency. Without an operative theology of the present action and speech of Jesus Christ (which means also, without an operative pneumatology) human acts of ministry threaten to assume his role. The danger is present with especial acuteness in those theologies of episcopal ministry which interpret the apostolicity of the church's ministry in terms of succession. Such accounts characteristically restrict the Christological dimension of ministry to a dominical mandate given in the past, and run the risk of converting the pneumatological dimension of ministry into a mystagogical power transmitted through historical sequence. The Christological inadequacy here is, very simply, an inoperative theology of the resurrection and the present activity of the glorified Christ; the pneumatological inadequacy is that of construing the gifts of the Spirit as manipulable possessions rather than as events of relation.

By contrast, an evangelical theology of ministry will be an 'account of the history of Christ's acts'.[11] Because of this, the critical questions concern the relation of Christ's acts to the ministerial activity of the church. Here a number of lines intersect.

First, the ministerial acts of Jesus Christ in the Spirit, by which he gathers, protects and preserves the church, are, properly speaking, incommunicable and non-representable. That is to say, if by 'communication' or 'representation' we mean the assumption of Christ's proper work by agents other than himself, we may not make use of such concepts in a Christologically and pneumatologically structured theology of ministry. The dogmatic premises of an evangelical ecclesiology – that, as the risen and ascended Lord, Jesus Christ is present

---

[11] J. Moltmann, *The Church in the Power of the Spirit* (London: SCM Press, 1977), p. 69.

and active – do not permit any such transference of agency. Christ distributes his own benefits through his Spirit, that is, by his own hand; they are not to be thought of as some treasure turned over to the church for it to dispense. Whatever else we may wish to say about the mediating acts of the church's ministry, the barrier between Christ and the church must not be breached, for it is at this point that the principle of *solus Christus* finds its ecclesiological application.

However, it would be illegitimate to deploy that principle in a way which disqualifies the real (though limited) ministerial activity to which the church is appointed by Christ himself as the vessel of his own ministry. For although the acts of Christ are incommunicable, non-representable, Christ himself freely chooses to represent himself through human ministry. He does so sovereignly, graciously and freely, that is, he does so as Lord; he is not delivered into the hands of his servants, who remain entirely at his disposal. But in his lordly freedom, he elects that alongside his triumphant self-manifestation there should also be human service in the church. In an especially fine and discriminating discussion, Calvin puts the matter thus:

> He alone should rule and reign in the church as well as have authority or pre-eminence in it, and this authority should be exercised and administered by his Word alone. Nevertheless, because he does not dwell among us in visible presence [Matt. 26.11], we have said that he uses the ministry of men to declare openly his will to us by mouth, as a sort of delegated work, not by transferring to them his right and honour, but only that through their mouths he may do his own work – just as a workman uses a tool to do his work ... 'Christ ascended on high,' Paul says, 'that he might fill all things' [Eph. 4.10]. This is the manner of fulfilment: through the ministers to whom he has entrusted this office and has conferred the grace to carry it out, he dispenses and distributes his gifts to the church; and he shows himself as though present by manifesting the power of his Spirit in this his institution, that it be not vain or idle.[12]

---

[12] Calvin, *Institutes of the Christian Religion*, IV.3.1, 2 (pp. 1053, 1055).

How, then, is this subordination of the church's ministry to be expressed? A modern Reformed theologian, T. F. Torrance, emphasizes that the church's ministerial acts are to be understood as *hypodeigma* (pattern or, perhaps, token), but not as *mimesis* (imitation) of Christ's own perfect work. What is secured by this or similar distinctions is the *indirectness* of the relation between Christ's ministry and that of the church. Indirectness is not a denial of the real participation of the church in Christ, for 'through the Spirit there is a direct relation of participation, but in the form of order the relation is indirect. The priesthood of the Church is not a transcription in the conditions of this passing age of the heavenly Priesthood of Christ'.[13] The real instrumentality of the church is thus neither self-generated nor self-sustaining; both its origin and its telos lie wholly beyond itself. And so the ministerial action of the church is not in any fundamental sense 'causative': it is simply appointed and empowered to present that whose accomplishment lies entirely outside the church's sphere of competence and responsibility.

Two things follow from this. First, ministerial activity shares in the asymmetrical character of the relation of Christ and the church. If an evangelical dogmatics of the church refuses to see the Christian community as co-constituted by Christ and the community as equal partners, an evangelical dogmatics of ministry similarly refuses to see the church's ministry as a co-ordination or co-operation between divine and human agents. Whatever else we mean by 'fellow-workers of God', that we cannot mean.

Second, and more importantly, however, positing a limit to the action of the church's ministry by reference to the principle of 'Christ alone' determines the task or content of the church's ministry. Ministry in the church 'points beyond itself' to the action of another.[14] Jesus Christ is not inert, but present with

---

[13] T. F. Torrance, *Royal Priesthood. A Theology of Ordained Ministry*, revised edn. (Edinburgh: T&T Clark, 1993), p. 97.

[14] Ibid.

force, active as prophet, priest and king. The task of ministry is thus not to complete that which he has done, or to accomplish that which Christ himself does not now do, but rather to indicate or attest his work both past and present. That to which the ministerial action of the church is ordered is the 'showing' of Jesus Christ's self-proclamation in word, baptism and the Lord's supper. As such, ministry is 'a *responsive* movement to the dynamic force of the Word of God'.[15] The ecclesiological principle here is that the community is defined by confession – that is, by dispositions and activities which give expression to the fact that the centre of the church is not within but without itself, constituted as it is by the free event of Christ's self-bestowal in the Holy Spirit. The ministerial principle is that, because the basic event of the life of the church is the event of Jesus Christ's self-communication, the task of ministry 'is simply to serve this happening'.[16] Ministry is thus *ostensive*, a work of testifying. Ministries in the church

> exist not as visible signs or representations of the ministry of Jesus Christ, but as *ministeria verbi divini* [ministries of the divine word], that is to say, as *offices of service* of the actions in which and through which the ministry of Jesus Christ is accomplished.[17]

IV

We now reach (at an appropriately late stage) the question of episcopal ministry. The church is a political society; that is to say, it is a sphere of human fellowship, though one created not by natural affinity or association but by the gathering power of the gospel. And the church is commissioned to the task of bearing witness to the gospel – of indicating in proclamation, sacrament and service that 'Jesus Christ . . . is the one Word of God which we have to hear, and which we have to trust and

[15] O. O'Donovan, *On the Thirty-Nine Articles* (Exeter: Paternoster, 1986), p. 120.
[16] Barth, *Church Dogmatics* IV/3, p. 833.
[17] I. U. Dalferth, 'Ministry and the Office of Bishop according to Meissen and Porvoo', *Visible Unity and the Ministry of Oversight* (London: Church House Publishing, 1997), p. 42.

obey in life and in death'. The ministry of the church is thus *ordered*. Because the church is a visible and enduring arena of common life and action, authorized to indicate the gospel, 'official' patterns of ministry are required. 'Office' does not usurp the work of Christ or the Spirit, or the work of the whole church in witnessing to that work. Rather, it has the task of overseeing the unity and authenticity of the testimony of the church, and so of being caught up into Christ's own formation of his community.

In this sense, *episcopé*, oversight, is the basic ministry of the church. Anterior to the functional differentiation of office (whether in the so-called threefold office or in some other pattern) is the primary task of office to envisage, safeguard and unify the church's fulfilment of its gospel mandate. This ministry 'is, under God, what draws together the community of faith and equips it to continue the mission and ministry of Christ in the world', and it is therefore a ministry which 'keeps alive the question of the community's integrity, by challenging its practice in the name of the gospel'.[18] What orthodoxy is in the realm of reflection, *episcopé* is in the realm of practice and order: an instrument through which the church is recalled to Christianness, to the appropriateness of its action and speech to the truth of the gospel. Episcopal ministry 'is that ministry whose special province is both to gather the believing community around the centre which it proclaims, the preaching of the resurrection, and *in* that gathering, to make sure that this community is critically aware of itself'.[19] The gospel requires this simply because Jesus Christ elects to manifest himself to the world not without a visible human, historical society with a specific calling. And so the task of an ordered ministry of oversight is, very simply, 'to minister to the Church's very identity'.[20] The issue is therefore not whether we can do without *episcopé*, but whether oversight can be exercised

[18] R. Williams, 'Women and the Ministry', in M. Furlong, ed., *Feminine in the Church* (London: SPCK, 1984), pp. 13f.
[19] Ibid., p. 15.
[20] Ibid.

in a way which is sufficiently 'loose' that 'all encroachment on the lordship of the One who is alone the Lord is either avoided or so suppressed and eliminated in practice that there is place for His rule'.[21] What shape of episcopal ministry will best serve this 'giving place' to the rule of Christ in the visible community of the gospel?

First, the dogmatic, Christological groundwork. There is properly one 'overseer' of the church, Jesus Christ, 'the bishop of our souls' (1 Pet. 2.25). To start from this point is immediately to make episcopacy contingent, relative to the headship of Christ. This, indeed, is part of the force of Calvin's rejection of primatial understandings of episcopacy: the church has no human head; Christ does not transfer his headship to another, and so there can be no single human primate. The church

> has Christ as its sole Head, under whose sway all of us cleave to one another ... Christ is the head, 'from whom the whole body, joined and knit through every bond of mutual ministry (insofar as each member functions) achieves its growth' [Eph. 4.15f.]. Do you see how he includes all mortals without exception in the body, but leaves the honour and name of the head to Christ alone?[22]

Or, as he puts in a comment on Cyprian, 'he makes the universal bishopric Christ's alone'.[23] This extension of the doctrine of 'Christ alone' is a significant counter to those rich theologies of episcopacy which expound the office of bishop as the sign or epiphany of Christ in the church. Rowan Williams, for example, in a suggestive essay, argues that the church as a whole is a 'showing' of that which lies at its heart: '"Showing" is an effective, catalytic and transforming event, which draws new boundaries ... And to belong to the Christian community is to accept the paschal symbol as decisive.'[24] As eucharistic

[21] Barth, *Church Dogmatics* IV/1, p. 723.
[22] *Institutes*, IV.6.9.
[23] *Institutes*, IV.6.17.
[24] R. Williams, 'Authority and the Bishop in the Church', in M. Santer, ed., *Their Lord and Ours* (London: SPCK, 1982), p. 95.

president, the bishop is 'the focal point around which the community gathers, overcoming its divisions, to affirm a single identity governed by the paschal symbol in its eucharistic shape'.[25] Such an account owes much to a strand of modern Orthodox theology, as well as to Ramsey's work.[26] If it fails to persuade, that is because it risks softening the distinction between Christ's self-presentation and the testifying acts of ordered ministry. Certainly Williams is insistent that 'no particular act of showing is of the same creative order as the paschal event itself, so that no act of showing has meaning independently of the generative event and the life of the community as a whole'.[27] But even the refusal of the bishop as mystagogue does not secure the incommunicability, the non-transferable status, of Christ's headship which is primary for an evangelical account of ministerial order. In short: the bishop is not an 'effectual sign', for

> to make the bishop an 'effectual sign' of the unity and continuity of the Church and thus to give him independent significance in the role of a mediator ... is to make the episcopate usurp the office of the One Mediator and to give it precedence over the Church which is His Body.[28]

Placed in this way by reference to Christ as the church's prophet, priest and king, episcopal order 'oversees' the Christian community. It is that official, ordered place within the life of the church as a whole where its oneness and genuineness are most directly addressed. But this only takes place in so far as episcopal office is indicatory or ostensive, and not epiphanic. Episcopal office may serve unity and the continuation of apostolic authenticity, but it cannot secure those goods by its own existence. If it were able to do so as *alter Christus*, then

[25] Ibid., p. 96.
[26] See J. Zizioulas, 'The Eucharistic Community and the Catholicity of the Church', *One in Christ* 7 (1971); J. Zizioulas, 'The Bishop in the Theological Doctrine of the Orthodox Church', *Kanon* 7 (1985), pp. 23–35; and Williams, 'Theology and the Churches'.
[27] Williams, 'Authority and the Bishop in the Church', p. 97.
[28] Torrance, *Royal Priesthood*, p. 108.

Christ would be pushed into inactive transcendence, and Spirit would be reduced to simply the immanent animating power of an institution.

This means, consequently, that the unity of the church is not generated or kept by the episcopate. Unity is pure gift; it is brought about by Christ himself, for '[t]he unity of the Church is not primarily the unity of her members, but the unity of Christ who acts upon them all, in all places and at all times'.[29] And so we must say that

> [t]he ministry of the church can neither create nor represent this unity, but only make visible through it that it points unmistakeably away from itself and toward that which it serves – the present action of Christ in the proclamation of the Gospel through word and sacrament.[30]

Unity is evangelical; it is to that unity, established and formed by the gospel, that the ministry of oversight directs its own attention and the attention of the whole church. The office of bishop is not constitutive of the unity of the church; if it were, then the church would indeed by 'episcopocentric',[31] and the sole headship of the one Lord Jesus Christ to some degree compromised. Nor does the office of bishop symbolize the unity of the church, at least if by 'symbolize' we mean 'realize' or 'actualize'. Nor does the office of bishop represent the unity of the church. Rather, the office of bishop *indicates* the unity of the church, testifying in a public manner to the oneness of the people of God as it is set out in the gospel. Episcopal office is thus a focussed, public and institutional place through which attention can be turned to the given unity of the people of God through Spirit, baptism and confession. As such, episcopal office serves the unity of the church as it takes form in the congregation of the redeemed as one body with one Spirit, one hope, one Lord, one faith, one baptism, one God and Father of all (Eph. 4.4–6).

---

[29] Schlink, 'Christ and the Church', p. 105.

[30] Dalferth, 'Ministry and the Office of Bishop', p. 37.

[31] Cf. Zizioulas, 'The Bishop in the Theological Doctrine of the Orthodox Church'.

Episcopal office undertakes this in a variety of ways, but most centrally through teaching, through presiding at the sacraments and at the commissioning of ordered ministry, and through the exercise of discipline. The point can be illustrated by reference to the bishop as teacher. The teaching task of the bishop consists in the proclamation and safeguarding of the truth of the gospel. Accordingly, this involves – positively – the celebration of the sheerly authoritative goodness of the good news which the church is appointed to declare. It also involves – negatively – the defence of the gospel, particularly its defence from arbitrary, selective or partial exposition. But as teacher, the bishop is not to be considered as in possession of something other than the truth of the gospel which is set before the whole congregation; it is the task of the office simply to encourage and defend by functioning as an exemplary instance of submission to the gospel's claim. Ignatius's *Letter to the Ephesians* is not reluctant to take episcopal office pretty seriously ('we should look upon the bishop as we would look upon the Lord himself', *ad Eph* 6); yet behind this is an important movement of deference. 'I do not issue orders to you as if I were a great person', he says (*ad Eph* 3): at the core of episcopal ministry is a renunciation, a following of the declared will of God which is the true content of Christian teaching:

> I have ... taken upon me first to exhort you that you would all run together in accordance with the will of God. For even Christ, our inseparable life, is the manifested will of the Father, as also bishops ... are so by the will of Jesus Christ. (3)

The bishop's authorization as teacher, in other words, is inseparable from submission to Jesus Christ, 'the manifested will' of God. If, then, it is the task of the bishop to 'form' the community, it is only by virtue of the fact that both bishop and community have already been formed by the divine self-manifestation of God in Christ and Spirit. As overseer, the bishop is one whose task it is to promote 'unanimous obedience' to the one faith' (*ad Eph.* 2).

In this way, the special task of the ministry of oversight with respect to the unity of the church is closely related to the church's apostolicity. Apostolicity has less to do with transmission and much more to do with identity or authenticity, with the 'Christianness' of the church's teaching and mission. Such authenticity cannot by its very nature be 'transmitted', because it is not capable of being embodied without residue in ordered forms. Forms cannot guarantee authenticity, simply because forms are themselves not immune to the critical question of their own authenticity. If this is so, then episcopal office is not some sort of condensation of apostolicity, or some means of securing the apostolic character of the whole church. Rather, episcopal office oversees the life of the apostolic community as a whole, presiding over the event in which the church becomes apostolic by consenting to the apostolic gospel of the resurrection and giving itself to the apostolic mission of proclamation and service. In particular, because apostolicity is so closely tied to mission, it is properly not merely an internal but an external orientation in the church's life. 'As an apostolic Church the Church can never in any respect be an end in itself, but, following the existence of the apostles, it exists only as it exercises the ministry of a herald.'[32] If the ministry of oversight is apostolic, it can therefore only be because it acts in relation to this mission. Episcopal order without mission is simply not the order of the church – that is, the order of the community which is simultaneously gathered around and impelled outwards by the uncontrollable compulsion of the Spirit of Christ – but mere form.

My suggestion is, then, that the office of oversight is best understood as a function of the unity and apostolic character which the church has by virtue of its election, gathering and sanctification, and its empowerment to know and speak the gospel. Episcopacy does not secure the life of the church, but is an office of deference to the life-giving power of Christ. Episcopal office forms the church insofar as episcopacy itself is formed by the one bishop of the church; and episcopal office

---

[32] Barth, *Church Dogmatics* IV/1, p. 724.

forms the church insofar as it testifies to the shaping power of the same Jesus Christ.

How is episcopal office, so conceived, to be ordered? Two basic principles are to be held together. First, there is a necessary distinction to be drawn between *episcopé*, a ministry of oversight, and particular, contingent orderings of the episcopal office. I have suggested that oversight is a necessary implication of the gospel through which the church is brought into being and which it is commissioned to proclaim. But this is quite other than a defence of – for example – a threefold order of ministry headed by a regional episcopate, or of a 'historic episcopate', whether maintained by laying on of hands or by succession of teaching office; nor, alternatively, does it necessarily entail a synodical or congregational episcopate. Such orderings are *adiaphora*. To claim this is not to claim, of course, that the way in which oversight is ordered is purely arbitrary or driven by the exigencies (and limitations) of context. If part of the function of *episcopé* is to indicate the church's unity and apostolicity, and therefore its catholicity, office cannot be simply reinvented at will. Rather, freedom is given to the church to order its life *appropriately*, that is the light of its evangelical calling and mandate. But such freedom is not the freedom to invent, but freedom responsibly to structure the life of the church in view of the fact that

> Christian believers *find themselves ordered* in a certain form of society precisely by the message which they believe and are charged to proclaim. And the decisive character of their order ... is that it maintains the teaching of the truth of the gospel.[33]

Hence the second principle: the particular shape assumed by the episcopal office must be *fitting* to the church's identity, for it is the structural expression of what it means to be the church living out of and testifying to the converting energy of the gospel.

---

[33] O'Donovan, *On the Thirty Nine Articles*, p. 118.

V

In sum: my suggestion is that – in the words of P. T. Forsyth – episcopal order is indicative of the 'self-organizing' power of the gospel.[34] A dogmatic case for episcopal ministry such as that offered here does not leave the exercise of that office undisturbed: evangelical dogmatics, we must recall, is an aspect of the church's self-interrogation. A dogmatics of episcopacy, because it sets the office and its exercise in the light of the Christological, pneumatological and ecclesiological principles of the gospel, is quite far from those serene Anglican accounts of the history and practice of episcopal ministry in which the emergence of the monarchical episcopate is shown to be an entirely natural and unproblematic development from the earliest Christian impulse. The naivety of such accounts is not merely their reliance on the apologetic power of historical reconstructions, but their incapacity to envisage the history of episcopacy as political and ideological.[35] The church makes a move against the threats of ideology, in this sphere as in any other, by simply being the church – attentive to word and sacrament, docile before the gospel, above all, prayerful for the coming of Christ and his Spirit. But theology, too, may have its part to play. Kierkegaard once famously remarked that 'there is nothing so displeasing to God as official Christianity'.[36] If, on balance, he was more right than wrong, one way of heeding his lament would be to make sure that the case for episcopal office be made with the right kind of dogmatic precision and robustness.

[34] P. T. Forsyth, *Lectures on the Church and the Sacraments* (London: Longmans, Green, 1917), p. 42.

[35] Cf. R. H. Roberts, 'Lord, Bondsman and Churchman. Identity, Integrity and Power in Anglicanism', in Gunton and Hardy, eds., *On Being the Church*, pp. 156–224.

[36] S. Kierkegaard, *Attack upon Christendom* (Princeton: Princeton University Press, 1944), p. 210.

7

CHRIST, CHURCH AND
RECONCILIATION

I

What follows is a half-way between a theological essay and a homily; but we should not be particularly troubled by its homiletic tone. The clear distinctions which some members of the academic theological guild draw between proclamation and critical reflection are part of the pathology of modern theology: our forbears would have been distressed by the way in which theology has succumbed to the standardization of discourse in the academy and the consequent exclusion of certain modes of Christian speech, and we should probably worry more about what Bernard or Calvin might think of us than about the way in which *wissenschaftlich* colleagues may shake their heads. Part of what is involved in talking Christianly about reconciliation (as about any other topic) is coming to see that forms of thought and speech, genres of discourse, can themselves alienate us from the matter which must be spoken: thinking and speaking themselves need to be reconciled to God by God. As Stephen Williams has put it in his perceptive analysis of the resistance to the gospel of reconciliation in modernity:

> Those convinced of the fact of divine reconciliation should thereby be convinced that intellectual conviction is not attained in a sort of spiritual vacuum. One must have bared one's soul, even reckoned onself as some kind of sinner ... [T]alk of such realities as sin and forgiveness may fail to commend itself to us because it cannot discover in us a disposition to receive it.[1]

---

[1] Williams, *Revelation and Reconciliation*, pp. 146f.

The main purpose of these remarks is, on the basis of some theological comments on 2 Corinthians 5.18, to ponder what is involved in the church's ministry of reconciliation, most of all in its ethical aspects. It has become something of a commonplace in some now dominant styles of modern theology and theological ethics (especially but not exclusively Anglo-American) to emphasize the coinherence of the divine work of reconciliation and the church's moral action, in such a way that the work of the ecclesial community can properly be considered an extension (fleshing out, realization, embodiment) of the gospel of God's reconciling act.[2] These various attempts to artic-ulate the concrescence of soteriology, ecclesiology and moral theology are by no means necessarily lacking on a theology of divine prevenience, for they are often quite explicitly directed against the individualistic moral heroics of modernity, and often root ecclesiology in considerations of the trinitarian relations in which the church graciously participates through the work of the Holy Spirit. Nevertheless, they are characteristically less drawn to expansive depiction of the sheer gratuity of God's act of reconciliation, and more commonly offer lengthy accounts of the acts of the church, sacramental and moral, often through the idiom of virtues, habits and practices. The success or otherwise of such proposals, I suggest, will depend in large measure upon the care with which they are able to accomplish two tasks. First, they must draw the right kinds of distinctions between the reconciling work of God and those acts of the

---

[2] Some (varied) examples: T. Gorringe, *God's Just Vengeance. Crime, Violence and the Rhetoric of Salvation* (Cambridge: Cambridge University Press, 1996), esp. pp. 248–71; M. Grey, *Redeeming the Dream. Feminism, Redemption and Christian Tradition* (London: SPCK, 1989); idem, *From Barriers to Community. The Challenge of the Gospel for a Divided Society* (London: HarperCollins, 1991); G. Jones, *Embodying Forgiveness. A Theological Analysis* (Grand Rapids: Eerdmans, 1995); M. Volf, *Exclusion and Embrace. A Theological Exploration of Identity, Otherness, and Reconciliation* (Nashville: Abingdon Press, 1996); R. Williams, *Resurrection. Interpreting the Easter Gospel* (London: Darton, Longman & Todd, 1982); idem, *The Truce of God* (London: Fount, 1983); idem, 'Resurrection and Peace. More On New Testament Ethics', *On Christian Theology*, pp. 265–75; W. Wink, *When the Powers Fall. Reconciliation in the Healing of Nations* (Minneapolis: Fortress Press, 1998).

church in which that reconciliation is present; and, second, they must achieve a properly theological specificity in their depiction of the acts which are considered to be the expression or consequence of the reconciling work of God. The questions to be asked, roughly phrased, are these: what is the content of the church's ministry of reconciliation, and how is it to be related to and distinguished from the reconciling act of God in Christ?

There is a danger that dogmatic moral theology may be excessively preoccupied with the question of who does what – with identifying the precise demarcations between human and divine action (many contemporary readers of Barth whose theological instincts are shaped by the ethics of ecclesial practice are understandably nervous on precisely this score). The danger of such preoccupation is not only that of forcing distinctions where there are properly none, or of making distinctions appear to be polarizations. It is more that we may fall victim to moral agonistics: in making such distinctions, we may remain trapped within a set of oppositions which derive not from the gospel but from modernity's acute sense that in order to talk of moral dignity we have to talk of human autonomy, and in order to talk of human autonomy we have to counter the thought of divine heteronomy. The range of Barth's thinking is such that (in my judgment) he only rarely failed to escape the problem of competitive accounts of divine and human action. But he also sounded the alarm about the danger of grounding human moral action in the wrong way and of subverting a proper understanding of the sovereignty of God. And he also, especially in the last two decades of his life, protested (sometimes in rather jaundiced tones) against the over-inflation of ecclesiology and ethics into quasi-independent theological themes. His protests went largely unheeded, and are still routinely passed over, especially by enthusiasts for *koinonia* ecclesiologies who judge him to be a tetchy Zwinglian who could not cope with the thought of any enduring divine action through creaturely media.[3] Part of what I want to open

---

[3]   One of the most recent (and very sophisticated) version of this critique is that by R. Hütter, *Evangelische Ethik als kirchliches Zeugnis. Interpretationen zu Schlüsselfragen*

up is the question of whether the recent luxuriant growth of
ecclesial ethics has not made it hard for us to see the force of
Barth's protest. And this, in turn, may lead us to ask whether
ecclesiology is, in fact, not such a self-evidently basic doctrine as
it has become in some modern Protestant dogmatics, and take
up a comment of Edward Schillebeeckx – who, after all, comes
from a tradition with a rather long track record in producing
industrial-strength ecclesiologies – suggesting that what we
need is not so much an ecclesial ethics of reconciliation but 'a
bit of *negative theology*, church theology in a minor key'.[4]

II

> All this is from God, who through Christ reconciled us to himself
> and gave us the ministry of reconciliation; that is, in Christ God was
> reconciling the world to himself, not counting their trespasses
> against them, and entrusting to us the message of reconciliation. (2
> Cor. 5.18f.)

First, what is 'all this' that is from God? Clearly it is the great
divine work of salvation, summed up in verse 17 as the establishment of a 'new creation', a work of God of such generative
force that its accomplishment spells the end of one mode of
existence (which thereby becomes 'the old') and brings into
being 'the new'. And all this is from God, ἐκ τοῦ θεοῦ. This
'from God', of course, is not to be thought of as if it were some
statement of distant origin; it does not merely furnish the
ultimate backcloth against which other more immediate or
available or manageable realities may stand out in relief. It is
utterly proximate; 'from God' is directly and presently constitutive of the reality of 'the new' which has come. To put it
slightly differently, the little phrase 'from God' has real work to

---

theologischer Ethik in der Gegenwart (Neukirchen-Vluyn: Neukirchener Verlag,
1993). For a milder account, see J. Mangina, 'The Stranger as Sacrament. Karl
Barth and the Ethics of Ecclesial Practice', *International Journal of Systematic
Theology* 1 (1999), pp. 322–39.
[4] Schillebeeckx, *Church*, p. xix.

do here, since it is an operative assertion, not merely a remote statement of something at the far end of our description of the present life of the new creation. Indeed, the entire presentation of apostolic ministry and activity in 2 Corinthians, most of all in chapter 4, is predicated on this directly and constitutively present and effective reality of ἐκ τοῦ θεοῦ: 'the transcendent power belongs to God and not to us' (4.7). 'Not to us': because apostolic existence is a matter of the manifestation, the ostensive indication, of 'the life of Jesus' (4.10). Jesus' life, as the embodied actuality of God's transcendent power, cannot be transferred to the apostle in any straightforward way without compromise to its gracious, eschatological character; in one (only one) very real sense the life of the risen one is incommunicable. 'To God': because at the heart of apostolic existence is new creation, which is by its very nature *ex nihilo* and therefore on the other side of creaturely competence or capacity. 'All this', therefore, 'is from God'.

What are the consequences here for the way in which we approach a theological ethics of reconciliation? Two remarks are in order, one material or dogmatic, and one more formal in character.

The material remark is that an operative notion of ἐκ τοῦ θεοῦ will require us to invest a great deal of theological energy in the depiction of the person and work of the reconciling God. Most of all, what will be required will be a rich description of divine aseity as it is manifest in the work of redemption. The chief task, of course, will be a trinitarian theology, above all, one which is able to talk of the purposiveness of the life and activity of Father, Son and Spirit without thereby collapsing the life of God into the economy of salvation. This is not to set 'immanent' and 'economic' against one another; but it is to claim that there is a proper order in which immanent has soteriological priority over economic, because the economy of salvation is the sphere of the *free* mercy of God. And it is also to lodge a protest against the kinds of elision of the distinction between the triune life of God and the moral community of God's creatures which can result from making *koinonia* a common term between the Trinity and the church. Finally, it is also to suggest that one test of the adequacy of an ethics of reconciliation will be the seriousness (and the joy) with which it pauses over this descriptive task, and the vigilance which it demonstrates to the possibility of an ecclesial ethics which has ceased to make its appeal all along the line to Trinity, election and grace.

The second, more formal remark, is that ἐκ τοῦ θεοῦ is to be the dominating feature of a Christian ethical geography, of a theological depiction of the space for the church's endeavour which is established by the action of the triune God, and which it is the chief task of Christian moral theology to map. Human moral action is subordinate to divine saving action; the church is subordinate to the Holy Trinity; and therefore the sociology of morals is strictly subservient to moral ontology. To see the point at work, we may pause to consider a couple of examples.

First, in Professor Timothy Gorringe's book *God's Just Vengeance* an approach is made to the ethics of reconciliation (Gorringe has in mind especially the reconciliation of criminal offenders) in which the church is envisaged as an 'imagined community', that is, as a group held together by a commonly held image of social communion which may provide resources through which different modes of social relation can be envisaged and practised.[5] 'The Christian Church', he writes, 'was from the beginning ... an "imagined community" ... whose purpose was to provide a messianic "home", or rooting, to human beings;'[6] 'the community called "church" contributes to that struggle and negotiation for forms of social life properly called human by faithfulness to and proclamation of [its] tradition, and ... by the creation of such communities'.[7] To the obvious question which this provokes – 'Do we need to talk about the church at all?',[8] since many strategies of reconciliation are secular – Gorringe replies:

[5] Gorringe, *God's Just Vengeance*, p. 263. The notion is adopted from B. Anderson, *Imagined Communities* (London: Verso, 1991).
[6] Gorringe, *God's Just Vengeance*, p. 263.
[7] Ibid., p. 264.
[8] Ibid.

the community of reconciliation (not the church, but the church sacramentally) is the means through which atonement is effected, which is the reason, presumably, Christ bequeathed to us not a set of doctrines or truths, but a community founded on betrayal and the survival of betrayal.[9]

What this opposition of 'truths' and 'community' signals is simply the absence of a metaphysics of morals, a theological ontology of the church's acts of reconciling. In the absence of such a dogmatic underpinning to morals, what rushes in to fill the gap is a strong sense of churchly causality: it is the church which is (sacramentally) 'the means through which atonement is effected'. The moral force of the Christological ἐφάπαξ is simply lost.

A second example, initially at least much more companionable with what I am proposing here, is Miroslav Volf's theological-ethical study *Exclusion and Embrace*, whose central proposal is that 'God's reception of hostile humanity into divine communion is a model for how human beings should relate to the other'.[10] Volf is entirely correct to urge the priority of reconciliation over liberation, and to suggest that, because of its orientation to freedom, the theology and ethics of liberation may often betray a 'tendency to ideologize relations of social agents and perpetuate their antagonisms'.[11] Hence the book's proposal that the primary need is for a 'theology of embrace'.[12] Yet there is a disabling slenderness to the Christology and soteriology which undergird this theology; whilst the book does not lack a theology of grace, it rarely succeeds in portraying grace with much vividness, and often does so as a concession rather than as a major preoccupation. Problems emerge initially with Volf's insistence that 'final reconciliation' is prospective, and that, therefore, a 'grand narrative' of reconciliation is not available to us: the right question, he

---

[9] Ibid., p. 268.
[10] Volf, *Exclusion and Embrace*, p. 100.
[11] Ibid., p. 105.
[12] Ibid.

argues, 'is not how to achieve the final reconciliation, but *what resources are needed to live in peace in the absence of final reconciliation*'.[13] This is well taken, if it simply means that we are to 'renounce all attempts at the final reconciliation: otherwise, we will end up perpetrating oppression'.[14] But there is a real loss here: the loss of a vigorously operative sense that human, churchly reconciling action is not only prospective but also, crucially, *retrospective*, looking *back* to a final reconciliation which – τετέλεσται – has already taken place. 'Both the modern project of emancipation and its postmodern critique suggest that a *nonfinal reconciliation in the midst of the struggle against oppression* is what a responsible theology must be designed to facilitate.'[15] But eschatological relativization of human action now must not be allowed to undermine the achieved sufficiency of the reconciling work of God; if it does, then human action once again threatens to become omnicompetent or omniresponsible.

Anxieties are not eased by the underlying account of the relation of God's action to that of creatures. Volf commends a life of 'self-giving modelled on the life of the triune God',[16] and urges engagement in 'the struggle for *a nonfinal reconciliation based on a vision of reconciliation that cannot be undone*'.[17] With 'model' and 'vision' we are in the sphere of *imitatio*: a useable concept, certainly, but only if it is grounded in a transcendental Christology. Yet it is just this sort of Christology which seems not to be at work, as Volf's account of repentance shows. The account is almost entirely immanentist and instrumentalist,[18] reduced to the task of removing psycho-social barriers to

---

[13] Ibid., p. 109.

[14] Ibid.

[15] Ibid. Responsible to whom? And can a truly responsible theology be 'designed'? Only if its task is reduced to that of 'facilitating' action (which is why, of course, Marx – correctly – perceived much theology to be ideology).

[16] Ibid., p. 101.

[17] Ibid., p. 110.

[18] 'Almost', because he does concede (p. 119) that '[f]or good reasons, Christian tradition thinks of genuine repentance not as a human possibility but as a gift of God'.

reconciled community. 'To repent means to resist the seduc-
tiveness of the sinful values and practices and to let the new
order of God's reign be established in one's heart.'[19] Is not this
too voluntarist, lacking in the backward reference of repentance? Is not repentance an act in face of an achieved act of
divine mercy which has already abolished the condition of
hostility and guilt and rendered its continuance absurd? Or
again, repentance is a matter of 'creation of the kinds of social
agents that are shaped by the values of God's kingdom and
therefore capable of participating in the project of authentic
social transformation'.[20] But how can repentance 'create'? And
what is 'capacity' in these matters? And does not such a
statement run the risk of reducing repentance to a useful
instrument in a process of social engineering? Volf's appeal to
the notion of the Christian as 'catholic personality' ('personal
microcosm of the eschatological new creation') brings the same
problems to the surface as it runs together Trinity, soteriology
and eucharist in an alarmingly Hegelian manner.

> In the Eucharist ... we celebrate the giving of the self to the other
> and the receiving of the other into the self that the triune God has
> undertaken in the passion of Christ, and that we are called and
> empowered to live such giving and receiving out in a conflict-
> ridden world[21]

This is a generalized and moralized account of the eucharist
which says little of Jesus and his death. 'Much of the meaning
of the death and resurrection of Christ is summed up in the
injunction, "Let us embrace each other"'.[22] It is, accordingly,
entirely characteristic that 'the drama of embrace'[23] is not a
Christological drama; it is a phenomenology of human
activities of embracing diversity and reconciling differences,
illustrated at the end by the parable of the prodigal, but left
Christologically unspecific.

[19] Ibid., p. 116.
[20] Ibid., p. 118.
[21] Ibid., p. 130.
[22] Ibid.
[23] See ibid., pp. 140–7.

Attempts at an ethics of reconciliation of this kind, with their basic conceptual equipment of community, education, embracing, vision and so forth,[24] are at best accounts of the moral application of the benefits of Christ in the social sphere; but without a robust theology of the *opus Christi*, they can scarcely resist the drift into immanence.

Over against this stands Paul's ἐκ τοῦ θεοῦ, the determinative divine action which generates the community of reconciliation. In verse 19, this determinative divine action is expanded in two ways: as incarnation ('in Christ God was reconciling the world to himself') and as justification ('not counting their trespasses against them') – the latter act being what Calvin finely calls the 'foundation and cause' of reconciliation.[25] Christian moral theology is required to give a vivid and sustained depiction of these realities: of the atoning work of the incarnate Son as the condition of possibility for human action. 'Whereas God had been before far distant from us,' Calvin remarks, 'He has drawn near to us in Christ, and so Christ has been made to us the true Emmanuel and His advent is the drawing near of God to men.'[26] More than anything else, a Christian depiction of the field in which human acts of reconciliation take place will want to insist on the wholly unique and perfect action of God in Christ. This act, as Barth puts it in a comment on 2 Corinthians 5.19, 'was a definitive and self-contained event'.[27] It is not just an incitement to human moral activity, still less a kind of cipher for what is properly a mode of human engagement; it is that without which reconciliation is groundless, lacking in any purchase on reality. Because this act was done by this one, there and then, acts of reconciliation are more than an attempt to

---

[24] Or 'facing' the other, as in David Ford's *Self and Salvation*, a book which in the end does not escape from moralizing the gospel.

[25] J. Calvin, *The Second Epistle of St Paul to the Corinthians and the Epistles to Timothy, Titus and Philemon* (Edinburgh: Oliver & Boyd, 1964), p. 79.

[26] Ibid., p. 78. It is one of the strengths of Pannenberg's treatment of reconciliation in volume II of his *Systematic Theology* (Grand Rapids: Eerdmans, 1994), pp. 397–464, that he insists on the priority of Christology over soteriology.

[27] Barth, *Church Dogmatics* IV/1, p. 76.

create reality by establishing imagined communities which offer a different sort of social space from that of the world's routine violence. Human acts of reconciliation are in accordance with the structure of reality which God in Christ creates and to the existence of which the gospel testifies; and therefore they are acts which tend towards the true end of creation which God's reconciling act establishes once and for all in Christ's person and work.[28] In sum: because of the ἐκ τοῦ θεοῦ, expounded here as incarnation and sin-bearing, there is an unbridgeable gulf between the reconciling activity of God and the church's ethical endeavour: his action forgives sin, the church's does not.[29] The church's acts of reconciling are no more than the repetition of the judgment of God which is established at the cross and resurrection from which the new creation comes: he reconciled us to himself.[30]

III

What, then, of the church's ministry of reconciliation? It is that which God *gave*. That is to say, it is a matter of election or appointment. It does not spring into being as an activity of a busy imagined community with a lively sense of the need for alternatives to oppression and marginalization. 'Reconciliation'

---

[28] For a magisterial depiction of this theme, see T. F. Torrance, 'Ecumenism. A Reappraisal of Its Significance, Past, Present and Future', *Theology in Reconciliation*, pp. 25–81.

[29] On this, see the brilliantly suggestive essay by G. Outka, 'Following at a Distance. Ethics and the Identity of Jesus', in G. Green, ed., *Scriptural Authority and Narrative Interpretation* (Philadelphia: Fortress Press, 1987), pp. 144–60, which offers an acute analysis of the correspondences and differences between the acts of Christ and the acts of the Christian, especially in relation to being 'for' others. Attention should also be given to the distinction drawn between Christ as sacrament and Christ as example by Eberhard Jüngel in 'The Sacrifice of Jesus Christ as Sacrament and Example', *Theological Essays II*, pp. 163–190.

[30] Here, at least, E. Käsemann was correct to protest against the way in which the notion of reconciliation can be expounded in such a way that Christology and soteriology are subordinated to ecclesiology: see 'Some Thoughts on the Theme "The Doctrine of Reconciliation in the New Testament"', in J. M. Robinson, ed., *The Future of Our Religious Past* (London: SCM Press, 1971), pp. 49–64.

is not a reality which is generally well known and understood, something to which the church also makes its particular contribution and lends its authority, but whose content is not strictly derivable from the content of the church's proclamation of salvation. The church is not simply as it were a volunteer, willing to spend itself in a task for which others are also suited but in which they decline to involve themselves. The church engages in actions which are given to it to do by its constitution as that gathering of humanity which confesses that in Christ God has reconciled the world to himself. No less than in the depiction of the moral space of the church, there is need also in our discussion of the moral διακονία of reconciliation to root what we have to say in divine election.

If the origin of this διακονια of reconciliation is the divine appointment, its content is primarily *speech*. What God has entrusted to the church is (in verse 19) the 'message (λόγος) of reconciliation'; we are 'ambassadors' through whom God 'makes his appeal'. Crucially, this emphasis on speech as primary in the church's ministry of reconciliation helps retain a sense of the proper transcendence and uniqueness of the divine act of reconciliation. Speech is in contrast here to 'ethical realization'. It helps counter the notion that through the moral life of the church reconciliation is first introduced into the anthropological sphere, first made real in the world. For apostolic speech is not a making real of the gospel of reconciliation, but a testifying to the fact that in Christ and Spirit it is already realized. The word of reconciliation is a word which witnesses to that reality which lies on the other side of our speech, which it may indicate or gesture towards but which it can never embody or present or realize in our midst. The apostolic word *indicates*, and that indication is the first great act of the ethics of reconciliation. What is the apostolic ministry? Barth puts it thus:

> It is a request for the openness, the attention and obedience which are needed to acknowledge that what has happened in Christ has really happened, to enter the only sphere which is now left to man, that of the new, that of the conversion to God which has taken place

in Christ. The ministry of reconciliation which consists in this entreaty is not of itself self-contained, but it begins only with this self-continued and completed event. This ministry is its first concrete result. The world ... needs this ministry. But reconciliation in itself and as such is not a process which has to be kept in motion towards some goal which is still far distant. It does not need to be repeated or extended or perfected. It is a unique history, but as such – because God in Christ was its subject – it is present in all its fulness in every age ... As this completed and perfectly completed turning, reconciliation makes necessary the ministry of reconciliation, giving to it a weight and a power to arouse and edify which no other ministry and indeed no other human activity can ever emulate.[31]

There is, of course, an objection near to hand: is not such an assertion of a 'perfectly completed turning' of human history merely ideological, a cloak for the self-evidently unreconciled state of human history? But the objection misses the real nature of the reconciliation which has been established and which is the content of the apostolic ministry. To see the point we might set these verses from 2 Corinthians 5 alongside Ephesians 2.14ff.:

He is our peace, who has made us both one, and has broken down our dividing wall of hostility, by abolishing in his flesh the law of commandments and ordinances, that he might create in himself one new man in place of the two, so making peace, and might reconcile us both to God in one body through the cross, thereby bringing the hostility to an end. (cf. Colossians 1.20–2)

These verses, we might say, offer a description of what Markus Barth called 'the political result of the Messiah's mission and work'.[32] We may try to put the matter thus. What the apostolic ministry of reconciliation indicates is the *existence* (not simply the *potentiality*)[33] of the 'one new man'. This new man, this

---

[31] *Church Dogmatics* IV/1, pp. 76f.

[32] M. Barth, *Ephesians 1–3* (Garden City: Doubleday, 1974), p. 266.

[33] The priority of actuality over potentiality in ecclesiology is (rightly) emphasized by D. Bonhoeffer, *Sanctorum Communio. A Theological Study of the Sociology of the Church* (Minneapolis: Fortress Press, 1998), p. 144.

reconciled existence in which human division and hostility have been put away, is not present to us simply as an imperatival goal. It is a divine creation, already made, already established as part of the new creation. The new creation establishes a form of human fellowship in which the dividing wall is broken down, and in which there is common 'access in one Spirit to the Father' (Eph. 2.18) through the Son; thereby, strangers become fellow-citizens. *Where* is this reality? In is *in him*; *he* is it; he does not simply figure it to us, or call us to fulfil what he initiates or instances: he *is* our peace.

But again, the question comes: if this is the doctrinal space of the church's life, what room is left for the activity of reconciliation? What kind of peace-*making* is left to us? Pannenberg asks: 'Do we not have to regard not merely God's reconciling act but also its human acceptance as constitutive of the event?'[34] A response might go along these lines: Human action is not constitutive of the event of reconciliation in the sense that the Christological 'once-for-all' is dependent for its completion upon those human acts through which reconciliation is accepted and lived out; in this sense, the event of reconciliation is closed. But that event is not closed in the sense that it eliminates all subsequent reconciling activity. It is an event charged with force to expand itself and establish conformity with itself, for it is an event one of whose agents is the Holy Spirit. And this expansion takes place as the risen Christ in the Spirit's power generates those human acts which seek to demonstrate conformity between achieved divine reconciliation and patterns of human life, and which refuse to act as if reconciliation had not, in fact, taken place. Truthful human action is action which is in conformity with the reality which is established in the resurrection of Jesus from the dead. It is 'truthful' because it presupposes that its *ratio essendi* (and therefore its *ratio cognoscendi*) lies outside itself in a reality to which it is conformed, but which it does not establish or actualize. The church, therefore, lives in that sphere of reality in which it is

---

[34] *Systematic Theology*, II, p. 415.

proper to acknowledge and testify to reconciliation because we have been reconciled; in which it is fitting to make peace because peace has already been made; in which it is truthful to speak to and welcome strangers because we ourselves have been spoken to and welcomed by God, and so have become no longer strangers but fellow-citizens. What is all-important is that an ethics, politics and spirituality of reconciliation should not be burdened with the task of doing God's work. Action is hopeful and unanxious if it knows itself to be action which is in conformity with how the world is *coram deo.*

All this should give us pause before deploying too swiftly the language of human action as a 'mediation' of the divine work of reconciliation. It would be superfluous here to rehearse in detail the constituents of the characteristic Protestant nervousness concerning ecclesial mediation: its apparent failure to state the sheer gratuity of the gospel; its potential compromise of the sole mediatorship of the risen Christ and of the Spirit's presentation of the *beneficia Christi*; its weakening of the backward reference of ecclesial action to the Christological 'once for all'; the danger that mediating agencies quickly become interesting in their own right; the assumption that the bridge between the 'objective' reality of the gospel and its 'subjective' realization must be built through human activity. It is, of course, more than ever an open question whether anxieties along these lines are well-founded, or whether they simply highlight the need for careful theological specification and refinement of language about ecclesial mediation. But behind the anxieties lies a fear that any account of ecclesial mediation can scarcely avoid becoming too dense, too humanly solid, and therefore insufficiently transparent towards – ostensive of – the self-presentation of God. The Western Catholic tradition developed its understanding of mediation in particular relation to questions concerning the significance of matter in sacraments and concerning the significance of institutional office in ministry. One result of such preoccupations (shared in many respects by the Reformers even as they struggled against this part of their heritage) was a strongly *kataphatic* theology of mediation. Later theologians, especially some strands of nineteenth- and twentieth-century Roman Catholic and Anglican theology, took up these developments and justified them by appealing to an 'incarnational' principle in which Christ, church, sacrament and ministry (and sometimes culture and ethos) threatened to become points on a continuum of God's 'embodied' saving activity. Contemporary ecclesial ethics often stands within this tradition, even if sometimes in a less dogmatic form owing as much to Hegelian theory of history as to theology.

By way of contrast, I suggest that the Christological ἐφάπαξ and its drastic curtailment of the *soteriological* significance of human ecclesial activity may best be safeguarded by a theology of mediation which is more *apophatic* in character. This is – emphatically – not grounded in a general principle of apophasis, whether philosophically or religiously derived; apophasis does not secure freedom from idolatry, and, indeed, may be itself a form of idolatrous resistance to the human vocation to positive speech and action.[35] Rather, an apophatic account of mediation draws attention, not so much to creaturely incapacity as to the utter capacity of God's self-communicative presence in Christ and Spirit, thereby entirely reorienting the task of creaturely witness. Apophatic mediation is at heart *indicative;* the mediating reality – object, activity, person, word – does not replace or embody or even 'represent' that which is mediated, but is as it were an empty space in which that which is mediated is left free to be and act. Such mediation is not *wirksame Handeln* but *darstellende Handeln*:[36] a 'showing' which

---

[35] On this last point, see two essays by Louis Dupré: 'From Silence to Speech. Negative Theology and Trinitarian Spirituality', *The Common Life. The Origins of Trinitarian Mysticism and Its Development by Jan Ruusbroec* (New York: Crossroad, 1984), and 'Negative Theology and Religious Symbols', *Religious Mystery and Rational Reflection* (Grand Rapids: Eerdmans, 1998), pp. 92–103, along with F. J. van Beeck, 'Apophaticism, Liturgy and Theology', in D. Cunningham et al., eds., *Ecumenical Theology in Worship, Doctrine and Life* (Oxford: Oxford University Press, 1999), pp. 33–9. Further, see the critique of negative theology in Jüngel, *God as the Mystery of the World*, pp. 255–61.

[36] For this distinction (taken from Schleiermacher) see E. Jüngel, 'Der Gottesdienst als Fest der Freiheit', and 'Der evangelisch verstandene Gottesdienst', *Wertlose*

does not effect but indicate and celebrate God's most proper effectiveness. Human mediation is not spontaneous; it is at its deepest level an ontological *passivum*. And the ontology of such mediation is therefore to be spelled out – over against the Western Catholic tradition – not in terms of an ontology of presence,[37] but in terms of what might be called an ontology of indication. Mediating realities have their being in the action of indicating that whose utter plenitude lies wholly beyond them. Once again, the grounds for this do not lie in general repudiations of the metaphysics of presence, but in a specifically theological critique which extends into ontology the force of the exclusive particles *solus Christus, solo verbo, sola gratia, sola fide*, behind all of which lies the great trinitarian principle of all dogmatics and ethics: *solus Deus*.

From this, two consequences of importance for an ecclesial ethics of reconciliation might be noted. The first concerns the concepts of virtue, habit and practice which of late have enjoyed much authority in theological ethics. In *Embodying Forgiveness*, Greg Jones writes that God's

> healing and re-creating is not God acting wholly without us. They also invite, and require, our practices, which – by the guiding, judging, and consoling work of the Spirit – enable us to witness to God's forgiving, re-creating work and to be transformed into holy people. To be involved in such practices is to engage the narrative of the triune God's creative and re-creative work as Father, Son, and Spirit; likewise, to believe faithfully in the Triune God is to have our lives formed and transformed through participation in Christian practices.[38]

Almost right; but the potential moral immanence of the language of practice may be troubling; talk of crafting

---

Wahrheit. Zur Identität und Relevanz des christlichen Glaubens. Theologische Erörterungen III (Munich: Kaiser, 1990), pp. 283–310.

[37] For theological critique of the application of the metaphysics of presence to the reality of God, see Jüngel, *God as the Mystery of the World*, for example pp. 182–4. I am not sure if the ontology in J.-L. Marion's *God Without Being* (Chicago: University of Chicago Press, 1991) is theologically derived.

[38] Jones, *Embodying Forgiveness*, p. 163.

forgiveness may run counter to its sheerly unassimilable character as the gift and work of God. Put differently: the region of Christian faith and practice is eschatological, and therefore notions such as practice can only be used if we allow that they will suffer some very considerable strain if they are to be bent to serve in a Christian moral psychology. The rule here, as for all ethics, is: *non nostri sumus, sed Domini.*[39]

The second is to suggest, accordingly, that before we need to speak of the church as a community characterized by reconciling practices, or by learned habits of peacemaking, we need to talk of the church as the creature of the Word, in order to retain the fundamental asymmetry between divine and human action.[40] To talk of the church in these terms is to insist that at its heart the church is passive, a community whose life has as its core activity the listening to the apostolic Word of reconciliation.[41] Ecclesiologies which centre on Word customarily have greater success in articulating the transcendent freedom of the object of Christian faith, and are customarily more resistant to moralization of the gospel, in which God's reconciling deed takes up residence in institutional forms or patterns of moral practice. If it was an assertion of the centrality of Word for church which drove much of the Reformers' unease about the structures of sacramental reconciliation in later mediaeval Christianity in the West, such an assertion may equally render us rather uneasy with an ecclesial ethics of reconciliation in which the task of indicating the gospel has been in some measure nudged to the sidelines. This is not, of course, to deny that the practice of the ecclesial community is of importance, nor to fall into the error of ethical nominalism in which human action *cannot* refer to divine action. It is simply to urge that what holds the

---

[39] On this, see my article 'Habits. Cultivating the Theologian's Soul', *Stimulus* 7/1 (1999), pp. 15–20.

[40] See Schwöbel, 'The Creature of the Word'.

[41] For a pungent recent reminder of this, see E. Jüngel, *Das Evangelium von der Rechtfertigung des Gottlosen als Zentrum des christlichen Glaubens* (Tübingen: Mohr, 1998).

ecclesial community together is not common moral activity
but attention to the gospel in which existing reconciliation is
set before us both as – shocking, revolutionary, unpossessable
– reality, and also as task. In morals, too, the figure of Jesus
the present one can be eclipsed and his work of self-demon-
stration be quietly assumed by others. But: he is present and
self-communicative, and needs no acts or speeches of ours to
do what is his to do.

> It might be asked, 'Where is Christ the peacemaker between God
> and men now? How far from us does He dwell?' He says that as He
> once suffered, so now every day He offers the fruit of His suffering
> to us through the Gospel which he has given to the world as a sure
> and certain record of His completed work of reconciliation.[42]

IV

'[O]nly in the sphere of the ethico-religious life, viewed from
the standpoint of the Kingdom of God, does the God-man find
His place, because that Kingdom, and nothing else, is the direct
correlate of the Divine self-end.'[43] Thus Ritschl. If he is wrong,
it is not only because of his near-identification of the Kingdom
of God and 'the sphere of ethico-religious life', but because
that near-identification corrodes Christ's transcendence of
moral community, the sheer freedom of his presence to the
church, and leads to a fundamentally non-dramatic
Christology, a Christology in which the sharp contours of the
identity and action of Jesus are not given adequate delineation
because they serve as little more than an ultimate whence of
human life and action. If an ecclesial ethics of reconciliation is
to commend itself as genuinely eschatological, and therefore
genuinely hopeful, it will have to demonstrate its concern to
resist what Ritschl failed to resist, in part by remembering the
dire fate of Protestant dogmatics and ethics when it adopted

---

[42] Calvin, *The Second Epistle of St. Paul to the Corinthians*, p. 79.
[43] A. Ritschl, *The Christian Doctrine of Justification and Reconciliation*, III (Edinburgh:
T&T Clark, 1900), p. 465.

'the *ethical apprehension of Jesus*'.[44] But modern theology has a very short memory.

---

[44] Ibid., p. 442.

ETHICS

8

GOD AND CONSCIENCE

1. Conscience and the Moral Field

Paul Lehmann once suggested that the tortuous history of the notion of conscience forces theologians to choose between two simple alternatives: '[E]ither "do the conscience over" or "do the conscience in"!'[1] Though there are good reasons for taking the latter option and abandoning conscience as part of the anthropological captivity of the church and its moral theology, I want to explore the first option. What kind of repair work is needed to accomplish the theological renovation of conscience? The suggestion upon which I want to reflect, both formally and materially, is that we best articulate a Christian theology of conscience when we refuse to isolate it and treat it as a phenomenon in itself. Instead, we need to expound it as one feature within a larger moral landscape. The kinds of things which the notion of conscience is after can best be appreciated when it is handled in the course of a more extensive depiction of moral reality. Conscience is not a foundational moral notion or an axiom from which we can proceed to positive moral doctrine, but a derivative notion whose force depends upon the functions which it is called to perform in a particular vision of the moral life.

Because of this, one of the important tasks of moral theology in this regard is dogmatic depiction of the moral field. By 'moral field' I refer to the space or arena within which human moral action and reflection on that action take place. Christian moral theology is in part the depiction of the moral field of the

[1] P. Lehmann, *Ethics in a Christian Context* (London: SCM Press, 1963), p. 327.

gospel. The gospel sets out the order within which human moral reasoning and action occur, an order which is properly understood as the history of the encounter between the God who graciously creates, saves and perfects, and the creatures who receive these graces and respond to them with grateful action. Theological reflection on that order will be resolutely dogmatic as it tries to give an account of the moral field of the gospel. It will therefore (1) talk of God and God's actions as the determining environment of human moral agency. For the gospel and its theology, 'God' is not to be construed as anonymous absolute value or inert criterion. Rather, God is self-manifesting agent, who through his acts names himself as Father, Son and Spirit. The moral field is thus defined as the arena of God's activity as creator, reconciler and perfecter, the one who brings all things into being, upholds them against all threats and enables them to attain their proper end. A Christian theology of the moral field will also (2) talk of the human person as one whose humanity is to be found in fellowship with this God, and therefore defined, not in terms of reason, will or consciousness anterior to God, but in terms of the good purposes of God, to which active allegiance is given in worship, confession and service. A Christian theology of the moral field will (3) try to spell out how episodes in the history of the encounter between God and humanity are part of a shapely, purposive history which, from origin to goal, is not merely a sub-plot in the wider passage of humanity through time, but the central, overarching history of human destiny. Finally, a Christian theological account of the moral field will (4) give particular attention to the church of Jesus Christ as the provisional yet real fruit of the reconciling and perfecting work of God, and thus as the anticipation (again, provisional yet real) of true human moral culture.

It is on the basis and within the terms of such an account of the Christian moral world that a theology of conscience can best be undertaken. Consequently, a theology of conscience will make extensive use of first-order Christian language about God, Christ, Spirit, sin, justification, sanctification, church and so forth, for only within the encompassing framework supplied by such language, and by the spiritual, dogmatic and moral culture which it bears, will reflection on conscience attain to a Christian determinacy.

This attempt to expound a theology of conscience within a larger framework ('the moral field') is very companionable to what in a philosophical context Charles Taylor calls 'moral ontology', that is, the description of the moral space within which human agents orient themselves and undertake acts of evaluation and discrimination.[2] In particular, a Christian theology of conscience will have much to learn from Taylor's critical analysis of the history of subjectivity and his attempts to reintegrate 'self' and 'world'. But the most magisterial theological attempt to map out the moral field in this way is, of course, that of Barth in the ethical sections of the *Church Dogmatics*. Thus, in the initial orientation of the ethics of creation in the opening pages of the *Church Dogmatics* III/4, for example, Barth is concerned to establish the possibility of what he calls '"formed" reference to the ethical event',[3] by which he means a description of human moral action as taking place within a sphere defined by the intersection of the horizontal by the vertical, an intersection which is not simply a point but something which 'must become linear'.[4] There is an arena within which human action has its place; that arena is constituted by the God who commands and claims and by the actively obedient human subject. What is thus described spatially can also be described historically, as the 'history of God and man from creation to reconciliation and redemption'.[5] And hence,

> since the ethical event as an encounter of the concrete God with concrete man does not take place in empty space but in that defined by the concreteness of both these partners and their

---

[2] C. Taylor, *Sources of the Self. The Making of Modern Identity* (Cambridge, Mass.: Harvard University Press, 1989).

[3] Barth, *Church Dogmatics* III/4, p. 18.

[4] Ibid.

[5] Ibid., p. 26.

encounter, ethics, too, does not stand before something which is general and cannot be expressed in particular terms ...[6]

Barth undertakes a similar task at the beginning of the ethics of reconciliation, as can be seen from the posthumously published paragraph 74 of the *Church Dogmatics*, 'Ethics as a Task of the Doctrine of Reconciliation'.[7] Picking up the threads of the earlier discussion in *Church Dogmatics* III/4, Barth once again describes the context of human moral action as the specific history of God and humanity which takes place in and as Jesus Christ. And so, the contours of the moral field can be mapped by asking four questions: Who is the God who commands? Who is the human subject responsible to this commanding God? What is the situation in which these two subjects encounter one another? What is the command that God gives to the human subject in this situation so depicted? The importance of Barth's material here is not simply that it highlights the inappropriateness of the charge of ethical actualism often made against him (a charge which cannot even be sustained against his early ethical writings, and is certainly without warrant with respect to the *Church Dogmatics*). It is also that Barth offers a striking example of moral theology oriented not to the reflective human subject as its transcendental condition but to the gospel's display of the *magnalia Dei*.

Equally interesting in this regard is Paul Lehmann's treatment of conscience. Where Barth describes the moral field by asking a series of questions about the encounter of God and humanity, Lehmann uses the notion of *koinonia*, that is, the ordering of divine and human activity in the history of salvation. 'In the context of the *koinonia* a transformation of the nature and function of conscience occurs in terms of which conscience acquires both ethical reality and the power to shape behaviour.'[8] *Koinonia* ethics, focussing on dynamic divine action ('the politics of God'), which 'sets up the conditions for

[6] Ibid., pp. 26f.
[7] Barth, *The Christian Life. Church Dogmatics* IV/4, pp. 3–46.
[8] Lehmann, *Ethics in a Christian Context*, p. 344.

human maturity and makes available to all men the power of human wholeness',[9] approaches the issue of conscience by undertaking

> an analysis of the environment of decision-making in terms of which the shape of behaviour can be concretely and conceptually described. Such an environment is one in which the ethical predicament of man is overcome in the formation of conscience for obedience in freedom through the dynamics and patterns of man's involvement in God's activity. The analysis of such an environment is one in which ethical generalization takes the form of indicative statements of the context, movement, and direction of behaviour, and behavioural acts are exhibited as concretely indicative of the divine and human dimensions of maturity.[10]

And so,

> Christian ethics in the tradition of the Reformation seeks to provide an analysis of the environment of decision in which the principal foundations and preceptual directives of behaviour are displaced by *contextual foundations* and *parabolic directives*. In a word, *the environment of decision is the context for the ethical reality of conscience.*[11]

Such a suggestion is, of course, rather counter-intuitive in view of some very deeply-held moral and spiritual ideals of modern culture. It involves extracting conscience from the curious mix of Stoicism, Thomistic moral anthropology (interpreted in a particular way) and post-Renaissance theories of human identity, consciousness and liberty in matters civil and moral. But, from the point of view of the gospel and its theology, taking this route has some distinct advantages.

First, it secures the point that moral action is properly action undertaken in view of how the world *is*. Acting morally involves reading the world as a particular place which by its very nature requires us to be certain kinds of persons who act in certain kinds of ways if we are to be and act *truthfully*. To say this does

---

[9] Ibid., p. 345.
[10] Ibid., p. 346.
[11] Ibid., p. 347.

not require that we convert culture into nature, ignoring the conventional character of our dealings with reality. Nor does it presume that we are in possession of the kind of certainty about what the world is like which we could attain by somehow being able to transcend culture and its traditions and check into its adequacy as a representation of what really is the case. For Christian theology, 'the good' and 'the true' are available spiritually, after the manner of God and God's self-giving, and not as inert, representable 'facts'. What is crucial is not some theory of ethical knowledge as representation but the refusal to collapse ethics into aesthetics, making morals into 'something like a creative fine art' in which we end up with an 'aesthetic-prudential conception of virtuous choice and action'.[12]

Second, the refusal to orient ethics around subjectivity is particularly important in a theology of conscience. Only by expounding conscience as one feature within a larger moral landscape, characterized by God's saving presence and action and the truthful human response which that presence and action evoke, are we able to extricate ourselves from one of the most potent of modern myths, namely, the idea of the virtual infinity or indefiniteness of the moral situation. We need somehow to shake our ideas of conscience free from the authoritative notion that the moral situation is an empty space, extending limitlessly outwards from my moral awareness, a space which it is my task to form or shape or colonize through the exercise of will or through deliberation. When conscience is severed from autonomy (and the instrumentalism with which it so readily forms alliances), then we are able to see that the ethical situation is 'limited', in the sense that it has a specific shape. In the moral sphere, that is, the human subject's 'encounter with God does not take place on his side in a sphere that is indefinite and infinite but in one that is fixed and limited'.[13]

---

[12] J. N. Finnis, *Moral Absolutes. Tradition, Revision and Truth* (Washington: Catholic University of America Press, 1991), pp. 102f.

[13] Barth, *The Christian Life*, p. 7.

Third, a Christian theological depiction of the moral field will give expression to the conviction that Christian beliefs about how the world is are constitutive of ethical reflection and practice. They are not incidental or peripheral; nor, crucially, are they symbolic of more common human states of affairs or experiences into which Christian convictions can be resolved. Whether such resolution be undertaken in order to establish foundations for Christian convictions, or to demonstrate their superiority to other symbolizations, or – by contrast – to demonstrate their merely contingent status, the method is to attempt to uncover some pre-thematic layer of human moral consciousness which precedes any one particular account of moral truth. Over against this, my suggestion is that the success of a theology of conscience will depend in large measure upon the confidence, vigour and sensitivity with which it appeals to, and makes use of, the spiritual and dogmatic traditions of Christian language, without being over-scrupulous to coordinate itself with general anthropology.

In sum: if, as Lehmann notes, the history of notions of conscience is about 'conscience in search of a context',[14] for Christian theology that context is supplied by forms of Christian speech and practice which articulate, bear witness to and celebrate the creative, reconciling and perfecting acts of God. Conscience does not supply the moral or experiential basis for what Christians say of God; rather, an account of conscience is a function of an account of the ways and works of Father, Son and Holy Spirit.

The priority of an understanding of reality over an anthropologically-oriented account of the experience of conscience was the chief burden of Pannenberg's critique of Ebeling in his 1962 Mainz inaugural lecture, 'Theology and the Crisis in Ethics'. Arguing that Ebeling (in, for example, 'Theological Reflections on Conscience')[15] is to be understood as standing in the tradition

---

[14] Lehmann, *Ethics in a Christian Context*, p. 344.
[15] G. Ebeling, 'Theological Reflections on Conscience', *Word and Faith* (London: SCM Press, 1963), pp. 407–23.

of Herrmann in so far as he makes reflection on conscience an anthropological prolegomena to theology, Pannenberg urges that

> theology cannot expect to demonstrate the reality of its subject matter in terms of ethical relevance or some presupposed ethical standard. On the contrary, the reality of God and of his revelation must first be firmly established if it is to have any ethical relevance at all ... The Christian ethical conscience presupposes the truth of the Christian message.[16]

Thus: 'Comprehensive knowledge of the reality of God, of the specific reality of the created world, and of our existence is the only possible basis for understanding the extent to which the ethical consequences we draw from that knowledge are applicable.'[17] In his open letter, 'An Answer to Gerhard Ebeling', Pannenberg continues to press 'the primacy of our understanding of reality for the task of providing a basis for ethics',[18] above all to ensure that ethics does not fall victim to the voluntarism characteristic of the Western tradition since the early modern period, in which central place is accorded to 'value-creating will'.[19] Thus, Pannenberg proposes the priority of meaning (here understood trans-subjectively):

> The specific meaning of what we experience through the conscience is valid only when its distinctive nature is honoured in the more comprehensive context of the question of meaning. When it is isolated, the appeal to conscience has, in the light of the present-day uncertainty of conscience concerning moral norms, only a subjective authority.[20]

Pannenberg is entirely correct to assert that the most necessary contribution which Christian theology can make to contemporary ethical reflection is 'to set forth the understanding of reality which the Christian faith implies in the context of the contemporary

---

[16] W. Pannenberg, 'Theology and the Crisis in Ethics', *Ethics* (Philadelphia: Westminster, 1981), p. 67.
[17] Ibid., p. 68.
[18] Ibid., p. 75.
[19] Ibid., p. 77.
[20] Ibid., p. 81.

experience of reality'.[21] Moreover, the correctness of his interpretation of Ebeling can readily be seen from J.C. Staten's use of Ebeling (who is here taught by Heidegger) to argue that 'in the experience given to man/woman as "conscience" we have a qualitatively unique ontological grounding for understanding the reality deemed "God"'.[22] Critical discussion with Pannenberg would only begin with consideration of the extent to which the reality of God which precedes experiences of conscience is mediated through the human historical life-world, and the question of whether such mediation may soften the unconditional character of the ethical question. In this regard, Pannenberg's exposition of conscience in *Anthropology in Theological Perspective* is important.[23]

Before proceeding to positive exposition, I may perhaps be forgiven for setting out four further delimitations of the idea of the 'moral field'. It is, of course, a sign of the times that, in order to undertake an account of conscience in frankly theological terms, we can no longer proceed with the cheerful sense that our presuppositions are already established; we must instead painfully and doggedly nail each one of them in place, and only in this way win our freedom from the axioms of an intellectual culture which threaten to subvert our task.

1. We need to meet the charge of idealism which might be levelled against this exposition by stressing that the moral field is not simply composed of ideas or moral notions. It is *history*. That is to say, the moral field in which conscience has its place, and which Christian moral theology seeks to describe, is composed of

---

[21] Ibid., p. 83.

[22] J. C. Staten, *Conscience and the Reality of God. An Essay on the Experiential Foundations of Religious Knowledge* (Berlin: Mouton de Gruyter, 1988), p. 24. A rather different account of Ebeling's account of conscience is offered by H. Schlögel, *Nicht moralisch, sondern theologisch. Zum Gewissensverständnis von Gerhard Ebeling* (Mainz: Matthias-Grünewald-Verlag, 1992), who suggests (with a particular eye to Ebeling's later work) that Ebeling's account of conscience is to be understood in the light of Luther's soteriological teaching.

[23] W. Pannenberg, *Anthropology in Theological Perspective* (Edinburgh: T&T Clark, 1985), pp. 293–312.

agents and their actions and interactions. Thus, on the human side, it is constituted by practices, conventions, roles and their associated structures of approval and disapproval – in other words, by the orders of human fellowship and common action. Of course, the history of agents and their actions includes deliberation, intention, patterns of thought and speech. Action, reflection and speech are not separable. But to say this is not to give priority to reflection; it is simply to ascribe to it a particular place in the history which we call the moral field. That field, we may say, is a sphere both of active moral reason and speech and of rational, articulate action. Only as such is it moral history.

2. To seek to expound conscience in terms of the wider moral field within which it occurs is to speak of more than the formation of conscience. Certainly, both the notion of the moral field and that of the formation of conscience work against the all-too-common assumption that conscience refers to 'that inmost citadel of the personality where the self is to reign in unmolested sovereignty, king of its own castle, uncorrupted by the compromises and pressures of the crowd'.[24] At its best, moral and pastoral theology has used the idea of formation of conscience to emphasize that individual moral judgment requires moulding by the believing community and its educative, pastoral, sacramental, disciplinary and therapeutic practices. This kind of formation is pathological only when it becomes a matter of securing conformity to community norms by the arbitrary imposition of authority and the internalization of prohibitions. Properly speaking, formation of conscience is not so much about policing moral conventions as it is a matter of consensual fellowship in moral truth. Moral maturity involves growth into such fellowship, and deepening sensitivity to, and appropriation of, the reasons for action which lie at its heart, as well as the practices in which it is expressed. In this sense, Grisez speaks of genuine formed conscience as 'an awareness of responsibility assessed by a judgement derived from some

---

[24] H. Chadwick, *Some Reflections on Conscience. Greek, Jewish and Christian* (London: Council of Christians and Jews, 1968), p. 5.

principle one understands in itself or accepts from a source
(such as the Church's teaching) to which one has intelligently
and freely committed oneself'.[25]

Understood in this way, however, formation of conscience is
an activity which necessarily presupposes the more comprehensive reality we have called the moral field. It presupposes,
that is, a vision of the human good. For the Christian
community engaged in the formation of its members, this
vision is definitively set forth in the history of God's election,
reconciliation and perfection of a people for himself.
Detached from this larger vision, indeed, formation of
conscience may quickly become either compulsion or mere
obligation to contingent traditional norms. An account of the
formation of conscience is only as good as the truthfulness of
the understanding of moral reality to which it gives expression.

3. To emphasize that the phenomena of conscience are part of
   moral culture is not to restrict theology to the descriptive
   exercise of mapping moral notions and practices. In its
   description of the moral field, Christian theology will want to
   resist any such restriction, above all because it will envisage
   the moral field as the arena of the history of God and
   humanity, and thus as a sphere of divine agency also, and not
   simply as an immanent cultural world. Accordingly, it will
   describe that field not through socio-pragmatic ethnography
   but through dogmatics.

   That a good deal hangs on this point can be seen from
   consideration of the very stimulating work of Wayne Meeks on
   early Christian moral communities. Like others who have
   sought to exploit the notion of Christianity as culture (notably
   George Lindbeck in *The Nature of Doctrine*[26] and Hans Frei in
   his later work, especially *Types of Christian Theology*,[27] both of
   whom are trying to disentangle theology from transcendental

---

[25] G. Grisez, *The Way of the Lord Jesus*, 1 (Chicago: Franciscan Herald Press, 1983),
p. 74.

[26] G. Lindbeck, *The Nature of Doctrine. Religion and Theology in a Postliberal Age*
(London: SPCK, 1984).

[27] Frei, *Types of Christian Theology*.

anthropology), Meeks owes much to the work of Clifford Geertz, especially to his classic essay 'Ethos, World View, and the Analysis of Sacred Symbols', where Geertz argues against analysis of ethos in terms of theory and in favour of a descriptive ethnography of moral notions and practices. Read ethnographically, the New Testament texts do not yield a formal moral theory but afford us glimpses of community and its 'idiom of morality'.[28] 'Morality' here means not a 'reflective, second-order reality' (for which Meeks reserves the term 'ethics');[29] rather, it 'names a dimension of life, a pervasive and, often, only partly conscious set of value-laden dispositions, inclinations, attitudes, and habits'.[30] Above all, this means giving attention to common moral life, and envisaging the emergence of Christianity as involving the formation of new moral community. 'We cannot begin to understand [the] process of moral formation until we see that it is inextricable from the process by which distinctive communities were taking shape. Making morals means making community.'[31] And hence, the historian of the New Testament and its world is trying to unearth 'something like a common moral sense, a set of moral intuitions'; the task is one of 'inquiry about the forms of culture within which the ethical sensibilities of the early Christians have meaning'.[32]

There are certainly considerable advantages in pursuing this kind of method. Above all, it helps break the tie between conscience and subjectivity by stressing the role of community in the development of moral notions and practices. The benefits of this at a purely historical level are certainly noteworthy, for it is only when we extricate ourselves from the

[28] W. Meeks, *The Origins of Christian Morality. The First Two Centuries* (New Haven: Yale University Press, 1993), p. 2.

[29] Ibid., p. 4.

[30] Ibid.

[31] Ibid., p. 5. See further the use of the idea of 'communities of moral discourse' in his earlier study *The Moral World of the First Christians* (London: SPCK, 1980), and his essay 'The Circle of Reference of Pauline Morality', in D. L. Balch et al., eds, *Greeks, Romans, and Christians. Essays in Honor of Abraham J. Malherbe* (Minneapolis: Fortress Press, 1990), pp. 305–17.

[32] Meeks, *The Origins of Christian Morality*, p. 11.

modern assumption that conscience is equivalent to universal moral reason that we can begin to see that the extraordinary historical plurality of understandings of conscience is most effectively mapped by attending to particular moral cultures in which such understandings have a home. Unless this is grasped, the history of conscience very quickly falls prey to a universalist anthropology which simply flattens out its variety.

Christian dogmatics, however, precisely because it talks of God, and of all other matters in the light of God, will not rest content with descriptions of contingent moral culture. Its concern will be with those cultural fields as fields of divine action. Consider, for example, Meeks's statement in *The First Urban Christians*:

> Paul and other founders and leaders of those groups [sc. of early Christians] engaged aggressively in the business of creating a new social reality. They held and elaborated a distinctive set of beliefs, some of them expressed in dramatic claims that proved pregnant with metaphor: "Jesus the Messiah, and him crucified". They developed norms and patterns of moral admonition and social control that, however many commonplaces from the moral discourse of the wider culture they might contain, still in ensemble constituted a distinctive ethos. They received, practised, and explicated distinctive ritual actions. None of these was made *ex nihilo*. All drew upon the common language and culture of the Greek-speaking, Roman provincial cities as well as upon the special sub-culture of Judaism, which had already over generations adapted to those cities. The result, nevertheless, was an evolving definition of a new, visibly different sub-culture.[33]

Maybe so. But, for Christian faith, and thus for Christian dogmatics, the life of the church is not only 'a new social reality' (though it is that) but a reality which is ingredient within the history of God's dealings with humanity and therefore something for whose description talk of God is primary. Such talk cannot be merely described as part of the moral culture under study. It must be operative in theological

---

[33] W. Meeks, *The First Urban Christians. The Social World of the Apostle Paul* (New Haven: Yale University Press, 1983), pp. 104f.

description and explanation. Moreover, lack of this element always leaves open the possibility of a relativistic account of the matter, so that the New Testament witness is thought to tell us 'This is how these early Christian communities construed the world' rather than telling us 'This is how the world *is*.' Readers of the postscript to *The Origins of Christian Morality* on 'History, Pluralism, and Christian Morality' will not necessarily be reassured that this possibility has been thoroughly excluded.

Another example may reinforce the point. Malina's account of the 'first century personality' in *The New Testament World* argues with some justice that, for the New Testament communities, conscience is not so much a uniquely personal centre of value but 'individualized common knowledge': 'Conscience ... refers to a person's sensitive awareness to one's public ego-image with the purpose of striving to align one's own personal behaviour and self-assessment with that publicly perceived ego-image.'[34] But the social immanence of this description is troubling. Malina continues: 'Conscience is a sort of internalization of what others say, do, and think about one, since these play the role of witness and judge. Their verdicts supply a person with grants of honour necessary for a meaningful, human existence.'[35] What of the divine verdict? For the New Testament, honour or dishonour are bestowed by the God who justifies; and unless this is the governing context of an account of conscience and its appraisals then its eschatological character, its orientation to the supremely critical and creative action of God, has become buried beneath moral convention.

It is crucial, therefore, that a theological depiction of conscience and its moral field be governed by the conviction that the Christian life is hidden with God in Christ. Owing its origin to the absolute creativity of God who brings into being the things that are not, manifest as a pattern of human activity only after the manner of God as mystery, known only in the miracle of divine self-revelation, the life of the people of God

[34] B. J. Malina, *The New Testament World. Insights from Cultural Anthropology* (Louisville: Westminster/John Knox Press, 1993), p. 63.
[35] Ibid., p. 64.

is more than simply a strand of moral culture. Unless this is stated with some force, then, as Barth noted, 'the holiness of the Christian character ... can be directly perceived', and theology becomes merely 'applied anthropology'.[36]

More help in this respect may be found in John Milbank's comment that a 'counter-ethics' has to be tied to a 'counter-ontology':

> [O]ne must describe the 'counter-ethics', or the different practice, which emerges. It is here that the qualification of 'counter' will especially be justified, because it will be emphasized that Christian ethics differs from both pre-Christian and post-Christian ethics, and differs in such a fashion that, by comparison, certain continuities between the antique and the modern are exhibited to view. Christianity starts to appear – even 'objectively' – as not just different, but as *the* difference from all other cultural systems, which it exposes as threatened by incipient nihilism. However, it is only at the ontological level, where theology articulates (always provisionally) the framework of reference implicit in Christian story and action, that this 'total' difference is fully clarified, along with its ineradicable ties to non-provable belief.[37]

4. More briefly, the same danger of social immanentism can sometimes disrupt moral theology when the predominant element of its account of the moral field is ecclesiology or liturgy. This need not happen, of course. Emphasis on the ecclesial character of the Christian ethos may enter a valuable protest against the hegemony of liberal individualism, whether in religious or civil dress.[38] It may reaffirm the location of moral selfhood in tradition; it may properly urge that moral renewal involves much more than improved moral knowledge or modes of reflection, and must include the renewal of forms of common life. Above all, ecclesial

[36] Barth, *Church Dogmatics* I/2, pp. 782f.

[37] J. Milbank, *Theology and Social Theory. Beyond Secular Reason* (Oxford: Blackwell, 1990), p. 381.

[38] See V. Guroian, *Ethics after Christendom. Toward an Ecclesial Christian Ethic* (Grand Rapids: Eerdmans, 1994). See also his essay 'Tradition and Ethics. Prospects in a Liberal Society', *Modern Theology* 7 (1991), pp. 205–24.

ethics is of value when it draws attention to the importance of common prayer as a locus of the formation of conscience: a description of the moral field which did not give attention to its doxological dimensions would be seriously flawed.

But worship – and, with it, ecclesiology – should not expand to occupy the whole moral field, and can only be kept within its proper limits when it is a function of language about God and God's acts in Christ and the Holy Spirit. In this respect Timothy Sedgwick's account of 'sacramental ethics' leaves much to be desired. Giving theological priority to the 'worshipping community',[39] Sedgwick consistently attributes to worship that which in the New Testament is attributed to the actions of Christ and the Spirit. Thus, 'worship is privileged because in worship conversion and reconciliation are both celebrated and effected'.[40] Or, more significantly, in worship the worshipper enters into the paschal mystery of Jesus in a way described thus:

> Jesus suffered the relations that constitute human life, even as those brought about his own death. Jesus' consent brought him into full relationship with the relations that constitute human life, what theologically we call the created order or, more simply, creation. Such reconciliation stands at the heart of redemption itself. What makes this story effective for us now, an experience of reconciliation, is that the church does more than tell the story of Jesus ... the church is the story of Jesus as it lives and celebrates that story in the world. In worship the paschal faith is enacted. The people do more than remember or recall the story of Jesus. In worship they enact the movement of Jesus' life.[41]

From the standpoint of a dogmatic depiction of the moral field, the difficulty with such a statement is not only that it does not appear to respect the finished, incommunicable character of Jesus' saving work, or to articulate our participation in him by talk of resurrection and Spirit. It is also that, in underemphasizing how church and worship are predicates of divine

---

[39] T. F. Sedgwick, *Sacramental Ethics. Pascal Identity and the Christian Life* (Philadelphia: Fortress Press, 1987), p. 14.

[40] Ibid., p. 15.

[41] Ibid., p. 106.

activity, it runs the risk of not making sufficiently clear the distinction in *kind* between 'church' and 'sociality', so that church comes to be a cultural and not a theological concept. In this frame of reference, conscience once again finds itself in relative detachment from the eschatological verdict of God.[42]

We may appropriately round off these initial orientations with some observations of the history of conscience. Delving into the literature on that history, one soon becomes aware both of the near limitless range and complexity of the materials, and of the temptation to make the complexity manageable by some kind of essentialist or progressivist theory. Essentialism afflicts those accounts which try to resolve the historical variety by establishing a criterion of a 'pure' phenomenon of conscience (usually on the basis of an anthropology). Progressivism reads the history of conscience as an ascent from muddled antique notions of shame and honour to the modern attainment of reflective moral individualism. Dictionary and encyclopaedia surveys do not always escape the temptation. Alasdair MacIntyre remarks aptly of the history of philosophy that for

the encyclopaedist this history is one of the progress of reason in which the limited conceptions of reasoning and practices of rational enquiry generated by Socrates, Plato, and Aristotle were enlarged by their successors ... and then given definitive and indefinitely improvable form by Descartes.[43]

With the substitution of suitable names, the same could be said of the history of conscience.[44]

---

[42] Theologically much more adequate is Paul Ramsey's account of the issue: 'A "people of God" proposes to understand the righteousness by which it judges performances among men according to the measure of the righteousness it believes God displayed in his word-deeds intervening in times past in men's deeds and moral talk. His were the master speech-acts; ours should be in character and have self-involving correlative force' ('Liturgy and Ethics', *Journal of Religious Ethics* 7 (1979), p. 145).

[43] A. MacIntyre, *Three Rival Versions of Moral Inquiry. Encyclopaedia, Genealogy and Tradition* (Notre Dame: University of Notre Dame Press, 1990), p. 58.

[44] See here the excellent *Forschungsgeschichte*, in J. G. Blühdorn et al., 'Gewissen', *Theologische Realenzyklopädie* 13, pp. 192–7.

It would seem that a successful account of the history of conscience will exhibit at least three features. (1) It will be free from the illusion that the history of conscience can be studied lexically, by simply tracing the history of terms. Not only are the terms themselves unstable and porous, but also they perform different functions in different moral worlds. (2) Accordingly, what is needed is careful enquiry into the determinants of meanings of conscience – conceptions of the human good, the nature of moral knowledge, and the religious and political ideals and practices by which such concepts are supported and which they in turn support. A history of conscience is thus not simply linguistic or conceptual but is also a history of 'manners' (social practices as they are embodied in roles, modes of approval, enforcement and punishment, and so forth). (3) This, finally, means that an account of the history of conscience needs to proceed from some very detailed examination of particular cases.[45]

Christian theology will, of course, want to make its own judgments about the history of conscience and its cultures. But it will do so on the basis of a due sense of the variety of that history, so that it is not trapped by the reductionist search for a common essence. The alternative to such essentialism is not, of course, only a pluralism without norms but a confident inhabitation of a particular world of meaning. For Christian theology, however, such confidence is inseparable from conviction of the catholic scope and truthfulness of its particular world.

We now turn to positive dogmatic exposition of the moral field.

---

[45] Some outstanding examples of such work can be found in the explorations of the interrelation of ideas of conscience with ideas of law, modes of moral education and Protestant and Catholic moral cultures in E. Leites, ed., *Conscience and Casuistry in Early Modern Europe* (Cambridge: Cambridge University Press, 1988). Other examples would include C. G. Davies's scrupulous analysis of modes of the self and their relation to linguistic change in *Conscience as Consciousness. The Idea of Self-Awareness in French Philosophical Writing from Descartes to Diderot* (Oxford: Voltaire Foundation, 1990), and H. D. Kittsteiner's wide-ranging history of conscience from the Reformation to the Enlightenment in *Die Entstehung des modernen Gewissens* (Frankfurt/M: Insel Verlag, 1992). All these works are alert to the permeability of the theological, philosophical and political traditions.

2. Conscience: A Dogmatic Exposition

Christian theology will be required to begin its talk of conscience
with talk of God, Father, Son and Holy Spirit. Conscience is an
aspect of our fellowship with this God; it is what it is in the
history of that fellowship, destroyed by human wickedness and
restored by divine mercy. Theology, therefore, will adhere with
some strictness and self-discipline to the 'very specific determination in which alone we can speak about conscience'.[46] What
Christian theology says here of God will proceed from God's self-
naming rather than from a project of speculation or
symbolization. God is not anonymous or indefinite, but named
and purposive; our speech proceeds from our being addressed.
And so, in conscience we do not relate to some Other, but to the
God and Father of our Lord Jesus, to the Spirit of the living God.

This refusal of anonymity sets a clear limit to the use of philosophical reflection on conscience as a prolegomenon to
Christian theology, as in the use of Heidegger's account of
conscience in *Being and Time*.[47] Moreover, the theological implications of Heidegger's thought are not best taken up by
elaborating an existentialist transcendental anthropology.[48]
Used in that way, Heidegger is absorbed back into the
philosophy of subjectivity for which he thoroughly criticized the
modern Western metaphysical tradition.[49] Paul Ricoeur's
reflections on conscience at the end of *Oneself as Another* much
better embody an appropriate use of Heidegger, precisely in
the reticence of their reference to God, and their modesty in
acknowledging the limits of philosophical discourse.[50]

In speaking of conscience by speaking of God, Christian moral
theology will emphasize (1) that conscience is a *created* reality. As

---

[46] K. Barth, *Ethics* (Edinburgh: T&T Clark, 1981), p. 477.

[47] M. Heidegger, *Being and Time* (Oxford: Blackwell, 1962), pp. 312–48.

[48] Examples would include Staten, *Conscience and the Reality of God*, or J. Macquarrie,
Three Issues in Ethics (London: SCM Press, 1970), pp. 111–30.

[49] On this, see the very fine essay by E. Jüngel and M. Trowitzsch, 'Provozierendes
Denken. Bemerkungen zur theologischen Anstößigkeit der Denkwege Martin
Heideggers', *Neue Hefte für Philosophie* 23 (1984), pp. 59–74.

[50] P. Ricoeur, *Oneself as Another* (Chicago: University of Chicago Press, 1992), pp.
341–55.

such, it is contingent, not necessary; limited, not infinite; first of all a hearing, rather than a form of speech. Above all, conscience is not a form of autonomy, a kind of moral *possessio sui*. We have conscience, as we have reason and will, in our creatureliness; and thus we have them spiritually, in the event of the grace of creatureliness. We have conscience by the gift of the Father.

Because our creatureliness is what it is in the history of our fellowship with God, Christian theology will (2) invest heavily in depiction of the acts of God in Jesus Christ, through which that fellowship is sustained against all opposition. Here – in Christology and not in a theology of created spirit – the key decisions will be taken. Everything beyond this point must be 'schooled by Christ',[51] for

> what [God] has now done in Jesus Christ, and what he is doing, ought now to become the one and only centre of man's existence before God. God has *now* showed thee, O man, what is good and what the Lord doth require of thee.[52]

In the broadest terms, this means that a theology of conscience will describe the ultimate context of conscience as the fact that, in and as Jesus Christ, God has acted to effect the entire reordering of human life, judging and excluding the hostility to himself which had issued in our ruin. In Christ he has restored us and enabled us to fulfill our human vocation by gathering us into fellowship with himself. The history of the work of God's grace, which is the history of Jesus Christ, is human destiny in which we, including our consciences, are enclosed. We do not transcend this history but are placed as figures within it. Human wisdom consists in the discernment and glad affirmation of that place. This history is also a moral history, that is, a history which cannot be told as if there were only one (divine) subject and agent; as the history of fellowship, it is also the history of human patience and action.

More particularly, a theology of conscience will pay especial heed to the role of God in Jesus Christ as judge. God in Christ is

---

[51] P. Ramsey, *Basic Christian Ethics* (Louisville: Westminster/John Knox Press, 1993), p. 85.
[52] Ibid., p. 84.

judge in that he is the comprehensive disclosure of human life and action; in and as Jesus, God sees, knows and declares the truth. In this, God is our unconditional accusation and our unconditional acquittal. On the one hand, this spells the end of the fantasy of being our own judges, finding a source of moral truth in ourselves independent of any reference to the presence and action of God. On the other hand, this liberates by setting us in the light of the one true judgment. Whatever is said about conscience has to respect the non-transferability of this judgment. Conscience cannot replace the divine verdict of condemnation and acquittal; it may not anticipate it, or convert it into steady and certain – or at least available – moral knowledge, on the basis of which we can finally, or perhaps merely provisionally, judge ourselves. It is for exactly this reason that conscience is not the site of our knowledge of good and evil but precisely its overthrow.[53] A theology of conscience thus starts from the confession that 'God is greater than our hearts' (1 John 3.20), a confession which is inseparable from the divine commandment 'that we should believe in the name of his son Jesus Christ' (1 John 3.23).

Again, as Christian theology speaks of conscience by speaking of God, it will (3) talk of the Holy Spirit as the repetition, the realizing and perfecting in us of the Father's verdict in the Son. This is by no means to collapse the Spirit into immanence, so that, in effect, Spirit *is* conscience, self-transcending moral awareness. Rather, Spirit and conscience are related in such a way that, through the Holy Spirit, Christ appropriates me to himself, displacing my self-will and desire for mastery of good and evil through reflection. It is through the 'secret energy of the Spirit'[54] that, in the exercise of conscience, I come to judge not on my own authority but only in the repetition of the authoritative judgment of God. Through the Holy Spirit, I appropriate (because I am appropriated by) the truth enacted and spoken concerning me by the

[53] See here Barth, *Church Dogmatics* IV/1, pp. 231–5; D. Bonhoeffer, *Ethics* (London: SCM Press, 1978), pp. 3–27; idem, *Creation and Fall*, pp. 128–30.

[54] Calvin, *Institutes of the Christian Religion*, III.1.i (p. 537).

Lord. 'To have a conscience is no more and no less than to have the Holy Spirit.'[55] To appropriate is not to possess. The judgment which I make my own in conscience is not a passive deposit or a proposal which I have to flesh out or activate, nor is my awareness of conscience a tabernacle to contain the Spirit. I have a conscience in the event of the Spirit's declaration of the work and promise of God, and so 'only in the prayer "Come Creator Spirit"'.[56] Conscience, then, serves as further confirmation of a basic rule of moral theology, namely that one of the fundamental characteristics of the moral field is prayer for the coming of God.

A Christian theology of conscience thus begins its task by talking of God. Such talk of God is to be operative. It is not to have the place of an axiom beneath the surface, to which appeal is only made *in extremis*, but which for most purposes can be left undisturbed. Talk of Father, Son and Spirit has work to do here, and not the least criterion of success for a Christian theology of conscience will be the trustfulness and readiness with which it lets that work proceed.

Next, a Christian theology of conscience is required to talk of the human creature who has conscience in fellowship with God. What is said theologically of humanity is said after what is said of God as creator, saviour and perfecter. The creature is simply not autonomous. Through Jesus Christ and in the Spirit I am a new creature, and therefore I exist and flourish solely within the miraculous history which God makes with me, the history of election, creation, justification, sanctification, preservation and glorification. Conscience is not simply a seat of personal authenticity where the latter is understood as self-wrought self-identity. Rather, it is a reflective practice in which I endorse the conclusion under which I am placed by my new birth, and to which I return with fear, wonder, gratitude and hope. Conscience is indicative moral reason before it is

---

[55] Barth, *Ethics*, p. 477.
[56] Ibid., p. 479.

legislative; it is the amazed acknowledgement of moral and theological truth before it is an awareness of obligation.

Securing this point at the present time requires some polemic with the conventions of modern theology and with the philosophical traditions to which it often is indebted. Both have encouraged anthropology to migrate from a derivative to a primary place. When that shift occurs, anthropology is no longer part of an assemblage of doctrines which seek to artic-ulate the history of salvation. Instead, it becomes assimilated to the tasks of apologetics and foundations, and acquires the status of a transcendental condition of possibility for all knowledge and action. And not only does its place or function undergo dramatic change; its content is also decisively altered as interiority comes to be co-terminous with moral selfhood. Here attention would need to be given to developments in the civil and philosophical traditions of modernity in which authority is accorded to conscience as an autonomous faculty of self-governance, increasingly detached from rational consider-ation of moral order.[57] Described by Montaigne as a mode of self-reflection ('I have my own laws and lawcourt to pass judgment on me and I appeal to them rather than elsewhere'),[58] and transformed by Descartes' account of conscience as affective rather than rational,[59] and by Spinoza's ethics of self-preservation,[60] conscience becomes the nucleus of

[57] Here particular attention needs to be devoted to developments in the very early modern period, and in particular to unravelling the detachment of morals from a Christian theological metaphysic. John Trentman notes 'the general shift in thinking about law and morals in the late scholastic period, a shift away from centring doctrines of natural law in an external order, in what had often been described as what nature teaches all animate being, towards finding a basis for natural law in thought and language' ('Mental Language and Lying', in C. Wenin, ed., L'Homme et son Univers au Moyen Âge (Louvain-la-Neuve: Editions de L'Institut Supérieure de Philosophie, 1986), vol. 2, p. 552).

[58] M. A. Screech, ed., Montaigne. The Complete Essays, III.2 (Harmondsworth: Penguin, 1987), p. 911.

[59] See R. Descartes, The Passions of the Soul, clxxvii, cxci, ccv, in J. Cottingham et al., eds., The Philosophical Writings of Descartes, vol. 1 (Cambridge: Cambridge University Press, 1985), pp. 392f., 396f., 401.

[60] B. de Spinoza, Ethics, IV.21–4 (Harmondsworth: Penguin, 1996), p. 127.

personal agency around which orbit other realities (authoritative teachings, public conventions) which furnish material for its deliberation. Conscience is akin to moral freedom construed as autonomy, in which the essential condition of moral selfhood is undetermination by nature or society. Such affirmations find political expression in the thesis: '[C]'est une Tirannie que de vouloir dominer sur la conscience',[61] which lies at the heart of liberal pluralism.

Post-Reformation Protestantism also weakened the association of conscience with soteriology and began the process of shifting its locus to the agent's awareness and review of self. Calvinists like Perkins or Ames make conscience the place of subjective certainty of salvation; it is a mode of intense self-examination against the norms of Scriptural commandments, casuistically applied. This incipient moralism, quite different from classical Reformation insistence on the priority of divine acquittal, can also be found elsewhere, for example, in Jeremy Taylor, where conscience is part of a scheme of Christian living which, if not frankly Pelagian, lays stress on the will's response to Christ's example. In time, these developments reinforced the individualism of conscience: only loosely related to soteriological doctrine, conscience concerns the conformity of the acting person to him- or herself. This concern for personal authenticity has other roots also: idealist philosophy of consciousness; pietism; and the rise of a religious culture of subjectivity in which moral selfhood is the place of divine immanence.

The article on conscience in *Sacramentum Mundi* is representative of much recent theological thinking. Starting from an analysis of what is called 'daily experience of conscience', that is, from 'a series of related phenomena of the soul, a kernel of which is an impressive basic experience reaching deep into personal consciousness', the argument is made:

---

[61] P. Bayle, *Critique générale de l'Histoire du Calvinisme*, xvii, cited by Blühdorn, 'Gewissen', p. 203.

In conscience man has a direct experience in the depths of his personality of the moral quality of a concrete personal decision or act as a call of duty on him, through his awareness of its significance for the ultimate fulfilment of his personal being.[62]

Conscience, we note, is different from moral knowledge and norms; it concerns 'the immediate attraction of value or its opposite',[63] and is therefore an expression of 'the ultimate capability of decision about one's personal being'.[64] However much it may stand in need of critical examination and formation, conscience is at heart a function of personal authenticity.

The human moral agent acts and reflects within the drama of salvation, a drama in which we – including our consciences – are put to death and made alive. Conscience is caught up by the struggle of God against sin; conscience, too, is overthrown. And so, for Christian theology, it can never be the location of a serene process of self-review which, even in self-reproof, is not exposed to any kind of *final* judgment. It cannot be simply internal moral auditing which never calls into question the project of me being me, but simply corrects, modifies or chastises without ever putting to death. Anxieties along these lines always underlie rejections of construals of conscience as a phenomenon of natural existence whose operations are reliable and of whose probity we can be justly confident. If such a natural account is to be rejected, it is because of the theological miscalculation involved: about human depravity, about the lack of transparency in human self-knowledge, about our incapacity for innocent and scrupulous enquiry into ourselves.[65] Conscience is caught up within the history of

---

[62] R. Hoffmann, 'Conscience', *Sacramentum Mundi* 1 (New York: Herder, 1968), p. 411.
[63] Ibid.
[64] Ibid.
[65] Paul Lehmann argues vigorously that, when moral theology reduces conscience to a 'built-in device for spot-checking right from wrong', it fails to grasp that '[t]he reality and resources of human renewal presuppose a context and direction of divine activity, within which man's activity is set and by which his behaviour can be guided' (*Ethics in a Christian Context*, pp. 323f.).

salvation, which sets before us the ethical question in its radical, absolute and disorienting force. In the *Ethics*, Barth describes how that question is not simply an interrogation of my actions but much more an interrogation of my assumption that in moral reflection I am safely in touch with moral truth:

> The superior truth in question here [is] the truth of my conduct (including my *theorein* and therefore the condition on which my assertions are assertions of the truth), the truth of my life and existence in the light of the good. All general and theoretical truths ... stand in the brackets of the question whether my life and therefore my action and therefore my *theorein* has a part in the truth of a basically different and higher order, in the truth of the good.[66]

Conscience does not lead us away from this question, out of the crisis, but is itself enveloped by that crisis and has its judgment announced.

But the judgment of conscience does not spell the end of conscience, any more than the judgment of our other idolatries spells the end of knowledge. In the moral reality of the covenant of grace, conscience is an affirmation of God's judgment and thus a knowing with God. Negatively, this means the setting aside of my hatred, superiority or sheer indifference towards the moral truth in which I stand. Positively, it means glad acceptance of that truth. This affirmation of God's judgment, precisely because it takes place in the history of salvation, is always the event of repudiation and acknowledgement. Like all knowledge of God, it is spiritual. But its spirituality – that is, its non-resolvability into a set of contingent material conditions – does not exclude the fact that it occurs as a mode of my reflection. What we must say, however, is that that reflection is not self-generated, arbitrary and finally responsible to nothing other than itself. It is an answer, a hearing, and thus a responsibility to truth. In conscience I attend to the call of my 'perfected' self; conscience is the presence to me in reflection of the moral effect of my new identity established in Christ

[66] Barth, *Ethics*, p. 64.

through the Holy Spirit. Conscience does not further my sinful disunity with myself but properly aims at my unity with what I am in Christ. Conscience is thus eschatological, oriented to that which I have been made through Christ and which, through the power of the Holy Spirit, I am becoming. It is for this reason alone that conscience is unconditional in the requirement under which it places me. The perfection and unconditional character of conscience has nothing to do with the inviolability of my ethical ego, and everything to do with the fact that, in conscience, I am accosted by the call of the future secured for me in Christ and held out to me as the only future in which I can be who I am. Yet, even this unconditional character of conscience is not a guaranteed condition. Conscience, like reason or will, is a field of desire, and my hearing of its call is always a matter of promise and prayer. Conscience remains 'very astonishing knowledge'.[67]

From this we may approach an understanding of the freedom of conscience. Conscience is my hearing the call of my perfected self; it may not, therefore, be controlled by those with authority over me, for authority does not guarantee truth. This is part of the force of the Reformation's assertion of the liberty of Christian conscience in face of the juridical power of sacramental order. But Christian liberty and modernity's ideal of unfettered judgment are simply different categories, and the ideal cannot be traced to the Reformation doctrine of *libertas christiana*. Christian freedom is freedom for the truth. The free conscience is absolutely bound to moral truth. Freedom of conscience is not freedom to 'choose' the good (a 'chosen' good no longer has the absoluteness of truth; it is a mere contingent reality, which I have annexed to my projection of

---

[67] Ibid, p. 475. The eschatological emphasis of the foregoing owes much to Barth's treatment of conscience (ibid., pp. 479–85) and to Bonhoeffer's reflections on conscience as my unity with my new being in Christ (see *Ethics*, pp. 211f.). More recently (and from a very different perspective), G. B. Hammond has drawn attention to conscience as 'the voice of the ideal self in the ideal community' in *Conscience and Its Recovery. From the Frankfurt School to Feminism* (Charlottesville: University of Virginia Press, 1993), p. 144.

myself in the world). The good chooses me; it annexes my projects to itself; it binds me, and thereby sets me free.

In this regard, the ecclesial character of conscience – its inescapable relation to formation – comes into its own. 'Formation' transcends mere 'socialization', assimilation into an existing social order. It is an ecclesial process of which the agent is ultimately the Holy Spirit and proximately the community of believers in which the baptized are shaped by moral truth. Formation is first and foremost a matter of discernment of how things are in the world as depicted in the gospel, and only secondarily about establishing social norms of what is permissible and forbidden.[68] Both moral and pastoral theology must not allow themselves to be trapped by the competing alternatives of either heteronomy (conscience as the internalization of moral codes or prohibitions of the social order overseen by guardians of community values) or autonomy (conscience as a necessarily undetermined centre of judgment). Conscience is formed by participation in social meaning and also in resistance to such meaning. But over and above that, in conscience we encounter the *viva vox Dei*, and do so as members of the community of faith whose common life includes hearing the Word, confession, encounter at the Lord's Table, mutual exhortation and – above all – the praise of the Lord Jesus.

We sum up the anthropological dimension with some reflections on the relation of conscience and faith. Faith is not simply an extension of antecedent subjectivity but rather that in which I first become subject. Faith defines my being; it does not modulate a being which I already have or am. In faith I am not my own. If this is so, then human being as such is not a core element of subjectivity to which we attribute certain activities or characteristics in a straightforward way. Human being *is coram Deo.*[69] Again, if this is so, then conscience is not a kind of inseity.

---

[68] See here Grisez, *The Way of the Lord Jesus*, 1, pp. 73–96.
[69] See here W. Joest, *Ontologie der Person bei Luther* (Göttingen: Vandenhoeck und Ruprecht, 1967).

Subsumed under faith, conscience is a matter of repeating and affirming God's judgment to which faith clings, and not a matter of self-accusation or self-absolution.[70] The tie of *conscientia* to *fides* is paradigmatic of the kind of description which will be involved in a Christian theological depiction of the moral field.

> [T]he Christian is not a moral man, not a man of good *conscience*, who acts *with* what he *knows* of death, scarcity and duty to totalities. He has a bad conscience but a good *confidence*: for he acts with what he does not know but has faith in. In absolute trust he gives up trying to be good, to sustain a right order of government within himself.[71]

This is why baptism is an appeal to God for a good conscience.

3. Conclusion

The most obvious conclusion to draw is that conscience is a derivative, not a primary, moral notion, and thus not the *inconcussum fundamentum* of morals that it often has been made out to be. It ranks well after 'prayer' or 'following Jesus' in the orderly arrangement of the Christian moral world. Seeing this simple point is not easy, perhaps because we are often mesmerized by the term and the rhetorical strategies which surround its invocation. Theology of all disciplines ought to be

---

[70] In his account of conscience in the early work of Luther, M. G. Baylor (*Action and Person. Conscience in Late Scholasticism and the Young Luther* (Leiden: Brill, 1977), p. 228) argues that, at this stage, Luther sees that 'it is faith which confers on the conscience the ability correctly to judge, as God judges, persons before actions and actions in the light of person. Or, perhaps more accurately, faith is the power of the conscience to accept God's judgments about the person rather than those which the conscience arrives at naturally, or by inference from actions.' Crucially, this means that conscience is not a natural activity of the soul or reason linking us reliably to God, but a hearing of the divine verdict. Baylor's interpretation of Luther draws on E. Wolf, 'Vom Problem des Gewissens in reformatorischer Sicht', *Peregrinatio*, 1 (Munich: Kaiser, 1962), pp. 81–112; see also Wolf's article 'Gewissen', in *Die Religion in Geschichte und Gegenwart*[3], vol. 2, pp. 1550–8. Both accounts are decidedly critical of Karl Holl's famous interpretation of Luther in *The Reconstruction of Morality* (Minneapolis: Augsburg, 1979).

[71] J. Milbank, 'Can Morality Be Christian?', *The Word Made Strange*, p. 231.

unafraid to break the spell and awaken our moral thinking from its 'anthropological slumbers'.[72] The turn to the subject which has so afflicted Christian thinking about conscience for at least three centuries is not a fate but a cultural convention. Disposing of it does not, however, mean a turn against humanity – quite the opposite. There is a proper evangelical humanism, which we may find among the ruins of our moral and civil and religious culture if we care to look, and which contains resources which, perhaps, we hardly dare to take into our hands.

---

[72] Cf. M. Foucault, *The Order of Things. An Archaeology of the Human Sciences* (London: Routledge, 1970), pp. 341f.

9

ESCHATOLOGY AND ANTHROPOLOGY

Christian theological anthropology is the dogmatic depiction of human identity as it is shaped by the creative, regenerative and glorifying work of the triune God. Dogmatic portrayal of human identity is thus determined both in its content and its procedures by the church's confession of the gospel, for the gospel constitutes the space within which Christian dogmatics operates. Dogmatics (of which anthropology is a part) is not a free science; although it requires of its practitioners considerable creative powers, it is not simply an imaginative construal of the human situation which draws heavily on Christian religious themes, symbols or practices; although in the accomplishment of its task it will inevitably make use of all manner of language, concepts and patterns of thought, it is not simply the result of a dialogue with whatever philosophical or social-scientific concerns are considered to have resonance with the Christian confession. Dogmatics is the focussed, modest and self-critical activity whereby the church seeks reflectively and systematically to give its attention to the gospel as it is announced in Holy Scripture: no more and no less.

Baldly expressed in that way, such an account of dogmatics seems fearfully unfriendly: closed, assertive, very far indeed from the conversational and interrogative mood which might recommend Christian doctrine to those who don't want to be scolded by catechesis. A recent and much heralded work on theological anthropology announces itself as an example of 'how to draw on various theological and other disciplines and genres without becoming stuck in any one', to avoid the way in which 'some theology and religious studies ... are inhibited from pursuing fascinating and appropriate questions by the fear of transgressing boundaries which are often quite arbitrary'; and so the book recommends 'the fruitfulness of thinking theologically in dialogue with phenomenological and hermeneutical philosophy'.[1] But *are* the barriers simply arbitrary? Sometimes, indeed, they may be; but I am unconvinced that in the present situation Christian dogmatics will have interesting and fruitful things to say without some quite firm marking out of its territory. In other situations – where, for example, wide familiarity with the traditions of doctrinal thought can be assumed, or where the tradition has become self-obsessed – theology might be able or might need to operate in a different, more extra-mural, way. But in the present situation, where dogmatics in English-speaking circles is at best a fragile enterprise in the academy and has almost completely lost its hold on the life of the mainline churches, what is needed more than anything else is a recovery of theology's exegetical and catechetical vocation. Christian theology will only be worthy of the title 'Christian' if it allows itself to be led all along the line by the witness of Holy Scripture, and if it modestly and humbly, and yet also with courage and astonishment, tries to indicate what it finds there. The essential task of Christian dogmatics, whether in postmodernity, modernity or premodernity, is one of patient, respectful attentiveness to the biblical testimony, allowing itself to be shaped by the hope which is there expressed, and quietly letting that hope disturb, shatter and remake human thought and action.

Christian anthropology is eschatological in two senses, only the second of which I propose to explore in this paper. It is eschatological, first, in the sense that central to its account of human identity is the regenerative work of God, effected in the life, death and resurrection of Jesus Christ, realized through the work of the Holy Spirit and signified in Christian baptism. Christian anthropology concerns the new creature of God; its

---

[1] Ford, *Self and Salvation*, pp. 12f.

ontology of the human is shaped by that eschatological event in which the creature's goal is confirmed even as the creature is put to death and made alive in Christ. Thus Christian anthropology, and especially Christian moral psychology, will be concerned with convertedness, that newness of life bestowed by the Spirit in which true human being is to be found. I am what in Christ through the Spirit I become.[2] However, it is a second sense of 'eschatological' which I want to take up here. Christian anthropology is eschatological in the sense that its account of human identity is possessed of a distinct teleology. It sets what it has to say about human identity in the context of the gospel's announcement of a comprehensive account of God's purposes for creation. It is important to stress this second feature of the eschatological character of Christian anthropology in order to prevent the first, more subjective, aspect from expanding to become the totality of what is said about eschatological humanity. The detachment of the eschatological aspects of regeneration from their wider teleological background, and the abeyance of the concept of 'nature' which this often entails, have been common enough in modern theology, especially of the more dramatically existential variety.[3] If these moves are to be resisted, it is because a theology of human identity and action needs to be supported on more than simply the rather narrow base of convertedness, which, however important it may be and however thoroughly it may pervade a Christian ontology of the human, cannot provide the whole scope of Christian anthropology. What is required is an understanding of destiny sufficiently sturdy and expansive to resist being collapsed into the psychological or ethical dramas of selfhood. And so a dogmatic account of converted human identity will be closely related to an account of the ends of creation.

How does this understanding of the dogmatic task of

---

[2] On these themes, see my article 'Eschatology, Ontology and Human Action', *Toronto Journal of Theology* 7 (1991), pp. 4–18.

[3] For a representative example, see Jüngel, 'The Emergence of the New'. My essay mentioned above falls into some of the same difficulties.

Christian anthropology relate to the claim that Christian
theology now is undertaken in the context of postmodernity?
By way of initial orientation, it is important that
'postmodernity' should not be allowed to become itself an
eschatological term, as if the advent of postmodernity were the
new age, such that the church and its theology now find
themselves in an entirely altered situation, which requires them
to rethink the fabric of Christian culture. Such epochal claims
are both historically and theologically deficient. Historically,
their weakness is that, far from enabling reflective awareness
of our present situation and tasks, they are often little more
than (rather specious) philosophical-cum-literary proposals
masquerading as historical-cultural analysis. Theologically,
their weakness is that they promote an account of the church
and its theological responsibilities which are largely unchas-
tened by the discipline of the gospel. Over against such epochal
thinking, in which church and theology are simply bit-players in
some larger cultural drama, I want to suggest that by the grace
of God it is given to the church (and therefore to its theology)
to discern the situation of humanity faithfully and truthfully –
in faith, not in sight, but nevertheless in truth – and therefore
to see the human situation now as that stretch of human history
which lies between the first and second advents of Jesus, in
whom and for whom all things are created and perfected.
Whatever else we may wish to say about the location of church
and theology, that, at least, must be said: church and theology
stand in the space between Jesus' coming in humiliation and
his coming in glory. That space – and not any cultural space,
postmodern or otherwise – is determinative of what church and
theology may and must be. Put differently: Christian theology,
and therefore Christian eschatology and anthropology, is
responsible *in* its context but not in any straightforward way
responsible *to* its context. For context is not fate; it may not
pretend to have a necessary character, to be anything other
than a contingent set of cultural arrangements which stands
under the judgment of the Christian gospel. And, moreover,
context – despite what we are often instructed – is not

transparent or self-interpreting. Truthful understanding of context requires the exercise of discernment, and, for Christian faith and theology, such discernment is a gift of the Holy Spirit, a mode of sanctification and a prophetic task; it is not simply a skill acquired through cultural immersion. We do not by nature know who or where or when we are; and if we are to come to know these things, our knowledge itself must be the Spirit's work, greeted with the obedience of faith.

The question, therefore, for Christian eschatology and anthropology in postmodernity is not what may still be said by Christian theology in the postmodern condition, for there is no such simple condition: 'the possibility of speech about God can be founded on nothing less than God's own speaking'.[4] That means that in one important sense, Christian theology in postmodernity must, as Barth once put it, carry on 'as if nothing had happened'.[5] In Barth's case, this was not because nothing had happened; indeed, what had happened in Barth's context was very grave indeed. But Barth knew better than almost anyone in his context that what that context required more than anything else was the service of a theology which was theological to the bone, which did not allow its context, however stringent, to distract it from the task of clarifying the Christian confession, precisely so that it could indicate to its culture the word of judgment and grace spoken to it by the gospel. Theology's task, in other words, is neither apologetic nor revisionary, but exegetical and dogmatic, busying itself quietly and confidently with its proper concerns, not in order to sidestep the exigencies of whatever its host culture may be, but precisely so as to be able to address them with the right kind of Christian specificity, determination and hope.

Our concern here is with the particular set of exigencies which have come to be termed collectively as postmodernity. The term is notoriously slippery, but can be thought of as a

---

[4] F. C. Bauerschmidt, 'Aesthetics. The theological sublime', in J. Milbank et al., eds., *Radical Orthodoxy. A New Theology* (London: Routledge, 1999), p. 201.

[5] K. Barth, *Theological Existence Today! A Plea for Theological Freedom* (London: Hodder & Stoughton, 1933), p. 9.

handy way of clustering together diverse ideas and styles of cultural and philosophical analysis which repudiate presence, the given, depth, order, identities and structures in favour of absence, surfaces, dispersal, the non-identical, plurality, play. In theological terms, postmodernity is often proposed as ushering in the end of 'onto-theology' – that is, of the mode of talk about God in which God and being are thought together in the kind of metaphysical mythology of absolute presence which Nietzsche and the genealogists finally scoured out of Western culture. Postmodern theology turns away from the substance metaphysics of selfhood, history and deity which have been considered ingredient within the world-view of Christian faith, replacing them by a style of theology which is non-identical, ahistorical and atheological. Christian eschatology and anthropology, set as they are within an overarching teleology of time and a particular commitment to the significance of human action in history, are points at which the sharpness of postmodernity can be felt with particular acuteness. Postmodernism is deeply hostile to teleological renderings of history, with their apparently unified trajectories and their emphasis on the preservation of identity. And it is similarly inimical to accounts of moral agency which tie human action to pre-given human identity or to an overarching order within which moral action is possible and meaningful. In short: once onto-theology is disposed of, then eschatology, and the framework which eschatology offers for generating and evaluating human action, requires radical reworking. In this paper, I want to explore some of the connections between eschatology and anthropology, suggesting that eschatology furnishes part of the teleological context for dogmatic depiction of human identity. Without such a context, accounts of the identity of human agents are difficult to sustain. In the first section I look at the postmodern dissolution of teleology; in the second at the dissolution of the human subject.

1. Eschatology and the End of History: The Dissolution of Teleology

One way of characterizing postmodernism would be to view it as a 'radicalization of historical consciousness'.[6] If modernity involves an account of being as time – as historical process rather than as unchanging substance – postmodernism dissolves the notion of history itself. That is, postmodernism characteristically rejects any idea that human existence in time constitutes an ordered whole; history is dispersed into a non-sequential, non-developmental, non-utopian, non-eschato-logical scatter of elements. History is 'a matter of constant mutability, exhilaratingly multiple and open-ended, a set of conjectures or discontinuities which only some theoretical violence could hammer into the unity of a single narrative'.[7] This, of course, lies behind the rejection of 'grand narratives' in postmodernity, famously enunciated in an essay on the nature of the university institution by Jean-François Lyotard: 'The narrative function', he wrote, 'is losing its great functors, its great hero, its great dangers, its great voyages, its great goal. It is being dispersed in clouds of narrative language elements.'[8] Lyotard's specific target is the emancipatory narrative of modern intellectual institutions, according to which the scientist – the hero of knowledge – is the central character in a story of liberation from myth and opinion into true science. But what Lyotard terms 'incredulity toward metanarratives'[9] has wide application: it signals a turn from any attempt to articulate a coherent shape to human history as having origin, ground or goal, any 'totalization' of history into a single, unidirectional and intelligible whole. Partly what comes to expression here is an attempt to display the link between narrative and the

---

[6] P. C. Hodgson, *God in History. Shapes of Freedom* (Nashville: Abingdon Press, 1989), p. 31.

[7] T. Eagleton, *The Illusions of Postmodernism* (Oxford: Blackwell, 1996), p. 46.

[8] J.-F. Lyotard, *The Postmodern Condition. A Report on Knowledge* (Manchester: Manchester University Press, 1986), p. xxiv.

[9] Ibid.

exercise of power: the process of telling a coherent story about history, making history into a whole, is itself an exercise of power – as Lyotard puts it, 'speech acts fall within the domain of a general agonistics'.[10] Totalizing stories erase otherness, by turns absorbing or excluding what is other in order to project a satisfyingly coherent temporal structure. It is important, however, to grasp that this postmodern critique of the narrative function is more than simply a further version of modernity's critique of ideology (contemporary versions of which we find in some kinds of feminist or liberationist thought, for example). Modernity, we might say, responds to the ideological potential of narrative by seeking to construct a better narrative – that is, a narrative of history which does not erase the counter-factual, but offers a better (more liberating, better founded, above all more *critical* and therefore more truthful) story. Postmodernism simply abandons the whole task of making sense: protology and teleology, and agents with stable or developing identities, are renounced, and history is dismantled into a jumble of heterogenous bits.

One obvious casualty of this process of dismantling in postmodern theology is, clearly, eschatology. The point can be seen in a couple of representative works, Mark Taylor's manifesto *Erring*, and John Caputo's more recent reflections on religious themes in Derrida's later work in *The Prayers and Tears of Jacques Derrida*.

Taylor's account of history in *Erring* is a somewhat amateurish attempt to break free of the inheritance of classical Christian theology (which he sketches in rather haphazard fashion from Augustine to Hegel), a tradition which, he believes, was organized around 'the conviction that a temporal course of events is plotted along a single line, which extends from a definite beginning, through an identifiable middle, to an expected end'. Or again: 'Between the "tick" of Genesis and the "tock" of Apocalypse, the history of the West runs its course. The line that joins beginning, middle, and end traces the plot

---

[10] Ibid., p. 10.

that defines history. History, as well as self, is a theological notion.'[11] All this Taylor expunges from the Christian imagination with appeal to Nietzsche, for whom any such comprehensive schemes are *poiesis*, fabrication, the imposition of comprehensible logic on scattered events, the fashioning of seriality. For the postmodern, Taylor writes,

> [t]he death of Alpha and Omega, the disappearance of the self, and the overcoming of unhappy consciousness combine to fray the fabric of history. When it is impossible to locate a definite beginning and a definite end, the narrative line is lost and the story seems pointless.[12]

On these terms, we should note, there can be no eschatology: destiny is invention, not temporal shape, and so what is left to us is (in the book's title) 'erring', undirected wandering (playful, carnivalesque, but entirely lacking in any point): 'the endlessness of erring discloses its unavoidable purposelessness'.[13]

If Taylor's account makes pretty plain that postmodernism doesn't offer much by way of soil in which eschatology might take root and grow, John Caputo's reflections on Derrida hint in a slightly different direction – namely, that it might be possible to redeem the notion of 'coming', the advent, without falling prey to the spectre of teleology. Caputo finds scattered in Derrida's writings occasional reflections on the theme of 'coming', 'in-coming', 'arrival' and the like which intimate a kind of eschatology which is on the far side of the manageable apocalypse of onto-theology. 'Derrida', he says, 'is dreaming and praying over an "absolute" future, a future sheltered by an absolute secret and absolved from whatever is presentable, programmable, or foreseeable'.[14] Still, however, there is a sort of extreme ascesis here, an extraordinarily scrupulous

---

[11] Taylor, *Erring*, p. 53.
[12] Ibid., p. 73.
[13] Ibid., p. 157.
[14] J. D. Caputo, *The Prayers and Tears of Jacques Derrida. Religion without Religion* (Bloomington: Indiana University Press, 1997), p. 73.

reluctance to associate coming with history and its goals. Partly this is because Caputo finds in Derrida a distaste for the apocalyptic theme of privileged access or vision; partly it is because the theme of coming has to be detached from the modern 'politics of invention' in which that which comes to us is managed by being integrated into the economics of the same, so that its sheer novelty is suppressed; above all, the reticence is a response to the stringent demand to resist the metaphysics (and the metaphysical theology) of presence. 'Every determinable telos is still "present", has already been anticipated within the horizon of what presently prevails'.[15] What Derrida is gesturing towards, therefore is 'the beyond, *au-delà,* the *tout autre, the* impossible, the unimaginable, un-foreseeable, un-believable, ab-solute surprise, which is absolved from the same'.[16] Over against the metaphysics (and political and cultural economy) of the classical traditions of the West, in short, what is needed (or perhaps what is left to us) is 'an apocalypse without vision, without truth, without revelation'.[17]

Is that all that's left to us? Has postmodernism simply chased from the field those traditions of thought and practice (both Christian and secular) which have struggled with the notion of destiny as an essential backcloth to human identity and action, to meaningful speech and action? To answer that question would be a lengthy business indeed; but we may, perhaps, sample some of the issues if we set ourselves a more restricted task of asking whether the target of the postmodernist's criticism is not so much an authentically Christian eschatology but rather its pathological substitute, sharing some of its outer form but lacking its inner substance.

In pondering this question, we need to bear in mind that in one very important sense Christian theology, spirituality and morals are such that we cannot abandon 'grand narratives'.

---

[15] Ibid., p. 73.

[16] Ibid.

[17] J. Derrida, *Raising the Tone of Philosophy* (Baltimore: Johns Hopkins University Press, 1993), p. 167, cited by Caputo, p. 71.

The proposal that '[t]he mythos of salvation history, with its logic of triumph and causality, its distinction of planes (profane and sacred), its special sequence of events, its linear teleology, and its supernatural, other-worldly eschatology must be allowed to die out'[18] is one over which we should pause long and hard before accepting. The structure of a single (though complex) line of history of redemption, stretching protologically to the divine act of creation out of nothing and eschatologically to the consummation of all things, with a centre in the life, death and resurrection of Jesus Christ as the ground and manifestation of its teleology, is one so deeply embedded in the canonical texts of the Christian faith that it is almost impossible to envisage forms of Christian belief and practice, forms of theology, prayer and pastoral nurture from which that teleology has been excised. In one sense, the Christian faith is irredeemably positive, singular, comprehensive and purposive. The suggestion that responsible Christian faith and practice can be envisaged without a 'God-given, pre-given order'[19] runs the risk of simply trimming Christianity to the shape of our cultural imagination (or lack of it). Christian faith and practice are or ought to be *responsible*, that is, *responses*, ways of making sense of the world and of acting truthfully in the world which are generated by a sense that reality and history have a nature, that they are not infinitely malleable, or mere projections, and that the economy of desire is not all that there is. Put differently: styles of Christian faith and practice which are purely constructivist are self-defeating, since they exclude from the beginning that whose denial leads them into hopeless self-contradiction, namely that to believe and act Christianly is to be transfigured by a gift of transcendent freedom, goodness and splendour.

But if we are thereby committed to some form of 'grand narrative', we are not thereby committed to the abuse of that narrative as if the future of God's coming were 'to hand', an available telos neatly completing whatever purposes we happen

[18] Hodgson, *God in History*, p. 235.
[19] Caputo, *The Prayers and Tears of Jacques Derrida*, p. 75.

to have arranged for ourselves. In this sense, postmodernism is quite correct to reject what Taylor calls 'the realized eschatology of the system';[20] authentically Christian eschatology needs to be distinguished from what we might call futurism, that is, the elaboration of a satisfyingly coherent narrative scheme on the basis of which we may come to possess and control the outcome of human history, assigning roles and predicting outcomes in what is no more than a kind of eschatological technology. Postmodernists rightly deplore the false homogenization and singularization of history which this entails.[21] But the protection against this predictive abuse of eschatology is not to abandon teleology, but to specify its character with the right kind of Christian precision. Two things above all are of critical significance here.

First, the fundamental content of Christian eschatology is the personal identity of the one who was and is and is to come, and only by derivation is it teleological. Its core is not the elaboration of a scheme of historical purposes, but the coming of Jesus Christ. His being, his presence and activity, now known in a hidden and yet real way in the activity of the Holy Spirit but to be manifest in the last day, is the content of Christian eschatological belief, and only on the basis of that coming as the transfiguring event of human history may we speak of history's *telos*. It is therefore supremely important that we 'concentrate *on the eschatos rather than on the eschata*: on Jesus Christ as he is described in Revelation 1:17f. ... as "the first and the last and the living one"'.[22] Eschatology is the forward expansion of the name of Jesus; it is the confession that he will be, that he will come; only as such is it also a confession of the future of humanity and its history. The object, therefore, of Christian eschatological speech is the perfect, that is, complete and

---

[20] M. C. Taylor, *Altarity* (Chicago: University of Chicago Press, 1987), p. 293.

[21] See the critique of Moltmann's millenarian strand in M. Volf, 'After Moltmann. Reflections on the Future of Eschatology', in R. Bauckham, ed., *God Will Be All in All. The Eschatology of Jürgen Moltmann* (Edinburgh: T&T Clark, 1999), p. 243.

[22] G. Sauter, 'The Concept and Task of Eschatology', *Eschatological Rationality. Theological Issues in Focus* (Grand Rapids: Baker, 1996), p. 146.

utterly self-sufficient, reality indicated by the name of Jesus. Once this point is quietly laid aside, and the Christological determinacy of eschatology is allowed to recede, the space so vacated is filled with all manner of substitutes. It may be replaced, for example, by large-scale immanent teleologies of human history in which talk of Jesus Christ becomes a mere ornament in what is, in effect, a theory of temporality or an ideology of human achievement. But, as Barth once remarked, '[r]edemption does not mean that the world and we ourselves within it evolve in this or that direction. It means that Jesus Christ is coming again.'[23]

Second, this coming of Jesus Christ, and thus Christian eschatological talk which tries to indicate his coming, is promissory, not possessive, in character. The centrality of promise for biblical eschatology is what distinguishes it from any kind of predictive futurism. This is not because promise indicates that Christian eschatology is ambivalent or even sceptical, lacking in definiteness or assurance. Quite the opposite: the creedal confession that 'he will come again' is no less assured than the confession that God is the creator of heaven and earth, that God's Son suffered under Pontius Pilate or that on the third day he rose again. But such assurance is the assurance of faith, and therefore quite different from that self-certainty which might be the basis for predictive control. Eschatological certainty takes the form of confidence in the promises of God, a confidence whose certainty cannot be replaced by an act of intellectual or spiritual or political possession of the object of hope. The negative aspect of this promissory character of Christian eschatology is the hiddenness of its object, that is, its unavailability for systematic comprehension and its resistance to be used as an instrument in some project of our own devising. God's promise

> is hidden because God becomes present as himself in his own way and in his own time but remains beyond human grasp. He remains hidden even as he reveals himself. His acts take place *sub contrario*

---

[23] K. Barth, *Church Dogmatics* II/1 (Edinburgh: T&T Clark, 1957), p. 78.

of that which humankind expects of him (instead of waiting for him and hoping in him!).[24]

If this suggests that Christian eschatology is more modest than postmodernism allows, it is not because the Christian shares postmodernism's extreme apophaticism, but because the object of Christian eschatological certainty is Jesus Christ himself, the unfettered risen one who shares in the absolute liberty of God. This divine freedom properly shapes both eschatological speech and eschatological spirituality.

One of the primary modes of eschatological speech is prayer for the coming of God. 'The Spirit and the Bride say, "Come" ... Amen. Come, Lord Jesus' (Rev. 22.17, 20); '*Maranatha,* our Lord, come!' (1 Cor. 16.22); 'Thy kingdom come' (Mt. 6.10). This prayerful mode of speech is to be retained with full seriousness, and not simply regarded as a liturgical decoration which can be translated without residue into propositional form. What does the idiom of prayer indicate about Christian eschatology? First, it gives expression to the personal specificity of Christian eschatology. Jesus is our hope: come, Lord *Jesus.* Jesus is not merely an emblematic figure in a larger historical canvas; he *is* the future. Second, in praying that he may come, Christian speech indicates that Jesus is not to be handled as an available object, something or someone to hand. As the one who will come, he is other than an object or figure within the horizon of the world. Third, we *pray* that he may come; that is, we look for the action of another, we implore him to take the initiative, to act in an affair where we cannot act. Here, in other words, Christian speech is quite other than some sort of apparatus for controlling destiny; it is supplication. In short: if Christian eschatology has prayer for Jesus' coming as one of its primary modes, then it is not to be confused with projection. If the postmodernist misconstrues Christian faith at this point, it is because of a lack of attention to some of its basic modes of speech, and a consequent misapprehension of the character of God's relation to the world.

[24] Sauter, 'The Concept and Task of Eschatology', p. 151.

Eschatological speech is never far from the language of prayer. An eschatological spirituality is therefore ascetical, eschatology in the desert.[25] That is to say, it involves the rupturing of ties and attachments, separation, processes whereby we are detached from belonging to a comprehensible historical order, on the basis of which we can assign roles to ourselves and others, above all, in which we can be safe. This is not to deny that Christian eschatology indicates a kind of security, even safety. But what kind? In his remarkable book *Expérience et Absolu*, the French theologian Jean-Yves Lacoste suggests a link between the ascetic's refusal of possession and location and the way in which 'the fool' (unlike the person of learning) is dissatisfied with that which is provisional. The person of learning, the sage,

> is satisfied with a happiness which bears every sign of being provisional (since speculative knowledge suggests that God is present other than through the Second Coming, since the promises made at Easter – which the sage is either unaware of or misunderstands – remain unfulfilled, etc.), and on the other hand he does not really try to situate in the present all the eschatological meanings that he may perceive. The fool, because he desires the final state ... more deeply than anyone, but can accede only to a fragile degree of anticipation ... is thus able to smile at those who hold that the *eschaton* is already here in the present.[26]

Once again, some vigilance is needed here. A spirituality of reticence ought properly to dispossess us of false objects of desire and the satisfactions they afford; it ought not to direct itself against those hopes which are, indeed, given to the saints. But with that caution, we may at least be reminded of the need to build into the fabric of Christian dogmatics the disavowal of those uses of eschatology which annexe it to the fertile processes of idolatry.

We may sum up this first section by reminding ourselves of what Barth once said about the doctrine of providence, and

[25] Cf. Volf, 'After Moltmann', p. 255.
[26] J.-Y. Lacoste, 'Liturgy and Kenosis', in G. Ward, ed., *The Postmodern God. A Theological Reader* (Oxford: Blackwell, 1997), p. 252.

which applies very aptly to the doctrine of the last things. '[T]he Christian belief in providence is faith in the strict sense of the term, and this means ... that it is a hearing and receiving of the Word of God'.[27] Belief in providence is not consent to a narrative projection. It is not 'an opinion, postulate or hypothesis concerning God, the world, man, and other things, an attempt at interpretation, exposition and explanation based upon all kinds of impressions and needs, carried through in the form of a systematic construction'.[28] And it is not this because the movement which the doctrine states begins with God.

> We can and must understand that the knowledge of this lordship of God can be compared only to the category of axiomatic knowledge, and that even in relation to this knowledge it forms a class apart .... It consists in a realisation of the possibility which God gives to man.[29]

In sum: in belief in providence we do not have to do with 'a so-called world view, even a Christian world view. For a world view is an opinion, postulate and hypothesis even when it pretends to be Christian'.[30] In Christian eschatology we do not have to do with a world view but with the confidence of faith, discerned through patient attention to faith's forms of prayer and speech. Yet what such prayer and speech presuppose is that the history over which Jesus Christ presides is directional and purposive, culminating in the day of the Lord. What does this have to say for dogmatic questions of human identity?

2. Eschatology and the End of the Subject: the Dissolution of Ethics and Politics

Postmodernism sometimes tells a story which runs something like this. The history of the modern age is the history of the invention of the self. Modernity is self-consciously a process of

---

[27] K. Barth, *Church Dogmatics* III/3 (Edinburgh: T&T Clark, 1961), p. 15.
[28] Ibid., p. 16.
[29] Ibid.
[30] Ibid., p. 18.

the emancipation of cognitive and moral selfhood from the encompassing orders of gods, societies, customs and texts, and all their attendant officials. In the course of this emancipation, the self finally emerges into the light as that which is axiomatically real, true and good. Postmodernity announces that this modern drama of emancipation is mere pretence. The transcendent subject is simply a fictive conglomeration of fragments. And so Kant's lonely, severely rational and utterly responsible agent becomes Musil's 'man without qualities' – either an empty space played upon by systems of differences, or an anarchic trickster figure lacking in form or definition. Whereas modernity stands under Montaigne's rubric 'I look within',[31] postmodernism more characteristically says: '[E]ach of us knows that our self does not amount to much'.[32] Like all such stories, the cogency of the postmodern version of the history of anthropology depends on not being too worried about the details and on being harnessed to a strong proposal in the light of which it acquires plausibility. This strong proposal – the so-called 'death of the subject' – is well described by Calvin Schrag at the beginning of one of the very best studies of the topic, *The Self after Postmodernity*:

> For the most part, questions about the self, and particularly questions about the self *as subject*, are deemed anathema. As there is no longer a need for the unification of the diverse culture-spheres, so the problem of the self, at least as traditionally formulated, is seen to evaporate. Questions about self-identity, the unity of consciousness and centralized and goal-directed activity has been displaced in the aftermath of the dissolution of the subject. If one cannot rid oneself of the vocabulary of self, subject, and mind, the most that can be asserted is that the self is multiplicity, heterogeneity, difference, and ceaseless becoming, bereft of origin and purpose. Such is the manifesto of postmodernity on matters of the human subject as self and mind.[33]

[31] M. de Montaigne, 'On Presumption', *Essays*, II.17 (Harmondsworth: Penguin, 1958), p. 220.
[32] Lyotard, *The Postmodern Condition*, p. 15.
[33] C. O. Schrag, *The Self after Postmodernity* (New Haven: Yale University Press, 1997), p. 8.

Postmodern theology has been especially interested in stressing the connection of onto-theology and subjectivity. In the Western tradition of metaphysics and theology, so the argument goes, God the supreme being is equally the supreme subject, the monadic, substantial, self-possessing bearer of a name. Mark Taylor writes,

> From a monotheistic perspective to be is to be one. In order to be one, the subject cannot err and must always remain proper. By following the straight and narrow course, the self hopes to gain its most precious possession – itself.[34]

Human subjectivity is thus the replication of divine self-possession: 'The self-presence of the self-conscious subject reflects the self-presence of absolute subjectivity'.[35] One could certainly argue that Taylor's pretty monochrome portrait of the Western theological tradition succeeds only by maximalising certain doctrinal aspects (divine absoluteness, mentalist accounts of human nature) and minimalizing other corrective features within the tradition such as the doctrine of trinitarian relations, or those traditions of ascetical theology which have given weight to dispossession (both spiritual and social) as a mode of authentic humanity. Indeed, to target the whole tradition as resting on 'the repressive logic of identity', or 'the "logic" of oneness [which] implies an economy of ownership',[36] is not much more than a crude pastiche. What it serves, however, is a proposal for a differential structure of human selfhood, which 'subverts the exclusive logic of identity' by seeing the self as 'a function of the intersection of structures and the crossing of forces'.[37] '*Desubstantialized* and deindividualized' the self is '*co-relative*' and '*co-dependent*':[38] not the centre

---

[34] Taylor, *Erring*, pp. 41f.; for further representative works here, see R. P. Scharlemann, *The Reason of Following. Christology and the Ecstatic I* (Chicago: University of Chicago Press, 1991), and C. E. Winquist, *Desiring Theology* (Chicago: University of Chicago Press, 1995), pp. 99–126.

[35] Taylor, *Erring*, p. 42.

[36] Ibid., p. 130.

[37] Ibid., p. 134.

[38] Ibid., p. 135.

of a set of given structures, but a trace, a point at which fluid lines of force play against one another (the link between postmodern theology and process theology is not incidental). 'Fabricated from transecting acentric structures, the deindividualized subject is never centred in itself.'[39]

Selfhood, in other words, shares the same fate as teleology in postmodernism: it is left behind in the migration to the fields of anarchic free play. By way of response, I want to suggest that there is a strong connection between Christian eschatology and a certain understanding of the human person, and that the severing of that link by proposing a strictly non-teleological anthropology does severe damage to our understanding of persons as moral and political agents. In short: postmodern turns from eschatology may constitute a (literally) hopeless amoral and apolitical account of what it means to be human.

Critics of postmodern thought have not been slow in pointing out that, when combined with the evacuation of the category of history, the repudiation of enduring selfhood or identity clearly renders any kind of account of meaningful or purposive moral and political action acutely difficult. At best, human action can only be seen as ungrounded, unattached to any depth, unfastened to any features of the world of history which might evoke, order, evaluate or bring such action to completion. At worst, action is anarchic, erratic, sheerly undirected play (though it hardly deserves the name 'play', since games are ruled, not random, behaviour). Thus Richard Rorty, who has been especially concerned with the political fallout of postmodernism, argues for the retention of some kind of moral teleology for human politics, but only 'as long as the point of doing so is to lift our spirits by utopian fantasy, rather than to gird our loins with metaphysical weapons'.[40] I want to suggest that, far from dealing in utopian fantasy, Christian eschatology furnishes a frame for moral-political

---

[39] Ibid., p. 139.

[40] R. Rorty, 'Cosmopolitanism without Emancipation', *Objectivity, Relativism and Truth. Philosophical Papers Volume 1* (Cambridge: Cambridge University Press, 1991), p. 212.

action, and thus for that resistance to evil which is part of the Christian's baptismal vocation.

In (rightly) discarding the sovereign, self-enclosed, self-identical subject of modernity, postmodernism 'leaves us with a subject too thin to bear the responsibilities of its narratival involvements': so Calvin Schrag.[41] The reference to narrative there is important: over against the postmodern dispersal of the self into fragments, it is rightly objected that a firm sense of human selfhood and agency requires some sort of account of enduring human identity, embodied in a life-story which moves towards an end in which it will be integrated. Thus Schrag argues for 'narrative self-identity borne by a process of character-formation'.[42] Accepting the demise of substance-oriented accounts of selfhood as changeless and fully formed in advance of the history of the self's performance, Schrag nevertheless affirms 'a species of self-identity' acquired through participation in a narratable history.[43] Crucially, such a temporal – and therefore teleological – self is *agent*, '[t]he who of action' that 'can make a difference in the world of communicative praxis'.[44] In slightly less elevated terms: one crucial requirement for being a self is to be able to see onself as a purposive participant and agent in story where what one does *matters*.

So far, so good. But Christian theology will want to go a good deal further than this. It will not be sufficient to respond to the postmodern dissolution of the self into unstructurable, utterly discrete moments by pressing, as Schrag does, the logic of narratival achievement of identity. Indeed, there is a real question whether Schrag's account of selfhood can distinguish

---

[41] Schrag, *The Self after Postmodernity*, p. 28.

[42] Ibid., p. 42. Schrag's account is heavily reliant on P. Ricoeur, *Oneself as Another* (Chicago: University of Chicago Press, 1992), and is also indebted to J. Kristeva (e.g., 'The System and the Speaking Subject' in T. Moi, ed., *The Kristeva Reader* (Oxford: Blackwell, 1986), pp. 24–33), as well as to aspects of the later work of Foucault; see now M. Foucault, *Ethics. Subjectivity and Truth* (London: Allen Lane, 1997).

[43] *The Self after Postmodernity*, p. 33.

[44] Ibid., p. 71.

itself sufficiently sharply from the later Foucault's aesthetics of the 'care of the self'.[45] The crucial difference from Christian anthropology will be this. Christian faith will not articulate the teleology of the self and its actions in terms of that *techne tou biou* recommended by Foucault, that 'intensification of the relation to oneself by which one constitute[s] oneself as the subject of one's acts'.[46] Such nominalism, lacking a sense of human nature as brought into being, sustained and perfected by the creative action of divine love, sits very uneasily with Christian theology. Instead, theology will talk of the self and its agency by offering an account of the 'field' or 'space' of moral selfhood and action. It will set its moral anthropology in the framework of an account of the drama of human nature, origin and destiny, a drama presided over by the triune God who will bring it to its consummation at the appearing of the Lord Jesus. That drama is the space of our action, the field within which what we do is possible and meaningful.

Postmodernism characteristically resists this kind of spatial or geographical language, since it seems to indicate constraint or closure, the establishment of boundaries which eliminate the heterogenous and eclectic.[47] But much depends on how the idiom of space is used. A Christian theological depiction of the field or space of human moral selfhood is not simply a portrayal of some determinate cultural district. It is an account of the identity of God (the triune creator, reconciler and perfecter); an account of the identity of the human agent as both a divine gift and a human task; an account of the encounter between this God and his creature; and an account of the differentiated teleology of their actions. All Christian language is, directly or indirectly, a depiction of moral space, for what it does is express one or other aspect of God or of God's creatures as agents in relation. This is – emphatically – not to fall

[45] Schrag himself admits as much: see p. 68.
[46] M. Foucault, *The History of Sexuality, volume 3: The Care of the Self* (Harmondsworth: Penguin, 1988), p. 41.
[47] Cf. K. Tanner, *Theories of Culture. A New Agenda for Theology* (Minneapolis: Fortress Press, 1997), pp. 93–119.

into the kind of wearisome ethical reductionism in which doctrines can be decoded into moral imperatives. But it is to say that, because the triune creator is the Lord of the covenant, and because the people of the covenant find themselves in obedience to God's gift and summons, then any talk of God is also talk of the identity of God's creatures. In particular, talk of God (and of humanity *coram deo*) is talk which – because it is talk of *this* God – effects at the same time the ascription of roles and the establishment of standards of role-performance. Precisely because and only because Christian talk of God is talk of God, it is also by derivation moral language. If that general rule holds true, then Christian eschatology is not some futurist projection; it is talk about the coming of Jesus Christ which also talks of the teleological aspects of the moral field in which human agents find their identity. Two things flow from this.

First, Christian eschatology is practical rather than speculative. It has an ethical character, in that one of its functions is to inform and evaluate the church's practice rather than offer a theory of universal history. Christian eschatology is what Jürgen Moltmann calls 'a theology for combatants, not onlookers'.[48] Eschatology informs moral practice by indicating that the field of human action (including the identity of the human agents in the field) is ordered, and ordered teleologically. Human moral action is therefore neither arbitrary, inconsequential behaviour (which scarcely deserves the title 'moral'), nor an attempt to create a goal for or impose a goal upon our lives. It is action ordered towards the telos of history, which is the coming of Jesus Christ. That telos both relativizes and incites action. It relativizes action, because the end of history is the manifestation of Jesus Christ, the one who was and is and is to come; the end of history is not within the sphere of human competence or responsibility, and is hence a matter of prayer. But it incites action, because the Christian's prayer. *Maranatha!* is an active, not an inactive prayer, a prayer which

---

[48] J. Moltmann, *The Coming of God. Christian Eschatology* (London: SCM Press, 1996), p. 146.

invites, expects, indeed, commands us to do in our sphere what is fitting in the light of the action of God to whom we pray. And so Christian eschatology is ethical, and Christian ethics are eschatological. The ultimate doctrinal grounds for this are, of course, trinitarian: the Christian is now empowered by the Spirit to act in anticipation of the final coming of the Son of God, in which the creative purpose of the Father will reach its ultimate goal.

Second, if all this is the case, then Christian eschatology, far from being the leaden metaphysics of historical sameness, is in part concerned with the manner in which God's action evokes and sustains patterns of human action. As such, it may, perhaps, furnish what postmodernism has found it acutely difficult to provide, namely an account of reality as the ground for true, good human action. The word 'ground' is deliberate: without a sense that moral-political action corresponds, in however fragmentary a way, to the nature and destiny of the world, then moral action will surely be unable to master its discouragements. Moral action, if it is to be hopeful, courageous and free from anxiety about its own possibility, requires a sense of its ontological depth, its being in accord with what is and will be. For Christian eschatology, we are able to move ahead and resist only because another – Jesus – has gone before us and has overcome and will manifest his triumph at the last. And we move ahead, we resist, because this one is present in the power of the Holy Spirit in which the future is sealed and the powers of the age to come are given in anticipation.

If all this sounds curiously antiquated, so be it . . . in one sense it is. But our age is neither (as Kant thought) the age of criticism nor (as postmodernism suggests) the age of the dispersal of all things. Our age is the present age of reconciliation, in which it is given to the church to taste the Spirit and know the presence and power of the risen Jesus, and therefore it is the space in which we may pray and act hopefully and in truth. 'Since all these things are thus to be dissolved', the writer of 2 Peter asks his audience, 'what sort of persons ought you to be?' His answer is an end to the mythology either of total responsibility or of its negation; in their place, he counsels a kind of passive activity and active passivity, 'waiting for and hastening the coming of the day of God'. And why? Because the truth of our situation is that we are those who occupy that place in history where the most truthful thing to do is this: 'according to his promise [to] wait for new heavens and a new earth in which righteousness dwells' (2 Pet. 3.11–13).

INDEX OF NAMES

Abraham, W. 25
Adriaanse, H. J. 46
Ames, W. 256
Appel, N. 24f.
Augustine 37, 78, 86, 139f., 150
Aulén, G. 143f.
Avis, P. 195

Balthasar, H. U. von 187f.
Barth, K. 6, 29, 33, 36, 39, 40, 42, 44, 60, 62f., 66, 68, 87–110, 117, 134, 147, 155f., 171, 178, 180, 187, 202, 204, 208, 213, 220, 222f., 235f., 238, 247, 253f, 258f., 267, 275, 277f.
Barth, M. 223
Bauerschmidt, F. C. 267
Baur, F. C. 142
Bayle, P. 256
Berkouwer, G. C. 34, 76
Bethge, E. 104
Bloom, H. 80
Bonhoeffer, D. 87–110, 116f., 120, 123, 183
Bruns, G. L. 55, 59
Buckley, M. 152
Bultmann, R. 101, 153f., 162f., 165

Calvin, J. 37f., 78, 81f., 91–4, 95, 200, 204, 220, 229, 253

Caputo, J. D. 271–3
Chadwick, H. 242
Charry, E. 83

Dalferth, I. U. 202, 206
Demson, D. 74
Derrida, J. 271f
Descartes, R. 255
Donfried, K. P. 60
Dupré, L. 49

Eagleton, T. 269
Ebeling, G. 165, 239–41

Finnis, J. N. 238
Folkert, K. 41
Ford, D. 264
Forsyth, P. T. 210
Foucault, M. 262, 283
Fowl, S. E. 23
Frei, H. 63, 69f., 127, 151f., 188, 243
Fuchs, E. 155, 179f.

Gadamer, H.-G. 53, 69
Galot, J. 136
Geertz, C. 61, 243
Geffré, C. 48
Gorringe, T. 216f.
Grisez, G. 242f.

Guillory, J. 14
Gunton, C. 175

Harnack, A. von 11
Haight, R. 126
Hegel, G. W. F. 174
Heidegger, M. 53, 156, 241, 251
Hodgson, P. C. 269, 273

Ignatius 139, 207

Jasper, D. 15
Jeanrond, W. 50f., 71f., 73f.
Jeffrey, D. L. 81
Jennings, W. J. 80
Jenson, R. W. 39f., 69
Jones, G. 227
Jüngel, E. 2, 75, 136, 151–90, 196

Kant, I. 114, 128f., 279, 285
Käsemann, E. 165
Kelsey, D. 19f., 73
Kenny, A. 84
Kierkegaard, S. 189f., 210

Lacoste, J.-Y. 277
Lehmann, P. 233, 236f., 239
Lyotard, J.-F. 269f.
Lindbeck, G. 42, 45, 62, 243
Luther, M. 195, 261

MacIntyre, A. 249
MacKinnon, D. M. 132, 134, 144f., 175f.
Malina, B. 246
Marcion 11
Marsh, C. 99
Marshall, B. 130
Martensen, H. 24
Marxsen, W. 15

McFague, S. 127
Meeks, W. 243–6
Milbank, J. 149f., 246f., 261
Moltmann, J. 199, 284
Montaigne, M. de 255, 279
Morgan, R. 76

Nietzsche, F. 268

O'Donovan, O. 202, 209

Pannenberg, W. 224, 239–41
Perkins, W. 256

Ramsey, A. M. 191, 194
Ramsey, P. 252
Ricoeur, P. 53, 59, 251
Ritschl, A. 143, 229f.
Rorty, R. 281

Sauter, G. 274, 275f.
Schillebeeckx, E. 192, 214
Schleiermacher, F. D. E. 36f., 53, 94
Schlink, E. 124, 195, 206
Schrag, C. O. 279, 282f.
Schwöbel, C. 146, 196, 197
Sedgwick, T. F. 248
Siegwalt, G. 29, 35
Smith, W. C. 13, 31
Spinoza, B. de 55–7, 146, 255
Spjuth, R. 175
Staten, J. C. 241
Steiner, G. 80
Surin, K. 43

Taylor, C. 55, 77, 235
Taylor, J. 256
Taylor, M. C. 15f., 138, 270f., 274, 280f.

Thiemann, R. 62, 65
Thiselton, A. C. 80
Torrance, T. F. 28f., 33f., 35, 70,
  79, 82, 136, 201, 205
Tracy, D. 51

Vanhoozer, K. 31f., 79
Vogel, H. 172
Volf, M. 198, 217–19

Westcott, B. F. 142
Wolterstorff, N. 59, 72f., 83

Watson, F. 27, 51f.
Weber, O. 39, 40
Wendel, E. G. 90
Werner, M. 15
Wiles, M. 17
Williams, R. 15, 20–2, 67, 72,
  122, 203, 204f.
Williams, S. 27, 211
Wood, C. 18f., 52, 59, 61

Zizioulas, J. 205